D1272897

DK
265.42   Pearlstien
.U5   Revolution in Russia
P4
(1)

Date Due		
JUL 1 1982		
NOV 1 2 1982		
MAR 1 5 1984		
DEC 1 4 1985		
DEC 1 2 1986		
MY 28 '88		
FEB 2 0 1992		
MAR 1 2 1992		
APR 4 1994		

LIBRARY-ALLEGHENY CAMPUS
808 RIDGE AVENUE
PITTSBURGH, PA.   15212

bdy PRINTED IN U.S.A.

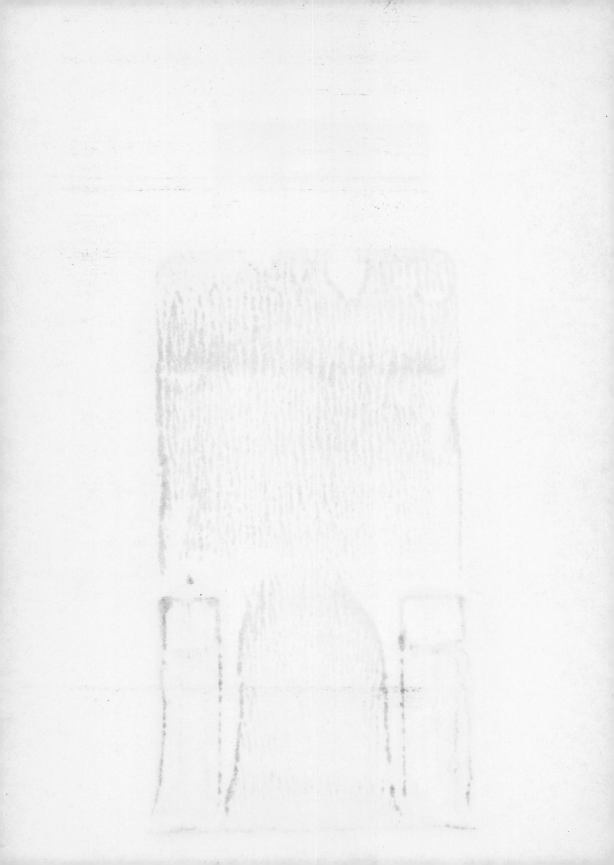

Revolution in Russia!

REVOLUTION

As reported by the New York Tribune

INTRODUCTION BY *Richard O'Connor*

NEW YORK

IN RUSSIA!

and the New York Herald, 1894-1921

EDITED BY EDWARD W. PEARLSTIEN

The Viking Press

COMMUNITY COLLEGE OF ALLEGHENY COUNTY

ALLEGHENY CAMPUS

808 RIDGE AVENUE
PITTSBURGH, PA.
15212

LIBRARY

Copyright © 1967 by Richard P. Cecil
Introduction by Richard O'Connor:
Copyright © 1967 by The Viking Press, Inc.

Extracts from The New York *Tribune*: Copyright 1906, 1907,
1914, 1915, 1917, by The Tribune Association;
Copyright, 1918, 1919, 1920, 1921, New York Tribune Inc.
Extracts from The New York *Herald*:
Copyright 1914, 1915, 1917, 1918, by The New York Herald Co.

All rights reserved

Published in 1967 by The Viking Press, Inc.
625 Madison Avenue, New York, N.Y. 10022
Published simultaneously in Canada by
The Macmillan Company of Canada Limited
Printed in U.S.A.

DK
265.42
. U5
P4
(1)

Preface

The purpose of this book is to present the unfolding of the Russian Revolution day by day (in so far as possible), as a reader of the time might have experienced it in his daily newspaper. The files of the New York *Tribune,* one of the great papers of the world, and those of the New York *Herald,* a paper of rare excitement, have been used. The reader of today will notice a somewhat more leisurely style of writing. During World War I the cable was very much in use, but many stories were still sent by ship. Perhaps the result was this more leisurely style, and also the thoughtfully interpretive articles of a kind rare today.

This book was conceived, planned, and contracted for while the undersigned was the head of WCC Books, the book-publishing division of the New York *Herald Tribune.* It is ironical that this is a *Herald Tribune* book, even though the period covered in it preceded the merger of the *Herald* and the *Tribune* (which took place in 1924), and even though the *Herald Tribune,* while this book was in process, became one element in the new *World Journal Tribune,* then passed away. The changes on the New York newspaper scene are not "revolutionary" in the sense of the revolution in Russia, but they are indicative of the relentless changes of the past half-century.

Revolution in Russia! consists primarily of the newspaper articles which are here reprinted. However, certain kinds of events, such as secret meetings held by then obscure revolutionaries, were not reported in any major newspaper, and so the narrative supplies additional information in these and other cases where it was needed to tell the story properly. Edward W. Pearlstien performed or directed the research into the newspaper files, organized the results, and wrote the connective narrative. Yet the undersigned has been responsible for seeing that this was a New York *Herald Tribune* book and has participated in the planning and editing stages, with the discerning help of his assistant, Jill Rosenberger, and must, therefore, be considered responsible for its final form.

Special thanks must be given to Professor Donald W. Treadgold of the Far Eastern and Russian Institute of the University of Washington, who has read the entire manuscript carefully and made many helpful suggestions. Gratitude is also in order to Professor Henry Huttenbach of the City University of New York, who has also read the manuscript and prevented errors. The assistance of Robert Grayson, Head Librarian of the *World Journal Tribune,* has been invaluable. Nevertheless, such errors that may remain are the responsibility of the undersigned.

The attentive reader will notice a number of inconsistencies. V. I. Lenin's name will sometimes appear in these early newspapers as "Lenine" or even as "Nikolai Lenine." In the narrative we have, with some exceptions, followed the style of transliteration of the very useful *Encyclopedia of Russia and the Soviet Union,* edited by Michael T. Florinsky (New York: McGraw-Hill Book Company, 1961), but we have not changed the newspaper dispatches to conform, feeling that we would lose some of the flavor of the period if we did. Yet, trying to be pragmatic, we have followed in the connective narrative the contemporary usage of "Czar" instead of the form "Tsar" simply because it appears so frequently in the articles.

Until February 1918 the Julian calendar was used in Russia. In the nineteenth century this ran twelve days behind the Gregorian calendar used in the West and in the twentieth century thirteen days behind. The date of the Bolshevik Revolution is October 25, 1917, by the Julian calendar, Old Style, but November 7, according to the New (Gregorian) Style. As the American newspapers naturally dated their stories in the New Style, the editors have used that system throughout.

Finally, the editors would like to note that while the newspaper articles have sometimes been abbreviated or combined for the sake of cogency and accuracy, we believe that we have avoided any distortions of fact or interpretation. An item–by–item listing of each article used appears at the end of the book.

RICHARD P. CECIL

March 9, 1967

Contents

Introduction

There is probably nothing that arouses our sense of the drama in history quite as much as picking up an old newspaper and reading the report of some world-shattering event. The impact is like that of a Greek play; we not only feel that we are living through a crucial moment in human affairs, but we see the implications and know the consequences. Indeed, the effect on us of the newspaper story is often greater than it was on readers at the time. Probably few people perusing their copy of the New York *Tribune* over coffee on the morning of November 8, 1917, paid more than scant attention to the modest one-column headline that announced, REBELS SEIZE 4 BUILDINGS IN PETROGRAD; ARMED BOLSHEVIKI BREAK UP PRELIMINARY PARLIAMENT. Yet the story turned out to be one of the most significant ever printed. To read it now makes our nerve ends vibrate. This was the beginning of the Bolshevik seizure of power in Russia. This, in a manner of speaking, inaugurated the contemporary era.

Journalism's method of enlightening us on history as it is being made is necessarily prismatic. The newspaper correspondent confronted with the necessity of making sense out of chaos for his readership is afflicted by insistent deadlines, quarrelsome censors, demanding editors, rivals who may beat him if he is slow in breaking a story or crow over him if he is too hasty and misinterprets what he has uncovered. His is the atmosphere of the pressure cooker.

The wonder is, as this book so admirably conveys, that anything cool, reasonable, and objective emerges from the process; that the coverage of the Russian revolution, necessarily handled in part from different European capitals and pieced together from conflicting reports, claims, and counterclaims, was not a welter of bulletins and fragmentary dispatches but often an accurate summary of what took place. With only a little use of scissors and paste and a narrative to integrate the reports from the New York *Tribune* and New York *Herald,* the editor of the book was able to construct a history of the background and day-to-day unfolding of the revolution.

For any diligent newspaper reader of half a century ago, the Russian revolution should have come as no overwhelming surprise, always providing that he subscribed to a newspaper as perceptive and objective as either the New York *Herald* or the New York *Tribune*. These two newspapers—and there were others, of course—quite accurately conveyed the sense of what was happening in Russia. It was not *the* revolution, but a series of political shocks coming from peasant masses, urban workingmen, the leaders of a slowly forming democratic impulse, as well as from anarchists, Marxists, and other revolutionists, that confused and weakened the grip of the Russian autocracy; the famous "ten days" were only the culmination. In the columns of the *Herald* and *Tribune* these events, and the almost incredible lack of comprehension with which they were met in the imperial palaces, can be clearly traced. They convey the awful feeling that if there had been just one man who possessed both the power to act and the political intelligence to act promptly and forcefully, Russia might now be a democracy.

It is particularly interesting to read the parallel interpretations of the New York *Herald* and the New York *Tribune* because of the difference in their journalistic styles. Both were fairly conservative in their physical makeup, not given to scareheads; there is not the contrast between them that one would find, for instance, in reading *The New York Times* and the exclamatory New York *Journal* with its six-inch headlines. But the two journals were guided by different philosophies, traceable to their founders.

The *Tribune* was the creation of Horace Greeley, the eccentric, idealistic, very liberal Republican. Before, during, and after the Civil War Greeley made his columns hospitable to almost every visionary with a dream of how America could be converted into a Utopia. After Greeley's death the *Tribune* was published by Whitelaw Reid, a former Civil War correspondent, who was a much more practical man—so practical, in fact, that he accepted financial assistance from the piratical Jay Gould and for a time parroted Gould's opinions. Reid finally managed to lift the mortgage and thereafter the *Tribune* was an independent journal of liberal Republican mold. Both in its typography and the way it presented the news, it cast an aura of dignity and elegance. The *Tribune,* a morning paper, was the one you would find at the breakfast table of a Fifth Avenue mansion. For all its impeccable taste, however, it was objective and open-minded, not merely an intellectual comforter for the stockbroker and the cotillion leader.

One quick way to contrast the *Tribune* with its morning competitor, the *Herald,* is to note that Karl Marx was once a *Tribune* contributor (before Jay Gould got his teeth temporarily into the property), while Mark Twain often wrote for the *Herald.*

The New York *Herald* was the brainchild of James Gordon Bennett, Sr., who, as the late Elmer Davis once remarked, "invented almost everything, good and bad, in modern journalism." Until the senior Bennett founded the *Herald* in a Wall Street basement in 1835, the American newspaper was principally a platform for its publisher's political opinions. Bennett, a hard-bitten Scottish immigrant, saw that the day of personal journalism was ending, that the reader was more interested in news than in the often rabid personal concerns and feuds of the editor. Bennett exploited court and police news, developed the coverage of sports, financial, shipping, and society news, and greatly speeded up the transmission of cabled and telegraphed news from other parts of the country and from abroad. He gave the newspaper its immediacy, its urgency, and ultimately its mass readership. Almost up to World War I, the New York *Herald* was not only the most entertaining but the most enterprising paper in America.

At the time of World War I, the *Tribune* and the *Herald* were being operated, respectively, by the heirs of Whitelaw Reid and of James Gordon Bennett, Sr. Financial control of the *Tribune* was vested in the widowed Mrs. Reid, but the paper's publisher was her urbane son, Ogden Reid.

The *Herald,* for many years, was edited and published by James Gordon Bennett, Jr., whom not even the youthful William Randolph Hearst could match in willfulness, caprice, or contempt for convention. Known as the Commodore for his yachting triumphs, the junior Bennett had been socially banished in New York for his behavior at a New Year's party (urinating on the grand piano at the home of his fiancée, who abruptly terminated the engagement). He was also notorious for driving a coach-and-four while stark naked in the coachman's box and for other antics, but all his waywardness could not quite obscure his genuine talents for venturesome journalism and his willingness to spend large sums of money to express them. Educated abroad, he was determined to broaden the provincial horizons of his newspapers (he had added the New York *Evening Telegram*, a pink-sheeted sensational journal, to the Bennett properties) and to build up a foreign news service then unrivaled in the American newspaper business. In 1870 he sent Henry M. Stanley to find Dr. Livingstone and incidentally change the map of Africa; later he dispatched a correspondent to cover the Russian punitive expedition against the Turkomans in Central Asia and in 1879 financed the *Jeanette*'s polar expedition, which ended tragically in the pack ice off the northern coast of Siberia.

Commodore Bennett in 1878 exiled himself to Paris, where he continued to operate the *Herald* and *Telegram* by cable and in 1887 founded the English-language Paris *Herald*, which for generations has been the solace of American tourists on the continent. At the same time he posted correspondents in all the European capitals and watering places—a highly costly service which no other American paper could match. Paris by night knew Bennett as a drunken playboy, but every hungover morning he concerned himself with every detail of his papers' management and particularly the movements of his corps of correspondents. The Bennett papers were the only ones in history ever to carry a copyright slug ("Copyright by James Gordon Bennett") not only over every telegraphed or cabled story but over the headline itself. He personally directed coverage of the Spanish-American War, including the hiring of the peerless Richard Harding Davis as his chief war correspondent, and despite the hysterical sensationalism of the *World* and the *Journal* the New York *Herald* topped the half-million mark in circulation and was undoubtedly the No. 1 newspaper published in the United States.

By the time World War I began, however, Bennett was aging and the New York *Herald* had slipped far behind Joseph Pulitzer's morning *World* in circulation and prestige. Bennett stuck it out in Paris even when most of his staff fled as the Germans approached the Marne and seemed to be on the verge of capturing the capital. His fortune was virtually exhausted, the New York *Herald*'s circulation had slipped below the hundred-thousand mark, but he continued to invest all the money he could lay hands on in maintaining the Bennett foreign news service, as the excellence of the reporting in this volume attests. A rigid conservative politically, he naturally kept an anxious eye on developments in Russia and posted one of his best men, Herman Bernstein, to act as his listening post in St. Petersburg.

Thus, as events in Russia approached their climax, the New York *Herald* was slipping badly but still an admirably informative newspaper, particularly on the political and military aspects of the European cataclysm, while the New York *Tribune* was still firmly established as, certainly, one of the most influential United States newspapers. Their comparative strengths may even be noted in their coverage of events in Russia from the 1890s onward. At the beginning of that period the *Herald*'s dispatches from Russia ("By the Commercial Cable," in which Bennett was a part owner and which contributed to his interest in foreign news-gathering) were the more complete, authoritative, and frequent. After the Russian-Japanese War and the premonitory uprisings that followed in 1905, however, it was the *Tribune*'s correspondence from Russia that was superior. In the columns of both papers it was made apparent that the Russian autocracy, its religious institutions, and its secret police were struggling to keep the lid on a revolutionary situation.

The readers of the *Herald* and the *Tribune* were kept informed day to day on the unrest which manifested itself in the formation of opposition parties, on the leaders of the peasant and laboring masses, on the reaction of the people to the October Manifesto by which the Czarist regime promised a measure of constitutional government.

It was the heyday of the foreign correspondent. Every youthful reporter yearned to be sent abroad, to swagger into chancelleries with the plenipotential powers of the representative of a great newspaper in the years when the power of the press was unchallenged, to interview kings and generals and prime ministers on a footing of equality, as was ordained by the lordly Richard Harding Davis, to whom an American journalist was at least the equal in standing of a Turkish vizier or a French ambassador. The correspondent would be sent to Paris or Budapest or St. Petersburg —then not only the seat of the Czars but the administrative capital of All the Russias—with a silk hat, morning coat, striped trousers, and expense account. He would be established in an office with a secretary and an interpreter to cull the news out of the native press. He would be consulted, courted, and flattered, because the news he sent out was of prime influence in a period when the press was unrivaled as a means of communication— long before television superseded it as what Marshall McLuhan calls the "cool" medium. All that attention may have been head-turning to a young man who a few months before had been covering the Tombs in New York, but the dispatches and the dispassionate analyses of the *Herald* and *Tribune* men on the Czarist Russian scene demonstrate that they kept their objectivity. They did not soften the picture of pre-World War I Russia, with all its strikes, riots, and sabotage against the industrial conversion which the Czarist bureaucracy was attempting to bring about in time for its predictable confrontation with the German war machine, nor did they conceal the dry rot in the Romanov dynasty and its dependent nobility. A faithful reader of either the *Herald* or the *Tribune* would not have been as optimistic as certain European general staffs and political leaders were about the ability of Czarist Russia to maintain an eastern front against the Central Powers.

The impressive status of the foreign correspondents, particularly the war correspondents, was greatly diminished by World War I. Hitherto they could go where they pleased, describe what they saw, and fear no interference from governments. American correspondents covering the Cuban and Philippine campaigns during the Spanish-American War had been uninhibited about describing military movements and merciless in exposing the ineptitude of individual commanders. All that was changed by censorship and other forms of intimidation, which the various European governments (and later the American) excused on the grounds of military necessity, wartime secrecy, and national survival.

Correspondents learned of the change in ground rules almost the moment war broke out. One tried to cable home the names of 5,000 Americans stranded in Europe by the outbreak of war and was forbidden to do so on the grounds that the list might contain a code. During the first battles, war correspondents were refused permission to go to the front, the French General Staff claiming that the Germans won the Franco-Prussian War partly because of all the information published by correspondents with the French armies. The correspondents would be kept informed through daily communiqués. One of the few who got a glimpse of the French war machine in motion—"There was nothing but confusion"— was the New York *Tribune*'s Paris correspondent, the elderly Charles Inman Bernard, who was driven by his friend the Duc de Loubat to Versailles, the mobilization center for the Paris district. Thereafter any newspaperman who wandered outside the city limits of the French capital was arrested by the field security police, held in jail, and eventually returned to Paris.

The same held true, even more so, on the eastern and Balkan fronts of the war. If a correspondent did manage to glean something far back of the lines, he had little chance of getting it through the censorship. The military, of course, controlled the cableheads and censored everything that went out, not excising merely that which might affect security but anything reflecting on national morale or political unity; the mails were also sealed off; and any correspondent who somehow managed to elude all the watchdogs was declared *persona non grata* and shipped home when an unpleasing story was published. All the dash had gone out of the business. War correspondents were not much more than transmitting devices.

As the war went on, and on, the regulations were relaxed to some extent, but as will be apparent from the stories published in this volume the bracketed notation [Delayed] was frequent testimony to the ubiquity of the censor. The best an alert correspondent could manage was a story about what was happening in a country other than the one in which he was stationed. Thus the able Arthur S. Draper, London correspondent for the New York *Tribune,* managed to round up from various diplomatic sources some of the most incisive articles on what was happening inside Russia; early in 1917 he was reporting how the "extreme Socialists" were promoting unrest and organizing riots with the aim of getting Russia out of the war, and later and quite accurately that the democratic Kerensky was prevailing over the monarchist General Kornilov.

Inside Russia, as the turbulent summer wore on, the American correspondents struggled to provide their readers with a sense of the doom that seemed to be hovering over Russian democracy in the brief hour before it was overwhelmed by the revolutionary left (with its spectrum ranging from Bolsheviks through Mensheviks to Social Revolutionaries), which was united only in promising to extricate Russia from a war which had cost eight million casualties. The internal conflict was a matter of crucial importance to the United States—now in the war and expected to fill the gap left by Russian withdrawal—and to her allies. If the Bolsheviks won the power struggle centered in St. Petersburg (which since 1914 was called Petrograd), the whole weight of the Austro-German armies could be hurled at the western front, probably before the A.E.F. was ready to move into the trenches. The *Tribune,* in particular, was enterprising about rounding up all available opinion on what Russia might do and somehow obtained an article by Lenin, who had recently been smuggled into Russia on a sealed train, courtesy of German malice. Possibly he consented to write the *Tribune* article because the paper had been hospitable to Marx years before. The article, which makes ironical reading today, strenuously denounced the "slanderous" reports that his Bolshevik faction would arrange a separate peace with Germany.

Earlier the *Tribune,* in its determination to cover all viewpoints regarding the developments in Russia, had published an article by John Reed, whose eyewitness account of the revolution (*Ten Days That Shook the World*) was to become a classic. Reed, a young Harvard graduate who had become famous for his reportage on Pancho Villa's revolution in Mexico, had first journeyed to Russia in 1915 and so irked the Czarist authorities that the Grand Duke Nicholas himself ordered that Reed be deported. A Marxist Socialist soon to become an American Communist leader, Reed anticipated the Party line by claiming the Kerensky government was not representative of the peasant and laboring masses and that its primary objective was to unite Russia against Germany and keep the war going.

Reed himself returned to Russia, and the American correspondents there hoped that he would be a great help in covering the revolutionary movement. He was on the inside, being not only the nominal correspondent of the Socialist daily, the New York *Call,* but a courier for the Bolshevik underground and the confidant of its leaders. Soon he would become friendly with Lenin and Trotsky, almost their protégé, and on his death from typhus in 1920 would be among the few Americans elected to the honor of being buried at the foot of the Kremlin wall.

Reed, however, was too preoccupied to share his special influence with his colleagues, for he was now more the revolutionist than the journalist. The old comradeship of the newspaper business didn't hold good in a revolutionary situation. Reed and his beautiful young wife, Louise Bryant, who accompanied him to Petrograd, immediately joined the small colony of Americans who sympathized with the Bolsheviks; it included Albert Rhys Williams, Bill and Anna Shatoff, Zorin Shatoff, Alex Gomberg, and Boris Reinstein, and also a visiting journalist named Bessie Beatty. Those happy few had the entree to the inner circle of the revolution-to-be. Reed not only shunned his old friends in the correspondents' corps but referred to them as "bourgeoisie," the standard Marxist epithet. According to one report received at the American embassy, which kept a fairly close watch on the American correspondents and what they sent out of Russia, Reed was responsible for having the Associated Press man thrown out of one Bolshevik meeting. The *Herald,* the *Tribune,* and most of the other papers represented in Russia relied on the A.P. when their own correspondents were away from the capital. Reed would be of no help whatsoever as what the correspondents called a "pipeline" or in helping them divine the intentions of the most radical element of the revolutionary forces.

The men back in New York concerned with estimating the effectiveness of those forces had to rely more and more on news leaking out of Russia through the capitals of surrounding countries, and their correspondents in Stockholm and Helsinki were quick to pounce on any American businessman passing through from Petrograd. Only a few weeks before the climactic "ten days" in November 1917 they were able to glean reports of Russian troops refusing to go to the front, railways cut by bands of deserters, factories closed by strikes. Isaac Don Levine, the foreign editor of the *Tribune,* was in charge of pulling together all the reports and rumors and making sense of them. Soon after Kerensky became chief of state, Levine correctly prophesied that if the Provisional Government refused to be controlled by the dissident workers and soldiers, particularly on the issue of bringing about a peace on the eastern front, Russia would be "split into two hostile camps," one that of Kerensky and the middle classes, including the military, and the other containing the working class and the soldiers in the ranks.

The revolution, when it came, took place mainly in the meeting halls of the Smolny Institute in Petrograd, where the All-Russian Congress of Soviets was in session night and day. Fourteen out of twenty-five members of its presidium were Bolsheviks, who, on November 7, with stunning speed and force assumed control of the revolution. The more moderate elements of the left, the Mensheviks and the Social Revolutionaries, were shouted down, bullied into silence, until Lenin took the podium and announced the Bolshevik program.

The Petrograd correspondents, sitting at press tables in the front of the auditorium at the Smolny Institute, heard and saw it all, but getting it out over the cables was another matter. By the evening of November 7, Kerensky and his followers had fled the city. The Bolsheviks were in control of the capital, except for a few pockets of resistance.

Correspondents rushing to the cable office in the Petrograd post office found Bolshevik censors trying to take over control of the cablehead but having a hard time with the cable company employes, most of whom were anti-Bolshevik. The means of transmitting news out of Russia were thoroughly snarled. Amid much quarreling over who had the authority, a few correspondents managed to clear their stories, though they were heavily blue-penciled.

In the next few days, with Kerensky reported rallying a cavalry corps to retake the capital and Bolshevik mobs running through the streets looting wine cellars and displaying themselves in finery taken from the sack of the Winter Palace, the correspondents found themselves in a hazardous situation.

Several were attacked by the mobs as representatives of the "capitalist oppressors." Charles Stephenson Smith, the A.P. bureau chief, was knocked unconscious by a Red Guard rifle butt. Another member of the A.P. staff in St. Petersburg was struck in the knee by a sniper's bullet. The situation grew so menacing that Guy Beringer, the Reuters correspondent, took his wife and fled to safety in Finland. Once he had found temporary shelter for his wife, Beringer returned to Petrograd, was immediately arrested by the Bolsheviks and thrown into prison, where he remained for six months under constant threat of facing a firing squad.

On the weekend of November 10–11, all possibility of cabling news out of Russia was closed off when the employes of the post office went on strike against the Bolsheviks and barricaded themselves in the building. The post office was under siege, and the correspondents could only take notes and hope to stay out of trouble.

For days after the revolution was an accomplished fact, at least in the capital, the correspondents were prevented from sending out any news. Even John Reed, with all his influence in the inner circle, had to wait until November 15 before he could cable a short statement from Lenin to the New York *Call*. It wasn't until six days later that his first, fairly complete story of the "ten days" was cleared through censorship and cabled to the *Call*.

Even when an intermittent outflow of news was resumed, the Bolshevik censorship remained capricious. The Soviet censors naturally tended to let pass anything favorable to the shaky regime and to blue-pencil anything that reflected the hazards through which it was passing. Thus the first graphic accounts of how the Bolsheviks met the most immediate threat —the counterattack of Kerensky's cavalry regiments from the south—had to be pieced together from diplomatic reports under a London dateline. In this task of patching together a story from undoubtedly conflicting and often misleading, always fragmentary reports, the cable desks in the *Herald* and *Tribune* cityrooms back in New York functioned with an expertise acquired in coping with the coverage of the war in western Europe. In less than twenty-four hours New York newspaper readers were informed of the fighting on the approaches to the capital, with the *Tribune* reporting under a London dateline: KERENSKY NEARS PETROGRAD; CIVIL WAR IS BEGUN. That dispatch told of the fighting around Tsarskoye-Selo, where the Czar and his family had spent their summers, and gave an accurate picture of how the Bolshevik volunteers were driven out of the town, which they recaptured a day later; also of how the Red Guards had been defeated in Moscow and the Cossacks far to the south were reacting violently against the Bolshevik attempts to seize control of the Ukraine. Similarly, New York newspaper readers were informed within hours of Kerensky's defeat and his flight from Russia.

During those bewildering days, the *Tribune* adopted a wait-and-see editorial stance. It warned, however, that Russia could no longer be depended upon to hold the eastern front against the Germans and published a cartoon showing the Russian bear being pursued by a pack of German wolves with the title "Food for the Pack."

The reaction from Commodore Bennett's crustily conservative *Herald* was swift and predictably acrimonious. On November 9, only two days after the Bolsheviks announced they were taking over, a *Herald* editorial claimed, mistakenly, that every prominent member of the Council of Soldiers and Workmen was either a German or of German origin. The whole revolution, in the *Herald*'s view, was a German plot to haul Russia out of the war. "If the country turns itself over to the Bolsheviks," it warned, "it will turn itself over to the Tsar—and that means to the Kaiser."

When large-scale fighting broke out between the Reds and the Whites, the swaying course of the campaigns in South Russia, Siberia, and elsewhere was reported with a fair degree of accuracy, though from a distance. No correspondents were permitted to go near the fighting. There were no war correspondents in the Russian Civil War. Anyone who had attempted to leave the capital and follow the Red brigades into action would have been shot as a spy. Yet the cable editors managed to compose a mosaic of reports from St. Petersburg and foreign capitals which conveyed a fairly accurate impression of the confused struggle. The drama of conflicting loyalties could be followed from day to day as first the Whites advanced from the south and east—and the names of Wrangel, Denikin, Kolchak, and other White commanders became household words—and then the Reds slowly pushed them away from Petrograd and Moscow.

Fragmentary and perplexing as that jumble of bulletins and sketchy dispatches must have been, the foreign desks at the *Tribune* and *Herald* provided a picture of the great Russian nation in turmoil. They showed that the battles taking place all over Russia—the cavalry charges of the Cossacks, the swarming of Red militia into captured towns, the grappling for control of the railroads by armored trains—were not simply military engagements in the classic pattern but part of a struggle for the political loyalty of the Russian people, which would be more decisive than any victory in the field. With a sophistication remarkable in that time half a century ago, when the revolutionary process was still a great mystery to most people, the two newspapers, and especially the *Tribune,* explained how propaganda, agitation, the struggle for people's minds, the spread of promises of social and economic reform, were more likely to influence the outcome of the civil war than a battle won or a city occupied.

Coverage of Russian events perceptibly improved, as the dispatches included in this book show, when the Allies intervened and sent in various expeditionary forces with the professed aim of restoring order—an Anglo-American force at Archangel, the British marching across Persia (now Iran) to occupy the oil port of Baku, the landing of an American force at Vladivostok ostensibly to protect a mountain of supplies that the U.S. had shipped to the Kerensky government but did not intend to allow to fall into the hands of the Red guerrilla forces trying to gain control of eastern Siberia. Through the columns of the *Tribune* and *Herald* could be followed the course of the abortive Allied interventions and the eventual withdrawal of the expeditionary forces to allow Russia to decide her own fate. With reports gleaned from the Siberian Expeditionary Force and other American sources channeled through Washington, American newspaper readers were given a clearer picture of what was happening in the Soviet Union.

By the summer of 1921, when the accounts of this volume end, it was clear that the Communists had extended their dominion from the western marches to the Pacific. A United States anxious, sometimes close to hysteria, over the radical elements in its own midst and the proclaimed intention of Soviet Russia to spread its revolution over the rest of the world could only view with distrust, through the newspapers, the establishment of the Communist International, the centralizing of the Soviet government, and the immediate suppression of all dissent within its borders.

Meanwhile, a revolution of sorts was occurring in the New York newspaper business and eventually it affected both the *Herald* and the *Tribune*. Commodore Bennett had died in France in May 1918 and his journalistic properties were up for grabs. The circulation of the New York *Herald* was an anemic 55,000, the New York *Telegram* was also losing money, and only the Paris *Herald* continued to prosper. Bennett's estate was a tangle of impossible bequests (including a home for old newspapermen) written when the Commodore was still well-heeled, and his executors decided to sell out to Frank A. Munsey, a horse-faced Yankee trader who was buying up and cannibalizing various New York papers. Munsey combined the *Herald* with the *Morning Sun,* which he had aquired a few years before, and the *Telegram* with the *Evening Sun.* The *Suns* had been published by Charles A. Dana, another vanished paladin of journalism. A short time later, after a dizzying series of transactions, he sold the *Herald* to Ogden Reid, who combined it with his *Tribune.* For forty-odd years the New York *Herald Tribune* was one of the best-edited of American newspapers.

In 1966, as newspaper after newspaper faded from the metropolitan scene, the *Herald Tribune,* which had been bought by John Hay Whitney eight years before, was combined with the New York *Journal-American* and the *World-Telegram & Sun.* But the new paper, on which had been grafted all the dreams and aspirations of the Bennetts, Greeley, Dana, Pulitzer, and Hearst, could not survive.

Shortly before this volume went to press, the newspapers from which it was derived wrote their own composite obituary and their latter-day manifestation, the *World Journal Tribune,* appeared for the last time.

This book itself was a product of the book publishing division of Whitney Communications Corporation, which was the parent company of the *Herald Tribune.* In its own special way it constitutes a valedictory to all the enterprise and professional skill which through the generations and perhaps most strikingly during the Russian Revolution made the *Herald* and the *Tribune* two of the greatest of this country's newspapers.

—RICHARD O'CONNOR

Chapter One

At the Eve

DEATH OF THE RUSSIAN CZAR.

At a Quarter Past Two Yesterday Afternoon Alexander III. Passed Peacefully Away in the Palace at Livadia.

CONSCIOUS TO THE LAST.

Looking from His Windows He Expressed Satisfaction at Dying on Russian Soil.

WIDESPREAD SORROW IN PARIS.

President Cleveland to Send an Appropriate Message of Condolence To-Day.

EUROPE'S PEACE OUTLOOK

Nicholas II. Will Make No Change in Russia's Relations with the Powers.

The stubborn autocrat whose oppressive reign had seemed like one long act of vengeance for the murder of his father finally succumbed in November 1894 to the kidney disease that for a year had been wasting away his powerful body.

St. Petersburg, Nov. 19 [1894]. The body of Czar Alexander III was placed today in the tomb of his fathers, beneath the Fortress Cathedral of St. Peter and St. Paul, eighteen days after his death. The funeral services were the most elaborate of any similar services that had ever taken place in Russia, and the last rites were performed in the presence of an assemblage of royalty and representatives of royalty such as has seldom or never congregated in similar circumstances under the roof of a sacred building.

The morning opened cold and foggy. There was no rain, but a thick mist overhung the streets, and the emblems of mourning everywhere displayed were dripping with moisture. The populace were astir before daylight, and all the morning lines of people kept converging upon the Fortress Cathedral of St. Peter and St. Paul, where the booming of a cannon announced the beginning of the funeral services.

The ceremonies were conducted with all the pomp of which the ritual of the Greek Church is capable, and with all the display that the Russian court could command. The streets were thronged with people throughout the day, and the utmost good order prevailed. No accidents were reported, despite the constantly surging crowd, and the troops charged with the duty of preserving order had nothing to do but to put themselves upon exhibition and endure the exactions of the cold, damp, and altogether disagreeable weather until the funeral was over.

At ten o'clock the large choir, which during service is sometimes grouped on either side of the altar or at other times retiring behind the ikonastas into the sanctuary, suddenly burst into an anthem.

3

In contrast to the uncouth and poorly educated Alexander III (center), the Czarevich Nicholas (standing behind his father), was reputed to be refined, charming, and quite well informed, which encouraged the liberals to expect democratic reforms when he succeeded to the throne. The other members of the imperial family, clustered around the gargantuan Czar, are (clockwise from the left): Michael, the Czarina Maria Fyodorovna, Xenia, George, and Olga. (*The Bettmann Archive*)

Prayers and responses alternated until half-past ten. . . . The Emperor and the imperial family then walked into the church, preceded by the Metropolitan and the Holy Synod, and were conducted to their places on the dais before the altar. . . . When the ceremony of absolution was reached the Metropolitan of St. Petersburg walked to the dais and bowed a number of times. The Emperor Nicholas stood upon the pavement, and the Metropolitan, making the sign of the triple cross and bearing that emblem, pronounced the formula of absolution:

"The Lord Jesus Christ, our God, who gave divine commandments unto His holy Disciples and Apostles to bind and loose the sins of the fallen, and from whom we have again received authority to do the like, forgive thee, O spiritual child, whatever has done in the life that now is, voluntarily or involuntarily, now and ever, and to ages of ages. Amen."

For the mourners inside and outside the Cathedral—the statesmen and Russian aristocrats in their stiff uniforms, the throngs waiting in the quiet fall mist, the troops and secret police apprehensively scanning the unpredictable crowd—these gloomy proceedings were fraught with anxiety. Their attention was fixed not on the remains of the departed monarch or on the Czarina prostrated with grief, but on the young man of twenty-six who tossed a symbolic handful of dirt on the casket before it was lowered into the imperial vault and then emerged from the Cathedral amidst a salvo of cannon fire. To this slight person with the soft features (so unlike his massively built, ursine father) had passed the dreadful power of the Romanov dynasty. His dominion extended over one-sixth of the land area of the globe, from Finland to the Caucasus Mountains and from Poland to the Pacific Ocean, and within it his word was unappealable law. There was no constitution to harness his sovereign will, no legislature to express the desires of the people. The courts were his creatures; the ministers of government, the officers of the army, and even the clergy were his servants. Every decision of any importance concerning Russia or Russia's foreign relations had either to be made by him or to receive his consent. Would he—and this, of course, was what most concerned the statesmen of other countries—abstain from asserting Russian national interests in the Balkans, in the Near East, in China? Would he maintain Russia's pivotal role in the delicate system of alliances and counterposed force by which the peace of Europe was being precariously kept?

Shortly after the death of his father, Nicholas II married Princess Alice of Hesse-Darmstadt, in Russia called Alexandra Fyodorovna. (*The Bettmann Archive*)

Europe's Peace Involved

Alexander's Death Lessens the Chances of International Amity

Herald Bureau, Paris, Nov. 1, 1894. [Alexander III's] death is the most important political event that has happened in Europe since the year 1870. The dismissal of Bismarck was an event of historical interest, the old Chancellor having already accomplished his utmost. But Alexander III was concerned in current politics, and in fact controlled the politics of Europe, where nothing could be done independently of him.

GENERAL REGRET IN EUROPE

His death will cause general regret in Europe, for the Czar was an excellent man. He was absolutely desirous of peace. When he spoke it was always in order to preserve peace.

It will be interesting to observe the effects of the succession in Russia and the course of action followed by the young Emperor Nicholas. It is alarming to reflect that a young man of twenty-six, wholly without preparation hitherto for the terrible greatness of his mission, is about to be the absolute ruler of one hundred and twenty millions of men.

But the question which preyed upon the minds of Russians themselves and on which to a large extent everything else depended was what policies Nicholas would adopt regarding Russia's manifold domestic problems. How, for example, would he respond to a liberal pamphlet clandestinely published (and, typically, seized by the secret police) on the eve of his father's death?

St. Petersburg, Oct. 31 [*1894*]. The police have seized a large quantity of literature consisting of pamphlets, entitled "The Fundamental Statute of the Russian Empire." The aim of the brochure is to unite all the parties which are opposed to the Government and enlist the sympathy of the Liberal public officials. The "Statute" proposes that there shall be two law-making bodies, one consisting of local councils and the other an Imperial Chamber of Deputies. The monarch is to have the right of veto. According to the scheme, Poland is to have her own legislative Assembly and Finland is to retain her autonomy. The "Statute" provides for freedom of conscience, freedom of speech and freedom of the press.

The local councils actually were already in existence. Nicholas's grandfather, Alexander II, conceding a whit to popular pressure, had established a network of elected county assemblies (called *zemstvos*) and municipal councils, which were empowered to administer, within limitations, local government. But Alexander III had emasculated them. Bureaucrats from the central government had been put in charge and all but the most minor decisions had to be made by the appropriate minister in St. Petersburg or by his representative. Then, during the terrible famine of 1891, Alexander had been forced to allow the zemstvos and town councils to take independent action for relief, medical care, and other urgencies. Their appetite for an extension of democracy had been revived, and now, with the accession of a new czar, they intended to press for it.

How, also, would Nicholas deal with the pitiful—and extremely combustible—agrarian problem? As the *Tribune* reported:

> The truth is that the Russian peasant, 100,000,000 of him, is . . . slowly starving to death. His diet consists of meal, flour and grits, cabbage and potatoes; no meat, except three times a year. His diet is insufficient, and less than in any civilized country. The hovel he lives in is two and a half yards long and one and one-half yards high, harboring the whole family and whatever cattle he possesses.

Alexander II had emancipated the peasant-serfs from their ignominious bondage to the great landowners, granting them the rights to marry as they chose, to buy and sell property, and to institute legal proceedings in the courts. The emancipation decree, promulgated in 1861, also instituted a complicated system for distributing large portions of the great landed estates to the peasants. However, the peasants were not free to move from their villages; they still did not enjoy full civil rights (even to the extent that any other Russians had these); and, most important, the redistribution scheme was woefully inadequate, partly because of the compensation payments required, partly because the land was to go to the village communes, not to individual families, and partly because of the resistance of the landlords. The emancipation had not done enough to alleviate the misery of the peasant's life or to satisfy his desire for land. Alexander III had added practically nothing to the inadequate reforms of his father.

In addition, there was the administrative problem.

> [*Dec. 6, 1896.*] The Russian bureaucracy as now constituted is a piece of machinery so vast and complicated that no one can readily understand the extent to which it crushes every element of the vitality and progress of the dominions of the Czar. The latter stands at the top of the pyramid and in the words of Peter the Great has "to give an account of his acts to no one on earth, but has power and authority to rule his States and lands as a Christian sovereign according to his own will and judgment." Im-

mediately below the Emperor are the Council of State, the Council of Ministers and the Senate. The Council of State is intrusted with the duties of examining the annual budget, but has merely a consultative character, and the monarch is in no way bound by its decisions. The Council of Ministers is not a council at all in the Western sense of the word, the Ministers being directly and individually responsible to the Emperor, and having no common responsibility or cohesive force. They are ten in number, and are at the head of the various branches of the Imperial Government. As for the Senate, it was originally intended that it should exercise a controlling influence in all sections of administration. But it has been deprived of its prerogatives and is at the present moment little else than a species of court of appeal.

In each of the forty-six provinces of the European portion of the Empire, as well as in Poland, Finland, the Caucasus and in the Baltic Provinces, the Ministers of the Interior, of Public Works, of Public Instruction, of Justice, of Finance and of State Demesnes, have each his own particular army of officials, each member of which, from the highest to the lowest, considers it to be his duty to rule the people—that is to say, the non-official class—with a high hand; the principle of the Russian Government since the days of Peter the Great having been to treat the citizens as minors, utterly incapable of understanding politics, and even incompetent to look after their own local affairs. Looking for direction and approbation merely to their superiors, the officials are accustomed to treat those over whom they are placed as a conquered and and inferior race.

To keep this vast machine in motion it is necessary to have a large and well-drilled army of officials. These are mostly drawn from the ranks of the nobility and the clergy, and from a peculiar class called "Tchinovniks." In Russia a man's social position nowadays depends not upon his birth, but upon his "tchin"; that is to say, upon the official rank he holds. There are fourteen grades of so-called "tchins," and although education certificates may exempt one from passing through the lower grades, a man, no matter how lofty his birth, is compelled to begin near the bottom of the administrative ladder and to remain a fixed time at every step. Moreover, he cannot receive certain dignities, honors and appointments unless he possesses "tchin" corresponding thereto, while the severest punishment that can be inflicted upon him is the loss of several steps of "tchin."

The difficulties of centralized administration are always in direct proportion to the extent and territorial variety of the country to be governed, and in order to understand how slowly and imperfectly it works it must be remembered that the whole vast region stretching from the Polar Ocean to the Caspian, and from the shores of the Baltic to those of the Pacific, is administered from St. Petersburg. The genuine bureaucrat has a wholesome dread of formal responsibility, and generally tries to avoid it by passing it on to his superior. As soon, therefore, as affairs are caught up by the administrative machine, they begin to ascend, and unless they get lost by the way, which fortunately happens in at least forty cases out of every hundred, arrive in the course of time in the hands of the Minister at St. Petersburg, or . . . in the Czar's hands. The consequence is that the Ministerial departments at St. Petersburg have . . . been flooded with papers, many of them of the most trivial import, from all parts of the Empire, the very number being sufficient to preclude the possibility of any proper attention being given them. This, of course, has the effect of facilitating dishonesty, venality and official corruption.

When Peter the Great one day announced his intention of hanging every official guilty of dishonesty the Procurator-General frankly replied that if His Majesty put his project into execution there would be no officials left. "We all steal," added the worthy official. "The only difference is that some of us steal large amounts and more openly than others."

Only Nicholas could correct this deplorable situation, and only by instituting representative and decentralized government.

So much, therefore, depended upon the decisions the young Czar would make. So much depended upon his personality, upon his disposition toward the statesmen and rulers of other countries, the quality of his intellect, his forcefulness or lack of it, his idiosyncrasies, his moods, his susceptibility to influence—good or bad. Information about his character which might provide clues was very limited. His youth had not been distinguished by the sort of extravagances that might either endear him to his subjects or give them special cause for alarm. He had never given public utterance to his views about outstanding domestic and foreign problems. Even highly placed persons—diplomats and journalists whose business it was to be informed about such things—had only vague intimations of what kind of ruler he would be. People who had been privileged to talk with Nicholas found him charming and not unintelligent, although they did note a certain stubbornness in his makeup and a petulant, rather childish expression that would appear in his blue eyes when he was annoyed. He had traveled quite widely in the West and had visited Egypt, India, and Japan. He was reputed to speak English, German,

French, Danish, and Greek with remarkable fluency. He was supposed to have been solidly tutored in the subjects important to his profession—history, administration, and law—even though his father had never allowed him to participate, except perfunctorily, in governmental affairs. Presumably, Nicholas would start out with the equipment necessary to consider his problems of state reasonably.

However, what was definitely known, not about Nicholas, but concerning him, did not augur well for the tranquillity and steady progress of Russia. One of his chief advisers would undoubtedly be his former tutor Konstantin Petrovich Pobedonostsev, the Procurator of the Holy Synod, that is, the lay minister in charge of the administration of the Russian Orthodox Church.

Personally M. Pobedonostseff is a thin, dry, bloodless, emotionless ascetic. He dresses with a clerical sameness. His conversation is full of emphatic commonplaces and dry unction. His habits are scrupulously methodical. His books, pamphlets, documents and letters are all arranged in apple-pie order. He has a ready-formed opinion on all topics—trustworthy so far as Russia is concerned; otherwise random. His features are pinched, his glance is cheerless, his manner jerky. He has none of the ease of the man of the world. The one deep channel in his shallow nature—his one idea—is Orthodox Autocracy.

He never makes or takes a joke. He never has been known to laugh. He eschews luxury, even in the guise of art. He is abstemious in his habits, simple in his tastes, affable and courteous to all. When he smiles his vis-a-vis suffers from the creeps. One notices his "inhuman incisors." Another shudders at his formidable tusks.

He never enters a salon, but has a Mercury or two who "like Heimdall, can hear the wool grow on a sheep's back and the grass sprout up in the green meadows." Orthodox profligacy in his eyes is infinitely preferable to the morality of evangelical Christianity. The carefully closeted skeleton of every Russian Minister is at his beck and call. He puts breath into their dried bones, and they come forth in terrible array. The most powerful of the Czar's advisers is afraid of him.

He is absolutely incorruptible. He is utterly sincere and single-minded. Injustice he recognizes and corrects, or tries to correct, promptly. The most heartrending appeals of the tormented Stundists [a dissenting religious sect] pass through his ears without speaking to his brain.

He believes that what he does is right and for the best. He is the only genuinely Russian statesman in the Empire. He is not a man. He is a machine.

The narrowness of his views makes M. Pobedonostseff fixed in aim, firm in purpose. He has twice saved Russia from Constitutionalism; once in 1881, when Loris-Melikoff [Minister of the Interior] had an approved charter in his possession, and a year later, when Ignatieff [Loris-Melikoff's successor] was on the point of introducing it under the name of Parliamentary Government.

His Orthodox Church is a mass of glittering forms, the rhythmical swaying of censers, the march and countermarch of cassocked acolytes, the pageantry of standard and crucifix and the shrill intonations of a foreign tongue. His most Holy Synod labored zealously in 1887 to solve the questions of the quality of the olive oil to be used in church lamps, and the length of an Orthodox wax candle.

Narrow, intense, methodical, mechanical, sincere, heartless, adroit, M. Pobedonostseff has constructed his polity somewhat in this fashion: One Church which shall tolerate no rivals; one autonomy of power, a Czar. Two principles, and yet one fact. No liberty of thought; liberty means the right to disagree. One altar throne at which all shall kneel.

Criticize it as you may, on altruistic and humane grounds, M. Pobedonostseff has created and maintains a clean, logical, successful policy. The Russian nation is a unity. The rudiment of its education is "to know the Czar"; its motto, "Let ignorance be bliss, 'tis folly to be wise."

What this frightening man represented—indeed, incarnated—were the stultifying traditions of the Russian political system, the leaden troika of autocracy, Russian Orthodoxy, and nationality which Nicholas was going to have to drive. Autocracy had been the cardinal principle of the Russian government at least since the time of Ivan the Terrible (1533–1584), who had consummated the domination of Russia by the Grand Duchy of Moscow by ferociously suppressing the higher nobility. He was the first Grand Duke officially to assume the bloated title of Czar (it is a corruption of the Latin Caesar), and it was Ivan who for the first time had the authority, gained by force and unutterable cruelty, to propound the doctrine of absolutism.

While absolutism was not peculiar to the Russian monarchy, it was marked in Russia by a uniquely oppressive element—the utter subordination of the Russian Orthodox Church to the government. Erastianism—

that is, the supremacy of the state over the Church—had been inherited, along with Orthodoxy, from the Byzantine Empire. However, it was carried to quite unprecedented extremes by some of the metropolitans in their passionate support of the Muscovite Grand Dukes' efforts to unify and dominate Russia. The theory of the divine origin of monarchy, which was also prevalent in the West, they reinforced with an extraordinary historical theory devised by a Pskov monk named Filotheus. It held that the universal authority of the Byzantine Emperors, which they inherited from the Roman Emperors after the fall of Rome, had been transmitted to the Muscovite rulers after the Turkish conquest of Constantinople in the fifteenth century. Moscow had succeeded Rome and Constantinople as the capital of Christianity. It was, so to speak, the Third Rome, but, unlike the corrupt Roman and Byzantine empires, Muscovy (Russia) was destined to last until the end of the world. The Czar, according to the theory, was the only true Christian sovereign. In his hands the Church placed the religious power of excommunication and interdiction, and it issued dire warnings to his subjects against disobedience to their divinely ordained ruler. Gradually, the Russian Orthodox Church became completely absorbed in the apparatus of the state. Political and religious values tended to become identified, with the result that political opposition was often confused with blasphemy. The will of the Czar was believed to be an expression of divine truth defining the obligations of conscience. The concept of government by the people was considered sacrilege.

Nationality (*narodnost*), a vague term more or less meaning "official patriotism" or "official nationalism," was an adaptation to the Russian tradition of the nationalism informing many of the ideologies current in the West. It included the mystique of ethnic characteristics, the glorification of national traditions, and inordinate national pride. But whereas in the West—for example, in the United States—these were often associated with individualism and the striving for the utmost personal liberty, in Czarist Russia, narodnost strengthened the forces of racism, parochialism, and reaction in general.

Considering these traditions, no one reasonably expected the new Czar to inaugurate suddenly any great social or political change. As the *Tribune* pointed out in an editorial printed on Oct. 4, 1894:

In one sense no ruler is less a free agent than the Czar, whose manner of governing is predetermined by dynastic considerations and race instincts. But while a Czar is a slave to traditions, he is also an autocrat by virtue of them. There may be governing cabals in St. Petersburg, but, powerful as they may become, they are dependent upon his sovereign will.

The appearance of [Nicholas] upon the scene . . . will not have any immediate effect upon Russian destiny. The governing cabal, with the army and the secret service behind it, will continue to direct with iron hand domestic and diplomatic policies. The ultimate end cannot be forecast, for the world does not know what manner of man the [Czar] is. If he be, like his father, a dull, indolent and apathetic ruler, there will be neither war in Europe nor political progress in Russia. His prejudices and presuppositions will be determining influences. Unless he is a man of original force and mind, he cannot emancipate himself from instincts and dynastic traditions which predetermine the reign of a Czar and impart to it a reactionary Asiatic trend.

Should Nicholas fail, from choice or through weakness, to lead Russia out of the darkness in which it had been closeted for so many centuries, the consequences could be very grim.

London, Oct. 31 [1894]. The following manifesto, promulgated by the refugee Nihilists * in Switzerland and bearing the usual red bomb, revolver and dagger, is being circulated in Switzerland and London:

To Our Brothers, the Oppressed in Russia.
The tyrant, Alexander, autocrat Czar, hangman and assassin . . . purveyor of the Siberian galleys, persecutor of the Jews, is on the point of expiating his crimes. He is dying of a mysterious illness, a well-merited punishment. Venal science . . . can do nothing to prolong a life which has been devoted to violence and oppression. At length the monster is going to disappear. Hurrah! The day had passed when a man ought to be able by right of birth to dispose of the liberty and lives of 100,000,000 men.
Let his son, the Czarewitch . . . thoroughly understand that every

---

* The term "nihilist" was often mistakenly applied to the revolutionists by American newspapers. Nihilism was a philosophical movement condemning tradition and inherited values and asserting that only scientific reasoning can enable man to achieve his true aim of self-expression and liberty.

hour and at every step [he will find himself] face to face with the inflexible will of the revolutionists.

Let us leave to the hypocritical Liberals the task of covering with flow-
ers the horrid corpse of the scoundrel who is leaving this world after
having too long dishonored it. So long as an infernal autocracy, served
by a rapacious and shameless feudality, makes Russia a disgrace to the
civilized world, we shall always applaud any blow of destiny or provoke
it. Long live Liberty and Revolution!

However extravagant the inflammatory tone, this manifesto was by no
means an empty bluff. It emanated from the remnants of the organization
responsible for the long series of political murders that culminated in
the assassination of Alexander II. This organization was the notorious
People's Will (*Narodnaia volia*), the terrorist wing of the populist movement. Populism had emerged as a significant political force in the 1860s,
largely as a result of disappointment and anger over the inadequacy of
Alexander II's reforms, and especially his land reform. The program of
populism (*narodnichestvo*) asserted that there was no recourse but to
overthrow the autocratic regime by a revolution—a revolution, though,
that would be utterly different from any that had occurred, or could
occur, in the West, because of the unique character of Russian society.
It would be led by the peasants, who constituted ninety per cent of the
population, and—here was the startling assumption—socialism would be
established immediately.

In Russia, the populists argued, the peasants had a long tradition of
cooperation, indeed of practical socialism. For centuries most of them
had been organized into village communes administered by elders who
were elected by the peasants themselves. Strips of land in the common fields
were assigned by the elders to the heads of the households; the use of
pasture lands and forests was shared; decisions on all sorts of matters
from personal problems to agricultural methods were made in common
or by the elders. The commune was responsible for the taxes of the individual villagers, and under the Emancipation Act of 1861 the communes,
not the individuals, were given the land. As to the workers, particularly
those outside of St. Petersburg and Moscow, the populists pointed to the
artels—the cooperatives of craftsmen and workingmen for the hiring out
of labor, purchase of machinery and raw materials, sale of commodities,
and so forth. The fact that Russian capitalism was still in its infancy—that,

for example, in 1854 there were only 9,944 industrial enterprises in the entire country and that barely twenty per cent of the peasants held their land in hereditary tenure—was an asset, not a weakness, as Marxian socialist theory maintained. It was not necessary for the Russian people to pass through a protracted, torturous epoch of free-enterprise capitalism and middle-class parliamentary democracy in order to learn the techniques of self-rule. Indeed, the establishment of capitalism in Russia would be a step backward. Moreover, there was a deeply rooted revolutionary tradition among the peasants, as demonstrated by the Pugachev rebellion of 1773 and numerous subsequent uprisings. The populists believed that it was only necessary to explain the causes of their misery to the peasants and they would rise against the government, overthrow it, and establish a socialist regime.

Fervently inspired by this conviction, the populists in 1873 undertook a concerted educational and agitational campaign in the countryside. Dressing themselves up as peasants (most of them were middle-class urban intellectuals), they began the arduous, dangerous, and often heart-rending task of explaining the populist creed to the peasants. Their slogan, which they adopted from the intellectual father of populism, Alexander Herzen, was "To the People."

However, they soon discovered that they did not understand much about peasant life or aspirations. To begin with, the centuries of despotism had had a terribly stultifying effect upon the peasants. Having no legal means of protesting, or expressing their grievances, or asking that their needs be met, they had become brooding, suspicious, and ineluctably superstitious. They listened dumbly, uncomprehendingly to the exhortations of the ardent and naive young populists. Swathed in ignorance (78.9 per cent of the Russian population was officially reckoned as illiterate in 1877), they politely accepted the populist pamphlets, then used them for cigarette papers. The peasants believed, as the populists discovered, that if only they could take their grievances to the "saint-Czar," to the "Little Father," their problems would be solved. Between the masses and the source of goodness and power, the Czar, lay an unbridgeable abyss, populated by bureaucrats and clerics. It was these whom the peasants hated, not the Czar or the Czarist regime.

But the most important error in the populist reasoning was more fundamental. The much-touted communal life was becoming increasingly onerous to the peasants, and when they were able or willing to articulate their real wishes, it turned out that the younger men particularly wanted private property, not socialist collectivization. Now that they were legally free, some of the peasants, either individually or in partnership, were beginning to buy up or lease land. Many bolder spirits, defying the law, were migrating to unsettled regions of Siberia, where they were able to carve out farms for themselves in the icy wilderness.

The movement "To the People" was therefore a miserable failure. As a result, the populists made an important change in their philosophy of political action. For all practical purposes they abandoned the assumption that revolution would surge from the masses themselves after only a certain amount of coaching and organized into a secret society, which was to act as a sort of vanguard of the revolution. They themselves would engage in the struggle with the government. A "disorganizing section" was established to fight the police if necessary, rescue members who were arrested, and punish traitors. This strengthened a tendency that had always been present in the populist movement. One group, inspired originally by the teachings of the anarchist philosopher Michael Bakunin, had long advocated terrorism as a means of weakening the government and creating an atmosphere of rebellion that would stimulate the revolutionary instincts of the people.

On the morning of February 5, 1878, a young woman populist not quite thirty years old, Vera Zasulich, acting on her own, shot the military governor of St. Petersburg, General D. F. Trepov, in retaliation for the flogging of a political prisoner. For some unexplained reason the government deemed the assault a criminal rather than a political act, so Zasulich was tried before a jury. She turned the trial into a political indictment of the regime, and to everybody's amazement the jury acquitted her. When the government, infuriated by the decision, ordered her rearrest, she was whisked away to safety under protection of the large crowd that had gathered in front of the court. The acquittal was taken by the group advocating terrorism as a reflection of popular approval for such acts, and not without justification. A grisly series of political assassinations ensued.

The sheer boldness of the attempts, whether they succeeded or not, gained widespread public sympathy, which further encouraged the terrorists. In June 1879 the populist party, which now called itself Land and Freedom, split into two sections: the terrorists, calling themselves People's

Will, and those who favored the traditional policies of education and agitation. The latter, who assumed the name Black Repartition (*Chornyi peredel*), proved no more effectual than their predecessors who had gone "To the People" and soon virtually disappeared. After the assassination of Alexander II in 1881, many of the terrorists who escaped arrest fled abroad, but during the reign of Alexander III their bloody handiwork remained much in evidence, as can be seen from the *Tribune*'s editorial comment on October 3, 1894 as Alexander lay dying:

> The career of Alexander III has been a melancholy illustration of the irony of a despot's fate. He was condemned to live in daily dread of the secret bullet and the exploding bomb. The most powerful of monarchs, he could not return through the Great Morskaia Prospect from a requiem service in honor of his father's memory without being a target for assassins; nor is he free to visit his capital unless an army is put in motion to protect him; nor can he make the rounds of his apartments in his secluded palace fortress without having detectives dogging his steps. Is there anything more ironical in the vicissitudes of royal fortune than this contrast between absolute sovereignty over millions and abject helplessness to enjoy a moment's peace of mind in an atmosphere electric with suspicion!

Would this also prove to be a description of Nicholas's reign?

Chapter Two

Prelude to Revolution

MANY WOUNDED
IN WAR RIOTS IN
ST. PETERSBURG

Mounted Gendarmes in
Ambush Charge Men
and Women, Who
Flee in Terror.

RED FLAG RAISED
IN BOLD DEFIANCE

Revolutionary Proclamations
Thrown in the Face of
Drawn Sabres.

GIRL STUDENTS SUFFER

Zemstvos and the Friends of Moderate
Reform Appalled by the
Turn of Affairs.

Nicholas early made known his intentions.

Berlin, Jan. 29 [*1895*].   Private dispatches from St. Petersburg say that the Czar was called upon today by delegations representing the nobility of the provincial cities and many provincial and district assemblies, who congratulated him upon his recent marriage. In replying to their congratulations the Czar said that he had learned that in some of the provincial assemblies voices had been raised proposing that the assemblies have a share in State affairs, and expressing other absurd desires. He therefore wished everybody to understand that he devoted all his powers to his dear country, but that he was firmly resolved, as was his dear father, to uphold the autocracy of the Czar.

The liberals were stunned. In reply they issued a manifesto in the form of an open letter to Nicholas printed in the *Tribune* February 14, 1895:

The most advanced zemstvos asked only for the harmony of the Czar and people, free speech and the supremacy of law over the arbitrariness of the Executive. You were deceived and frightened by the representations of courtiers and bureaucrats. Society will understand perfectly that it was the bureaucracy, which jealously guards its own omnipotence, that spoke through you. The bureaucracy, beginning with the Council of Ministers and ending with the lowest country constable, hates any development, social or individual, and prevents the Monarch's free intercourse with representatives of his people, except as they come in gala dress, presenting congratulations, icons and offerings.

Your speech proved that any attempt to speak out before the throne, even in the most loyal form, about the crying needs of the country, meets only a rough and abrupt rebuff. Society expected from you encouragement and help, but heard only a reminder of your omnipotence, giving the impression of utter estrangement of Czar and people. You, yourself, have killed your own popularity and have alienated all that part of society which is peacefully struggling forward. Some individuals are jubilant over your speech, but you will soon discover their impotence. In another section of society your speech caused a feeling of injury and depression, which, however, the best social forces will overcome before proceeding to the peaceful, but obstinate and deliberate, struggle necessary to liberty. In another section your words will stimulate the readiness to struggle against the present hateful state of things with any means. You were the first to begin the struggle. Ere long it will proceed.

The zemstvo leaders, around whom the liberals rallied, now became aggressive. In accordance with an old demand for a central organization of zemstvos, a number of leaders met in Nizhny Novgorod in August 1896, ostensibly to discuss mutual problems but in reality to lay the groundwork for political cooperation. Another conference was scheduled for the following year. The doctors, nurses, veterinarians, teachers, and other professionals who were hired by the zemstvos began meeting, with the tacit permission of their employers, to discuss political subjects and the formation of unions. And the zemstvos began defiantly to pass resolutions on matters distinctly out of their legal purview. But the government was equally aggressive in its obstinate repression. The scheduled 1897 meeting of the zemstvo representatives was forbidden, as were the conferences of professionals. The elections of recalcitrant zemstvo members were nullified. Zemstvo finances were restricted. In consequence the liberals were pushed toward a critically more radical position. Subterranean conferences of the leaders began to be held regularly, and in September 1903 a secret organization, the Union of Liberation, was formed. The demands of this first liberal organization in Russian history for constitutional government, with or without a monarch, met with an eager response, and branches proliferated.

The flowering of liberalism was due in large measure to the extraordinary progress made by Russia during the last half of the nineteenth century. Between 1854 and 1896 the number of industrial enterprises had quadrupled. The most rapid progress came in the 1890s, when the cotton, coal, iron, and steel industries bounded ahead. The output of coal, oil, and iron ore tripled. Railway construction, which, considering Russia's vastness and deplorable system of roads, was crucial to the country's economic development, spurted forward; about 15,000 miles of Trans-Siberian railroad were built in the 1890s alone. In addition, peasant

The village of Kurejka (now called Turukhansk) was typical of the Siberian frontier settlements in the late nineteenth and early twentieth century. (*Sovfoto*)

migration to the beckoning lands of the Asiatic provinces reached proportions comparable to the westward movement in the United States; an estimated 1,078,000 peasants settled in Asiatic Russia between 1891 and 1900, as compared to a total of 461,000 during the previous three decades after the emancipation. This migration did not substantially relieve the pressure for land in European Russia; it merely intensified the peasants' craving for land of their own and hastened the breakdown of the communal system.

The peasants' chances of getting some schooling had also improved; in 1895 there were approximately 60,000 elementary schools compared to about 1500 a half-century earlier. Although schools were far too few and the teaching was often quite rudimentary, there was visible progress.

All these changes began to affect the psychology of the Russian people. Hope began to wedge its way into that melancholy resignation to suffering which the centuries of despotism and deprivation had created. Among the intellectuals the change manifested itself in an eager embrace of modern Western thought, much of which implicitly or explicitly dealt with the spiritual, political, and moral problems of commercially and industrially dynamic societies. Before, there had been at most an atmosphere of receptivity born of desire, desire for the personal liberty, fluidity, and material creativity that the Western nations had achieved. It was evident, for example, in the Nihilists—the real Nihilists—those young men and women, intellectuals, who turned their backs on tradition (sometimes quite excessively) and exalted scientific method and individualism. In general, however, Westernism, particularly those ideas of individual liberty, of the sanctity of the person, of liberal democracy and unfettered competition, were rejected as not in keeping with the special needs of the Russian "soul," or with the Russian historical experience. But by the end of the nineteenth century economic conditions similar to those of the capitalism of the West were well established. The desire for personal liberty could perhaps be fulfilled, because the economic wherewithal was there; creativity could find an outlet in material pursuits; class distinctions were beginning to be defined less by birth than by wealth. Many intellectuals who twenty years earlier might have flocked to the populist movement now joined the camp of the liberal constitutionalists, the advocates of Western-type parliamentary democracy.

However, the liberals were still comparatively few in number and weak in influence, and, as the liberal manifesto had predicted, another section of society prepared to struggle "against the present hateful state of things" in another manner.

In the summer of 1900 representatives of various populist groups scattered throughout the country met at Kharkov and formed the nucleus of a new organization calling itself the Socialist Revolutionary party, and within a year and a half most of the larger independent sections of the populist movement had been brought together in a loose association under the aegis of the new party. While the main body of the party attempted to organize mass action, an ultra-secret band of militants, the *Boevaia organisatsiya,* or Terrorist Organization, was established to wage a guerrilla war against the government. A writer for the *Tribune* managed to ferret out information about the Socialist Revolutionaries, whom he still incorrectly called Nihilists.

[*Mar. 31, 1901.*] It is now about twenty years since the Russian Nihilists instituted that memorable reign of terror which culminated in the assassination of Alexander II on March 1, 1881. Whether or not the present trouble is as widespread and deep rooted as was that of former years probably nobody within or without Russia is in a position to declare. For the Nihilist movement is necessarily unorganized. The rule of not letting the right hand know what the left hand is doing is, by compulsion, their principle. In all parts of the empire are little groups of revolutionists who know that they have many comrades; the government knows that the Nihilist clubs dot Russia from end to end, but the true extent of the movement is known neither to the one nor to the other. Among the Nihilists themselves communication involves a risk too great to be lightly undertaken, while the government, for all its costly spy system, can obtain only vague information regarding the condition of the great volcano on the pinnacle of which is enthroned the conscientious and unhappy Nicholas. The mystery which surrounds the movement naturally serves to add to its terror for the Russian, and to increase its fascination for the student of political conditions.

While the Nihilists are not an organized body, there is a central committee which makes communication with the scattered clubs the object of its existence. The whereabouts and doings of the societies are known in great part to this little circle of men. They do not always dare to make ordinary use of the mails, but send messages to their . . . comrades, keeping up a system of secret service as elaborate as the vigilance of the government will permit.

Nihilists are in a minority, but their sympathizers, undeclared revolutionists, are doubtless many. To become an avowed Nihilist requires courage, and, again, there is a liberal element which is thoroughly dissatisfied with existing conditions, while deprecating violence in bringing about change. For a Nihilist is, properly speaking, one who despairs of bettering present conditions by peaceable means, although he is not at all times a terrorist.

However, it was neither the liberal groups nor the Socialist Revolutionaries who inaugurated the eruptions that were to culminate in revolution.

Students' Protests in Russia

[*St. Petersburg, March 1, 1899.*] The strike which recently broke out here among the university students as a protest against the conduct of the police, who had used whips to disperse the student gatherings on the recent festival of the University of St. Petersburg, has increased to such an extent that almost all the colleges and schools are now participating in it, including the theological college and the high school for girls.

There have been no disturbances, but students in uniform are constantly parading the streets, and all their balls and entertainments have been countermanded by them in token of mourning.

The precipitating incident was trivial. University officials had warned the students that this year the rowdyism usually accompanying the annual festival would not be tolerated. The students had already been bridling under the restrictions imposed upon them by the university charter of 1884, which forbade them to hold meetings or organize clubs. There had been ominous incidents, and it was evident that a contagion of restiveness had infected the schools, where radical political philosophies were hotly debated in secret. So the official warning became the occasion for a protest demonstration. The brutal way in which the police broke it up enraged the students, who called a general strike, with such success that every university in the country was shut down. The government replied with oppressive measures. Hundreds of students were not only expelled from their schools but also drafted into the army. The result was to antagonize the students further and to make them even more susceptible to revolutionary notions. Then on February 27, 1901, a former student, a Socialist Revolutionary, shot the Minister of Instruction, N. P. Bogolepov. The students cheered.

Students Roughly Handled

Gathering in St. Petersburg Broken Up with Great Severity

St. Petersburg, March 4 [*1901*]. To-day was the fortieth aniversary of the emancipation of the serfs. The students had been planning for some time to keep the day as a holiday and perhaps make some demonstration, but no particular plans were made. At noon a thousand or fifteen hundred students of both sexes gathered in and around the cathedral and the Nevsky Prospekt [the Kasan Cathedral], where mass was celebrated for the repose of the soul of Czar Alexander II. After the mass the students began singing, and the police gathered in great numbers, including a force of mounted men. The students were surrounded and driven in a crowd toward the City Hall, not far away, and also on the Nevsky Prospekt. For no special reason the police began beating the students and trampling them under the feet of their horses. The Nevsky Prospekt, which is the principal street of St. Petersburg, four miles long and 130 feet wide, and one of the finest in Europe, was filled with spectators. The banks and business houses were nearly all closed, with shutters fastened and doors locked. The spectators and the women students screamed with horror, but the police kept up their attack on the students until four hundred of the latter were driven into the courtyard of the City Hall, the others escaping into the crowd. The entire city was horrified by the conduct of the police.

The clashes between the students and the police became increasingly violent.

Moscow in a Ferment

Students Threaten Barricades and Street Fighting

London, March 16 [1901]. "The students' agitation in this city," says the Moscow correspondent of "The Daily Mail," "has become extremely serious. Bloodshed has occurred, and the students threaten barricades and street fighting. It is not safe for individuals to cross the streets in the daytime. The schools are closed and the city is virtually in a state of siege."

Student Troubles in Russia

State of Siege Proclaimed in Several Cities

St. Petersburg, March 17 [1901]. In consequence of the riotous disturbances following the demonstrations promoted by university students, the government has proclaimed a state of siege at Odessa, Kieff, and Kharkoff. It is reported here that a student died at Kharkoff from injuries sutained in the disorders of March 4, in that city.

Eight hundred students of the University of St. Petersburg . . . met last Friday and resolved not to attend further lectures. The police subsequently arrested sixteen.

Four hundred students of the Technological School entered the courtyard of the Institution to hold a meeting, and the police inscribed all their names.

The Mining Academy is already entirely closed.

Students Defy Russian Troops

Demonstration in St. Petersburg Quelled After Cossacks Used Whips

Fatalities Are Reported

Women Students Leaders in Riot

More than 300 Taken Prisoner in Disturbances in St. Petersburg Sunday

Alarm at the Capital

Many Workmen Involved in Demonstration and Their Presence a Dangerous Omen

It was the participation of workers in the demonstrations that began to impart to the inchoate turmoil a revolutionary character. With the surge of economic growth in the late nineteenth century came a terrible dislocation for millions of Russians. Workers were needed in the new factories, and of course they had to be brought from the countryside, where there were many peasants only too glad to move in the hope of improving their lot. A *Tribune* correspondent described one of the slums that were beginning to proliferate in St. Petersburg.

The bulk of the people are peasants and artisans. They are also drunkards, but I did not feel that it was as such that they had drifted into the slums. They seemed to me to be largely victims of city life, pitiful emigrants from the country for whom the fierce competition of the town had proven too much. Russia is still a distinctly agricultural country, but its cities are continually growing larger, and factories are springing up with considerable rapidity. All this reacts upon the rural population, and many have begun that march upon the towns, both in European and Asiatic Russia, in which hundreds are tramped down in every country. There is something particularly pathetic, however, in this movement in Russia, for the simple peasants have almost no idea of what they are doing when they leave the village, and many of them fancy that gold lies waiting for them in the city streets. In the house Viazemski I saw a number who had sold everything they had, and, of course, at a great loss, in order to get to St. Petersburg where they hoped to better their condition, and had honestly intended to work hard with that end in view. But all they knew was farming, and they had drifted and drifted and drifted until extreme poverty drove them to where I found them.

The effects of the dislocation were visible in almost every town with a concentration of industry—Moscow, Odessa, Kharkov, Kiev, Baku. Many were chronically unemployed, and as a result of the abundant labor supply, wages were exceedingly low while the hours were exceedingly long. Trade unions were few, but there were many strikes, often chaotic affairs, spontaneously organized mostly (and with extraordinary skill), but frequently unsuccessful, leaving the workers worse off than before. The atmosphere in these industrial towns was highly combustible and the student demonstrations set off an explosion of strikes unprecedented in the extent of the violence used both by the workers and the police.

Riots at Russian Cotton Mills

St. Petersburg, May 17 [1901].   Strike riots have occurred in the cotton mills on the Viborg side of the Neva. It is reported that many have been killed.

London, May 31 [*1901*]. According to a dispatch received from St. Petersburg to-day it appears that the conflict at Alexandrovsky, in the vicinity of St. Petersburg, between the workers at the Obuchoff Iron Works and the authorities on May 20, when about thirty-five hundred rioters attacked the police, had much more serious results than were admitted in the police report of the affair issued on May 21. It was then said that after twelve of the police had been injured they were reinforced by soldiers, who fired three volleys, killing two men and wounding seven. The relatives of the strikers declared that forty of the men were killed and that 150 others were wounded. A trustworthy witness says he saw four vanloads of wounded persons covered with blood, and another spectator declares he saw two tugloads of wounded taken to the hospital.

Strike Riots in Moscow

Fifty Persons Reported Killed or Wounded

Riots at Batoum and Baku

Disorder Suppressed by Troops—the Vice-Governor Hurt

St. Petersburg, March 29 [*1903*]. "The Official Gazette" at Tiflis announces that rioting took place recently at Batoum and Baku, the centre of the petroleum industry in Russia.

Russia Strikeridden

Quarter of a Million Workmen Affected

On the whole, the strikers' demands were economic—higher wages, the eight-hour day, abolition of the system of fines imposed by factory owners as punishment—but workers were highly susceptible to radical influence. The Socialist Revolutionary party continued with fair success to proselytize among the city workers, but it was primarily agrarian-oriented and, moreover, put much of its energy into terrorist activities (there were hundreds of political murders and attempted murders during these years). This, in effect, left revolutionary organization of the workers to comparatively new groups of radicals, whose philosophy was focused almost exclusively on the urban laborers. These were the Social Democrats, the Marxists.

The first Russian Marxist organization, called the Liberation of Labor, was founded in Switzerland in 1883 by four exiled and disillusioned populists—Vera Zasulich (the woman whose assault on the military governor in 1878 precipitated the populist reign of terror), Leon Deutsch, P. B. Axelrod, and G. V. Plekhanov. Plekhanov, who had been the leader of the Black Repartition wing of the populists, was its intellectual father and political leader. It remained small and quite uninfluential until the 1890s, when Marxism began to attract a large number of Russian intellectuals for very much the same reason that other intellectuals became constitutional democrats. Revolutionary Marxist groups sprang up in many of the industrial centers of the Empire. In St. Petersburg in 1895 The Union of Struggle for the Liberation of the Working Class was organized by two young Marxist revolutionaries—Vladimir Ilyich Ulyanov, who in the underground revolutionary tradition of adopting pseudonyms called himself Lenin, and J. O. Tsederbaum, who took the name L. Martov. In 1897 the General Jewish Workers' Bund of Russia and Poland was established; in addition to the ordinary Marxist demands it advocated autonomy for the Jews within a Russian socialist commonwealth. At the instigation of the Liberation of Labor the various groups joined together in 1898 to form the Russian Social Democratic Labor Party. (The Marxist parties of the late nineteenth century, beginning with the German party, called themselves "Social Democratic" rather than "Communist.")

Marxism, as it emerged from the voluminous writings of the Germans Karl Marx and Friedrich Engels, is based upon two assumptions, one leading to the other. The first is the concept of dialectical materialism. It holds that the only objective reality is matter, which has always existed and always will exist. There is no Creator, no supernatural force. But there is an increate natural force that is the essential attribute of all matter—the quality of motion, or change, which occurs according to a definite pattern. Every phenomenon creates its opposite (the thesis creates the anti-thesis), and these then combine into a higher form (the synthesis). The synthesis in turn becomes the thesis of the next step.

This early photograph of Lenin adorned the police card made after his arrest in 1895 for his activities in the Union of Struggle for the Liberation of the Working Class.

Posing with Lenin (seated at the table) and L. Martov (seated at Lenin's left) in 1897, are four other members of the Union of Struggle for the Liberation of the Working Class, (left to right) V. V. Starkov, G. M. Krzhizhanovsky, A. L. Malchenko, and P. K. Zaporozhets. (*The Bettmann Archive*)

Development from lower forms to higher forms is thus a law of nature. This leads to the second assumption.

Since man is a material being, his needs and actions are shaped by the material conditions of his existence, whether or not he realizes it or wants it to be so. Therefore, the way men earn their living and their relationship to each other as a result of this is the essential aspect of history. Societies proceed from lower forms to higher and more complex forms as the needs of production and the resulting social relationships change. European civilization thus developed from the tribal system, with its rudimentary economic system based upon the communal ownership of moveable chattel (such as cattle and slaves), to feudalism, which was based entirely on landed property dominated by the nobility, to capitalism, in which the means of production, the goods produced, and the labor of the workers are owned by individuals. The transition from stage to stage invariably involves great turmoil, because the ruling class in each epoch resists change and must be dislodged, despite the fact that the system it upholds is actually crumbling of its own accord. As Marx and Engels put it in the *Communist Manifesto,* "The history of all hitherto existing society is the history of class struggles." The concept of the class struggle is an essential part of political Marxism.

European capitalism, Marx argued, was in its last stages. The prime elements of the free-enterprise private-property system—anarchistic competition and wage labor—were rapidly destroying it. With the profits that had accrued during the earlier stages, the capitalists had expanded their production, flooding the market with goods. Profits consequently declined, making competition for markets all the more fierce and plunging the system into ever-deepening crises in the form of depressions. As a result smaller concerns were driven out of business and the means of production were becoming concentrated in the hands of fewer and fewer people. More and more people were thus driven out of the property-owning class into the class of workers, who are characterized by the fact that they own nothing but their labor power, which they sell for wages. The worker is thereby "alienated" from the forces of production. He has sold his labor power to the capitalist and is excluded from sharing the fruits of his labor. The work itself is unsatisfying; the worker is unable to fulfill himself; he is prohibited from determining the course of the productive process which occupies his life; and he is disassociated from the end product. But in addition to the psychological misery, Marx insisted, the physical misery also would inevitably mount. As the working class increased, the competition for jobs would become more severe, with the result that wages would fall to the subsistence level. In the process, though, the workers were becoming increasingly aware of themselves as a class in conflict with the capitalist class. They were becoming aware that unionization, reforms, better wages, shorter hours, would not solve the essential problems. Capitalism, which was being weakened by continual crises anyway, would have to be overthrown.

The new system, socialism, was essentially in existence already within the womb of capitalism, because the workers were already socially organized as a result of the division of labor within the factories. Moreover, industry itself in advanced countries was already concentrated and noncompetitive, Marx believed, because of the elimination of competitors. With the revolutionary destruction of capitalism, socialism would thus spring forth. The state, which in Marxist theory is always an instrument of the ruling class for the suppression of the exploited classes, would no longer be necessary and would wither away, since after a short period of transition

G. V. Plekhanov, founder of the first Russian Marxist organization, Liberation of Labor. (*Sovfoto*)

Lenin as he appeared in 1900.

Lenin's wife, Nadezhda Konstantinovna Krupskaya. (*Sovfoto*)

there would be no classes. Society would become communistic; each person would give according to his abilities and receive according to his needs. Men no longer would govern men. All mankind's energy would now be turned to the conquest of nature and the fulfillment of the unlimited creative potential of the human being.

On these basic points of theory the Russian Marxists (indeed, Marxists everywhere) were in agreement. But the application to Russia was a different matter altogether. A substantial group, the so-called Economists, insisted that at such an early stage in the development of Russian capitalism it was pointless to think of the workers as leaders of the revolution. They were, after all, so few in number. All efforts, therefore, should be directed toward winning economic and political reforms and helping the liberals to establish a bourgeois constitutional regime. The moderate view, in one form or another, gained many adherents, and for a while the fervent revolutionism represented by the Liberation of Labor was overshadowed in the Social Democrat Party by it.

Then in 1900 Lenin, having returned from Siberia, to which he had been exiled after his arrest in 1896, joined Plekhanov and his followers in Switzerland. Considerably younger than the now well-ripened leaders of the Liberation of Labor, he was relegated by them to a subordinate position in the councils of the hierarchy, as befitting a talented neophyte. But Lenin's encyclopedic intelligence, incredible vitality, and uncompromising Marxist orthodoxy won the allegiance of the younger members of the group and soon fired even the older comrades. At his instigation a newspaper called *Iskra* (The Spark) was founded, and the organization of the Social Democratic Party along more militant lines was begun.

In 1903, the editorial board of *Iskra,* which consisted of Lenin, Plekhanov, Vera Zasulich, Martov, A. N. Potresov, and P. B. Axelrod, summoned a second congress of the Social Democratic Labor Party. (The first had been an abortive affair held in Minsk in 1898.) Its purpose was ostensibly to bind and unify the scattered, ideologically diverse constituent groups. But the Congress had not proceeded very far when it became clear that the now guiding light of the *Iskraites* (as the members of the Liberation of Labor were called), Lenin, meant not to conciliate differences through compromise but to mold both doctrine and organization firmly by ridding the party of politically uncongenial groups and compelling the rest to bend to militant revolutionary policies by winning majority votes. Debate soon came to center on what at first glance seemed to many to be an obscure and not very significant point.

Two drafts of the proposed party constitution had been submitted to the party membership, one by Lenin and one by Martov, his old associate in The Union of Struggle for the Liberation of the Working Class. The first article stipulated who might become a member of the party. Martov's proposal was that membership should be afforded to one "who recognizes the Party's program and supports it by material means *and by regular personal assistance under the direction of one of the party organizations.*" (The italics, of course, are added.) Lenin's draft, which was mostly the same, simply changed the italicized words to read: "and by personal participation in one of the party organizations."

Heretofore, Lenin had sat back listening to the debate, pursing his lips characteristically at speeches or actions of which he disapproved but contributing only occasionally. Plekhanov, the most prestigious man there and a notable speaker, had carried the brunt of the Iskrist attack on the Economists, the Bundists, and others. But now Lenin sprang into action. His striking, somewhat Mongolian face tensed. As he argued he stuck his middle fingers in the armholes of his vest and bent the top of his short body slightly forward as if he were casting his points from the depth of his soul. Most of the delegates were dumfounded at what seemed a disproportionate concern with a minor difference of opinion.

Gradually, the crucial principles became clear. In the party program adopted at the congress the delegates agreed that the revolution had to be led by the working class, perhaps in alliance with the peasants, and that there would have to be a "dictatorship of the proletariat" in order "to suppress all attempts at resistance on the part of the exploiters." But Lenin's argument was that left to themselves the workers would dissipate their revolutionary potential by attempting to organize unions for the achievement of economic concessions. They would, therefore, have to be led. This was the role of the Social Democrats, who would be the vanguard of the working class. To be effective the Social Democrats would have to organize in a highly centralized, military manner, and the party must therefore consist of dedicated revolutionaries, not a large number of supporters. Discipline, fervor, self-sacrifice were what was needed.

In the vote on this section of the constitution, Lenin was narrowly defeated. It was agreed to have the broad party open to all who believed in it, which Martov had proposed. But there was still the rest of the constitution, with many similar differences in the drafts, to be voted on. At this point Lenin gained a critical advantage by the withdrawal from the party of the Economists and the Jewish Socialist Bund, the former in protest against the aggressively revolutionary doctrines adopted by the Congress, and the latter because their plank of Jewish autonomy had been turned down. Both groups had supported Martov. When the vote came on Lenin's proposal for a reorganization of the *Iskra* staff, he won by a majority of two. The Social Democratic Party, instead of being unified, was now divided into two factions, Lenin's calling itself Bolsheviki (the Majority), and Martov's accepting the name Mensheviki (the Minority).

Ironically, soon after the congress the Mensheviks actually became the majority, and it was their more flexible policy in enlisting support and cooperating with the more liberally minded revolutionaries that prevailed in the Social Democratic agitation and organization of the workers.

Partly as a result of the influence of the Social Democrats and Socialist Revolutionaries, but probably more because of the brutal obstinacy of the government, the strikes began to assume a recognizably political, revolutionary character.

Leon Trotsky began his career as an active revolutionary in 1897, when he was seventeen years old, and celebrated his nineteenth birthday in prison. This police photograph was taken at the time of his arrest late in 1898. (*Sovfoto*)

London, Aug. 8 [*1903*]. "The Times" [of London] prints a dispatch from Kieff . . . which says that the disaffection among the workingmen is widening, and that disturbances have occurred at Kharkoff, Ikaterinoslaff and other centres. Work over a vast area is stagnant, and the situation is becoming dangerous, the anti-government [parties] being furnished with an excellent handle for their whip by the military rigors shown in the suppression of the right of free speech. The correspondent computes that in July in various parts of Russia two hundred strikers were killed outright and fully two thousand wounded, and says it is agreed on all hands that M. von Plehve [the Minister of the Interior] has a labor problem which will tax all his strength. A considerable portion of industrial Russia is already in a condition bordering upon wholesale anarchy.

"The Morning Leader's" Odessa correspondent asserts that M. von Plehve . . . has availed himself of the labour troubles to institute a system of wholesale arrests of political suspects by the secret police in all Russian industrial centres, and that six hundred were arrested at Odessa alone.

Inevitably, the reverberations of the mounting unrest in the cities added to the tremendous unrest already existing in the countryside.

Over Eighteen Thousand Ravaging Estates—Fear for Kharkoff

———◆●◆———

Peasant Revolt in Russia

They Burn the Chateau of the Duke of Oldenbourg and Ruin His Estate

———◆●◆———

Fear Rising of Peasants

St. Petersburg, Feb. 20 [1903]. A deputation of land owners from the government of Simbirsk, commonly known as "Darkest Russia," arrived here to-day to warn the government that the peasants of Simbirsk, who are among the most enlightened in the empire, have organized a rising which promises to surpass far that of Poltava or Kharkov. The peasants propose to confiscate the land and distribute it among themselves. The landlords appealed to Finance Minister Witte to divert a disturbance by adopting financial measures. But M. Witte referred them to the Department of Police. The landlords therefore departed, declaring that the police were incapable of coping with the emergency.

It was at this juncture, when the conflagration was spreading rapidly and becoming more revolutionary, that public attention was diverted, not without design, by a call to patriotic national unity. For years Russia had been lusting after the peninsular kingdom of Korea, partly as an extension of Manchuria, where Russia had established herself, partly to secure an all-year-round ice-free port on the Pacific, and partly as a blow against Japan, which was rapidly emerging as the most powerful nation in East Asia. The *Tribune,* quoting a report to the United States Government, described the situation as it was in 1901.

The Russo-Japanese War.

Cavalry skirmish at
Anju (Korea).

March 28th, 1904.

The humiliating outcome of the Russo-Japanese War helped precipitate the Revolution of 1905. This portrayal of a skirmish at Anju, Korea, on March 28, 1904, was made by the Japanese artist Koto Okura.

[*July 29, 1901.*] Corea [Korea] is the storm center [of the Far East], if there is one just now. The government of the [Korean] Emperor is a greedy, cruel and rapacious personal despotism, and Russia is playing with the territory as a cat does with a mouse. She is perfecting her railway system in Siberia and Manchuria, and when she is ready she will come down through the Corea peninsular and plant her military and commercial establishments in the magnificent harbor of Masanpho [Masan] in the southeast, whence she can descend upon Japan, and which lies between the British interests in the north and their base in Hong-Kong. To this end Russia seeks to control, or build and control, a railway from the northwestern frontier of Corea, near Mukden, to Masanpho, but her agreeement with Japan forbids her seeking such concessions in Corea.

Despite the agreement, which confined Russian interests to Manchuria and left Korea to Japan as a sphere of influence, the Russians penetrated the peninsula. Relations between Japan and Russia reached a crisis at the beginning of 1904. Negotiations achieved no result, largely because the Russians were convinced that they could easily defeat the "little apes," as some high-ranking officials were reputed to have called the Japanese.

[*Tokio, Feb. 7, 1904.*]   The severance of diplomatic relations between Russia and Japan was confirmed. The Japanese Minister at St. Petersburg informed Count Lamsdorff [the Russian Foreign Minister] of his government's decision . . . and will leave the capital as soon as possible for Berlin.

Japan will unquestionably seize Corea. The indications are that there will be no formal declaration of war. Japan has publicly defined her position and purposes.

The next day, Japan invaded Korea, and the war was on. For the moment at least, public sentiment in Russia rallied to the government, and there was a marked subsiding of demonstrations. Many Russians probably indulged the belief that once victory was secured a change in the government's attitude would be forthcoming. But the war turned out to be an immediate and unending series of disasters.

Japan's Ships Sweep Sea

Two Russian Cruisers Destroyed at Chemulpo and Large Transports Taken

Manchuria Invaded in Force

Japanese Seventy Miles East of New-Chwang— Battle Expected at Liao-Yang

Japanese Win on the Yalu

New-Chwang Taken

Kwan-Tung Heights Stormed

Japanese Take Position Thought Impregnable After Sixteen Hours of Fighting

Russians Depressed

Internal Troubles Likely to Follow Port Arthur's Fall

London, June 6 [1904]. Various special correspondents in St. Petersburg report increasing depression in Russia over the prospect of the fall of Port Arthur. "The Daily Mail" gives prominence to a statement "from a Russian correspondent" declaring that Russia will stand or fall by Port Arthur as far as "the government's prestige with the lower classes is concerned."

The terrorists of the Socialist Revolutionary Party punctuated the disillusionment with one of their boldest strikes.

Assassin's Bomb Kills Tsar's Chief Minister In St. Petersburg

Minister of Justice, M. Muravieff, Proceeding to Emperor to Tell of the Crime, Is Stoned by the Populace in Thoroughfare of St. Petersburg

St. Petersburg, Thursday [July 28, 1904]. M. von Plehve, Minister of the Interior, the most influential member of the government and admitted to be the greatest statesman in Russia . . . was blown to pieces this morning about ten o'clock, while on his way to Peterhof to make a report to the Emperor.

His life had long been threatened, consequently elaborate precautions had been taken to protect his movements.

The unfortunate Minister had reached a point within a minute's drive of the Baltic Station, when, just before reaching the bridge over the canal and in spite of many police, a tall, pale, young, bearded individual rushed out of a common hostelry, the Hotel de Varsovie, the lower part of which was a beer house, and with great force and precision hurled a bomb on the cobblestones exactly under M. von Plehve's carriage.

The detonation was terrible and the concussion was such that all the windows of houses were broken within a hundred yards. Out of the dense smoke could be seen black objects being hurled upward.

When the smoke cleared nothing remained but the wheels, springs, frame, pole and a few fragments of the woodwork of the carriage. The unfortunate Minister was literally blown to pieces. His entire face had disappeared. The coachman and likewise the horses were dead.

Lying on the ground was the assassin, wounded in his stomach by pieces of the bomb. He and an associate who had given a signal on the arrival of the Minister were arrested. Five other people were hurt.

The assassination worked as a catalyst. In September representatives of the Union of Liberation, the Socialist Revolutionaries, and other opposition groups met in Paris to form a united front against the regime, and in November leaders of the zemstvos gathered at an informal conference in St. Petersburg.

Russians Ask Freedom

People's Voice Heard

St. Petersburg, Nov. 19 [1904].   Despite the refusal of the Emperor to authorize a meeting, about a hundred representatives of the zemstvos assembled privately here this afternoon and discussed a carefully prepared memorandum, practically embodying a recommendation for a national representative body to have a share in the government. This memorandum will be presented to Emperor Nicholas.

[The document declares] that the "abnormal system of government in Russia is the result of the complete estrangement of the government and people," that the conditions make necessary freedom of conscience, speech and press and the privilege of holding meetings, and asserts that the peasants must be placed on an equality with the other classes. "In order to secure the proper development of the life of the State and the people, it is imperatively necessary that there be regular participation of national representatives, sitting as an especially elected body, to make laws, regulate the revenue, and expenditure and determine the legality of the actions of the administration."

This document . . . is all the more striking and impressive because the [102] zemstvo presidents who signed it, while elected by zemstvo organizations, are confirmed by the government. The signatories also include five marshals of the nobility, whose elections are also confirmed by the government.

The interest in the meetings is intense. The war and all other questions are temporarily forgotten. Liberals from all parts of the Empire are flocking hither, including many from Poland and Finland. The hotel lobbies are crowded, almost resembling convention times in American cities. The most able men in the assembly are counselling moderation and are doing everything possible to prevent demonstrations which might compel interference.

As one prominent member of the zemstvo delegation put it in an interview with newsmen:

[*Nov. 22, 1904.*]   We have put into concrete form our opinion that the present system in the end must spell ruin or revolution. The Emperor knows the character of the men whose names are attached to the memorial. They represent the best blood and thought of the Empire.
WE ARE NOT REVOLUTIONARIES. WE DO NOT BELIEVE THE PEOPLE ARE PREPARED FOR A REPUBLIC. WE SUPPORT THE MONARCHIAL IDEA. BUT WE BELIEVE IT MUST

BE A CONSTITUTIONAL MONARCHY, AND THAT THE EM-
PEROR MUST CHOOSE BETWEEN THE MODERATE PRO-
GRAMME WE OFFER AND EVENTUAL REVOLUTION.

Nicholas did not interfere with the conference.

St. Petersburg, Nov. 25 [1904]. Late this afternoon the Emperor received at the palace at Tsarskoe-Selo . . . four prominent members of
the zemstvo congress, the "First Russian Congress" as it is now called,
and listened to their views. It develops that when the Minister of the
Interior presented the zemstvo memorial and resolutions on November
24 the Emperor was so deeply impressed, both by the contents of the document and by the character of the signers, that he immediately expressed
the desire to receive a deputation of four.

The zemstvo leaders, therefore, went to Tsarskoe-Selo by imperial
command. At their audience, it is understood, they explained fully their
position and reiterated the views expressed in the memorial that the salvation of the empire from ruin by revolution lay in the adoption of the
general ideas expressed in the memorial. The Emperor was greatly impressed by what he heard and asked many questions. While it is understood that he gave no indication of his purpose, the members of the
deputation, when they returned to St. Petersburg, were in high spirits.

The Socialist Revolutionaries and the Social Democrats, now dominated by the Mensheviks, rallied behind the liberals. They all joined in
calling for a constitution, not necessarily a formal document of the
American sort but at least a body of law guaranteeing personal freedom,
to be promulgated by a democratically elected national assembly. However, while the zemstvo leaders courteously submitted their memorial, the
workers and the students demonstrated.

Rioting in Russian Capital

An Immense Throng Gathers to Denounce the Autocratic System and the War—Red Flags Displayed— Charge of Gendarmes

All Russia Stirred by Demand for Constitution

St. Petersburg, Dec. 11 [*1904*]. Over a hundred persons were injured and more than a hundred arrested in riots which began here this afternoon, and which were at last quelled by the police and mounted gendarmes. The authorities last night got wind of the big anti-government demonstration planned for to-day by the Social Democratic Labor Party to demand an immediate end to the war and the convocation of a National Assembly, and leading every paper this morning in black-face type was an explicit warning to the people at their peril to desist from congregating in the Nevsky Prospect near the Kazan Cathedral.

The newspapers' warnings, however, by giving notice to those not apprised of the prospect of a demonstration, defeated the very object for which they were designed, attracting seemingly the whole population of this vast city to the broad thoroughfare.

Long before the hour fixed, despite the pleading of the police, who literally lined the sidewalks, the throngs on the pavements were so dense that movement was almost impossible, while the snow covered boulevard was black with a tangled mass of sleighs, filled mostly with the curious. In the throngs on the sidewalk was practically the whole student body of the capital, including many young women who have always been prominent in Russian liberal and revolutionary movements, and also thousands of workmen belonging to the Social Democratic Labor Party, which had planned the demonstration.

When there was not a single mounted policeman in sight, on the stroke of 1 [o'clock], from the heart of the thickly wedged crowd a blood red flag, like a jet of flame, suddenly shot up. It was the signal.

Other flags appeared in other parts of the crowd, waving frantically overhead; and they were greeted with a hoarse roar, "Down with autocracy!" The students surged into the street singing the "Marseillaise," while innocent spectators, seeking to extricate themselves, crowded into doorways and hugged walls.

Dismounted police made a single attempt to force their way into the crowd to wrest flags from the demonstrators, but the students and the workmen, armed with sticks, stood close and beat back their assailants.

Then like a flash, from behind the Kazan Cathedral, came wheeling a squadron of gendarmerie. The main wedge of the crowd stood fast only a moment or two. There was a sharp rattle of cudgels and sabres, though the wounds showed the police struck principally with the flat of their sabres. The women were especially fierce in their resistance. Many were struck and trampled down, blood streaming from their faces.

While the mob stood, those within managed to throw hundreds of revolutionary proclamations over the heads of their fellows. The police urged their horses fiercely into the crowd, driving those who resisted into the courtyards, the Hotel Europe and the Catholic Church. The intense excitement lasted about ten minutes, after which mounted squads of gendarmerie patrolled the streets and the policemen devoted themselves to keeping the crowd moving.

Two weeks later the Czar gave his reply to the memorial.

St. Petersburg, Dec. 26 [*1904*]. Emperor Nicholas's long expected reform ukase was issued tonight. The document deals, under eight heads, with almost all the subjects brought to the Emperor's attention by the memorial of the congress of zemstvo presidents held here last month, and while not specifically pledging the government to carry out the various reforms in their entirety, as demanded by the memorial, promises that each shall be referred to the Council of Ministers, with orders to report promptly on the fullest measures of relief which can be afforded on the various subjects.

One question not touched by the ukase is that of the Constituent Assembly.

While Emperor Nicholas's manifesto on Russian reforms, coupled with [a] government note of warning on the same subject, leaves no doubt that it is the firm intention of the Emperor to maintain unimpaired the autocratic principle, and not to yield to the zemstvos' plea for a national assembly, the programme of reforms outlined is a broad one, and if it had not been preceded by the agitation of the last few months would probably have been accepted with universal acclaim in Russia as extremely liberal. The [contemplated] raising of the peasants to an equality with other citizens of the empire is practically second only to the emancipation of the serfs, but hardly less important is the [proposed guarantee] of the personal liberties of the people. The proposed increase in the independence and scope of the doumas [municipal councils] and zemstvos, as well as the creation of small zemstvo units, the [suggestions for] the definite protection of the Jews, Armenians and other unorthodox sects and the revision of the press laws are all in line with the zemstvo petition.

The Extreme party, of course, is not satisfied, and many of the Moderate Liberals are disappointed. The government note, threatening drastic measures in case of a continuation of the agitation, is resented deeply by them, and, it is feared, will inflame rather than allay the present agitation.

It was at this moment of bitter dismay that the news arrived of the fall of Port Arthur.

Russians Stunned

St. Petersburg, Jan. 3 [*1905*].   The public seems stunned by the announcement of the fall of Port Arthur. . . . Little had been done to prepare the people, and the impression, despite the heroic nature of the defense, almost produced stupefaction. What will be the immediate effect of the announcement on the internal situation remains to be seen, although it is fully expected to be followed by big demonstrations on the part of the elements which spare nothing to embarrass the government.

Almost immediately after the news came, a strike involving thousands of steel and iron workers broke out at the Neva Works in St. Petersburg and quickly spread to other factories. A mammoth demonstration was scheduled for Sunday, January 22, to be led, not by Social Democrats or by Socialist Revolutionaries, but by a young priest, Father G. A. Gapon, who had won wide popularity among the workers.

Chapter Three

The Revolution
of 1905

Tsar Grants Constitution, Free Speech and Press; Witte the First Premier

---

Imperial Manifesto Announces the End of Autocratic Government in Face of Popular Demand.

LEGISLATIVE ASSEMBLY IS MADE SOURCE OF LEGAL AUTHORITY

Electoral Rights To Be Extended to Classes of the Population Now Deprived of the Privilege of Choosing Members of the Douma.

INVIOLABILITY OF PERSON AND HABEAS CORPUS

In Granting These "Immutable Foundations of Civic Liberty" Emperor Nicholas Calls Upon All Faithful Sons of Russia to Do Their Duty to the Fatherland.

PARADING THOUSANDS SING THE NATIONAL ANTHEM

Count Witte, Through Whose Strength and Persistence the Mighty Result Was Wrought, Will Lead in Coming Reforms — Says America Will Rejoice to Hear the News.

The immense procession of workers and their families, chanting hymns and carrying ikons and portraits of the Czar, wound through the snow-covered streets of St. Petersburg toward the Winter Palace. At its head was Father Gapon,

> the leader and idol of the men, in his golden vestments, holding aloft the cross and marching ahead of thousands of workmen through the Narva Gate.

The marchers brought with them a humble petition addressed to the "Little Father."

> Sire: We, workmen, inhabitants of St. Petersburg, of all classes, our wives, children and indigent parents, come to you, our sovereign, asking for protection. We are poor, persecuted, burdened with labor beyond our strength. We are insulted, treated not as men, but as slaves who ought to bear their cruel fate in silence. We have suffered, but we are being plunged deeper in the mire and deprived of our rights. Uninstructed, stifled by destitution and injustice, we are perishing. We have no strength left.
>
> Sire, we have arrived at the extreme limits of endurance; we have reached the terrible moment when death is preferable to a continuation of our intolerable sufferings. We have left our work and informed our employers that we will not resume until our demands are conceded. . . .
>
> Our first request is that our masters should investigate our case. They have refused. We have been denied the right to put forward our claim, it being held that such right is not recognized by law.

After listing demands for the eight-hour day, wage adjustments, and the correction of a host of abuses, the petition continued:

> Any one of us who dared raise his voice in the interests of the people of the working classes has been thrown into prison or transported. Kind-

51

LIBRARY — Allegheny Campus

The priest Georgy Gapon, who led the massive procession of workers and their families on "Bloody Sunday," was in fact an agent of the Russian secret police, although his work to improve the conditions of the poor was probably sincere. (*Photo from European*)

ness and good feeling have been treated as a crime. The bureaucracy has brought the country to the verge of ruin by a shameful way. It is luring it to its downfall. We have no voice in the heavy burdens imposed; we do not know for whom or why this money is wrung from an impoverished people, and we do not know how it is expended.

This state of things, contrary to divine laws, renders life impossible. It were better that we should all perish, we workers and all Russia. Then good luck to capitalists and exploiters and poor, corrupt officials, robbers of the Russian people.

Assembled before thy palace, we plead for our salvation. Refuse not thine aid, and raise thy people from their tomb. Give them means of working out their own destiny. Rescue them from intolerable officialdom. Throw down the wall that separates; free thy people; order that they rule the country with thee. Create for thy people the happiness wrenched from us, leaving us nothing but sorrow and humiliation. . . . Russia is too great and her needs are too varied and numerous for officials only to rule. National representation is indispensable, as only the people themselves know the country's real needs.

Refuse not thine aid, but order a convocation of representatives of all classes, including workmen. Let all be free and equal in the elections, and to this end permit the election of a constituent assembly by a general secret ballot. That is our chief demand, in which all else centres. It is the sole balm for our wounds, which will otherwise speedily bring us death.

Rebellion in Russia

Hundreds Shot Down by Troops in the Capital

St. Petersburg, Jan. 22 [*1905*]. This has been a day of unspeakable horror in St. Petersburg. An ominous insurrection, which in European capitals is likened to the opening days of the French Revolution, has begun in St. Petersburg. The striking workmen, led by Father Gapon, were swept away by volleys, after a vain attempt to reach the Winter Palace and present their grievances to the Emperor. The workmen have been infuriated by the action of the troops, and in accordance with the decision of their leaders are arming to renew the struggle to-day. Though soldiers guard the principal quarter of the city, the strikers have erected barricades . . . and further bloodshed is expected.

The Minister of the Interior, Sviatopolk-Mirsky, presented to his majesty last night the invitation of the workmen to appear at the Winter Palace this afternoon and receive their petition, but the Emperor's advisers already had taken a decision to show a firm and resolute front.

Palace Square early this morning . . . presented the appearance of a military encampment. Several companies of the Pavlovsky and Preobrajensky guards had piled their arms, while the men were sitting around campfires or stamping on the snow to keep warm. Beyond the infantry stood squadrons of the Chevalier Guards and the Horse Guards, without their lances, cuirasses or the usual gay trappings. The men carried carbines slung across their shoulders, and their stirrups were covered with felt or straw to keep off the cold. All the soldiers wore bashliks or hoods, to protect their ears from the keen wind. A field kitchen was steaming. Many of the men wrestled or boxed, cracking jokes as they rolled on the snow. A long row of ambulances drawn up near the palace served as a grim reminder of the stern business at hand.

Meanwhile [troops] were stationed at all the entrances to the Palace, and cavalry patrols kept promenaders moving along the sidewalk. Sleigh traffic continued uninterrupted. The crowd of strikers in and outside the Admiralty Gardens continued to grow hourly, swelled by arrivals from the Nevsky Prospect, which debouches upon the boulevard skirting the gardens. Barred from the bridges and gates, men, women and children crossed the frozen river and canals on the ice by twos and threes, hurrying to the palace square, where they were sure the Emperor would be present to hear them.

The strikers manned and held a small edifice at the corner of the Gardens and poured out constant objurgations and reproaches at the troops. It was in vain that officers requested them to disperse.

"We have come to present our homage and grievances to the Emperor."

"Let the Emperor come out and hear us; we do not wish to do harm."

"Long live Nicholas II! If he only listens to our grievances, we are sure he will be just and merciful!"

"We cannot longer endure our sufferings. Better die at once and end all!"

Such were the cries repeatedly heard from many strikers.

Many strikers brought their wives and children. "You soldiers are our brothers; you cannot shoot these little ones," they exclaimed. As the pickets and patrols continued driving off the people the demonstrators began to give way, and the bitterest insults and oaths, in which the Russian vocabulary is particularly rich, became frequent.

Every time the troops moved the crowds hissed them. Strikers also gathered at the entrance of the Grand Morskaia and to the avenue leading to the Molkay Canal. The crowd at the latter place swelled to huge proportions, blocking the bridge across the canal.

The order came at 1:30 p.m. to clear the street. The colonel commanding the Horse Guards uttered a short, sharp command; the troopers drew their swords and advanced at a quick trot, and then broke into a gallop, heading straight for the Molkay, where they were lost in a cloud of snow. Shrieks from the wounded resounded. Then came silence, broken only by the galloping of ambulance horses.

The next twenty minutes passed without incident. Nothing indicated the approach of the horrible butchery which was destined to stain the corner of the Admiralty Garden with human blood. The crowd there persisted in refusing to move on, clamoring for the Emperor and continually hurling abuse at the troops, but attempting no violence. Two companies of the Preobrajensky Guards, of which Emperor Nicholas himself was formerly colonel, which had been standing at ease in front of the palace, formed and marched at double quick toward the fatal corner.

Events followed with awful swiftness. The commanding officer shouted: Disperse! Disperse! Disperse! Many in the crowd turned to flee, but it was too late. A bugle sounded, and the men in the front ranks sank to their knees and both companies fired three volleys, the first two with blank cartridges and the last with ball. A hundred bodies strewed the sidewalk.

The priest Gapon, marching at the head of thousands of workmen through the Narva Gate, miraculously escaped a volley which laid low half a hundred persons.

Men and women, infuriated to frenzy by the loss of loved ones, cursed the soldiers while they retreated. Men harangued the crowds, telling them that the Emperor had foiled them, and that the time had come to act. Men began to build barricades in the Nevsky Prospect and at other points, using any material that came to hand, and even chopping down telegraph poles.

Fighting, meantime, continued at various places, soldiers volleying and charging the mob. The whole city was in a state of panic. Women were running through the streets, seeking lost members of their families. Several barricades were carried by the troops.

Toward 8 o'clock in the evening the crowds, exhausted, began to disperse, leaving the military in possession. As they retreated up the Nevsky Prospect the workmen put out all the lights.

Maxim Gorky, the Russian novelist, expresses the opinion that to-day's work will break [the] faith of the people in the Emperor. He said this evening:

"To-day started revolution in Russia. The Emperor's prestige will be irrevocably shattered by the shedding of innocent blood. He has alienated himself forever from his people. Gapon taught the workmen to believe that an appeal direct to the 'Little Father' would be heeded. They have been undeceived. . . . The first blood has been shed, but more will follow. It is now the people against the oppressors, and the battle will be fought to the bitter end."

The events of "Bloody Sunday" touched off strikes and armed clashes between workers and troops throughout Russia.

St. Petersburg, Jan. 26 [1905]. National conditions in Russia appear to be steadily growing worse. The strike has spread to Saratoff, Riga, Narva and Reval, and in Moscow Cossacks dispersed a body of 3,000

Some of the elite corps of the Russian army were made up of Cossacks from southern Russia. Formerly frontiersmen, they were granted privileges in return for military service. (*Photo from European*)

workmen, many persons being wounded. Zemstvos in various parts of the country are sending to the Czar messages urging popular representation in the government.

Torch in Russian Capital

London, Jan. 26.   A dispatch from St. Petersburg, timed 9:26 p.m. to a news agency reports that Pahl's factory and a large cotton mill have been set on fire and are burning fiercely.

The turmoil spread to the subject nations of the Russian Empire—the Poles, the Finns, and the Latvians, among others.

Anarchy in Polish Capital

Wholesale Pillage at Warsaw by Frenzied Throngs of Workmen

Warsaw, Jan. 29 [*1905*].   The strike disorders are becoming more serious. The ordinary life of the city is entirely suspended.

St. Petersburg, Jan. 30 [*1905*].   The situation in Poland is increasingly threatening, especially in Warsaw and Lodz. In the latter place, it is reported, 100,000 men are out on strike.

Fighting in Finland

Thirty Persons Reported Wounded at Helsingfors

Revolt More Menacing

All Russia in Tumult

Riga Beyond Control—Civil War in Caucasus—Strikes in Siberia

The terrorists struck at the government in their usual fashion.

Czar's Uncle, Leader of the Russian Autocracy, Assassinated at Moscow

Grand Duke and His Carriage Blown to Pieces—The Assassin Captured —Consternation at Court

New Impulse Given to the Popular Agitation

Moscow, Feb. 18 [*1905*]. Within the walls of the far famed Kremlin, and almost underneath the historical tower from which Ivan the Terrible watched the heads of his enemies falling beneath the axe on the famous Red Square, and within a stone's throw of the great bell of Moscow, Grand Duke Sergius, uncle and brother-in-law of Emperor Nicholas, and the chief of the reactionaries, met a terrible death shortly before 3 o'clock this afternoon. The deed was committed by a single Terrorist, who threw beneath the carriage of the grand duke a bomb charged with the same high explosive which wrought Minister Plehve's death.

The assassin belongs to the noted "fighting group" of the Socialist Revolutionary Party, which has removed other prominent officials, and long ago passed sentence of death upon Grand Duke Sergius.

Even moderates who ordinarily disapproved of terrorist tactics welcomed the removal of the despised Sergius. The government was shaken— by the assassination, by the upheaval in general, by its own inability to deal with the situation. Nicholas now displayed a crucial indecisiveness. He had condoned the dispersal of the "Bloody Sunday" demonstration with troops, but he had not ordered the actual firing on the workers and was upset by it. In order to make amends, he received a delegation of workmen a few days after the massacre and promised to remove the causes that led to the strike, "in so far as they are economic." He also donated $25,000 in the name of the imperial family for the relief of the families of the victims. His paternalistic concern for the people was not a pretense, but he was unable to comprehend the qualitative difference between the strikes and agitation that had marred his entire reign and the nascent revolution occurring now. He continued to listen to Pobedonostsev, who inflexibly insisted that no concessions whatsoever should be made. However, the consistent battering with simple, clear-cut demands for which people were dying could not fail to impress him. He tarried, listening to advice, wondering, giving contradictory orders, until he finally reached a half-hearted decision.

St. Petersburg, March 3 [*1905*]. At the Alexandra Palace at Tsarkoe Selo, surrounded by the Ministers and a few members of the Court, and with the Empress at his side, Emperor Nicholas this afternoon affixed his signature to a rescript containing his majesty's decree to give elected representatives of the people an opportunity to express their views in the preparation of the laws of the Empire.

This is the autocracy's final response to the agitation which has brought Russia in the last few months almost to the brink of revolution. Its import must not be misunderstood. For the present, at least, it involves no change in the system of autocracy, and it means neither a constitution nor a national assembly. At the same time it recognizes the principle of the people's right to be heard regarding laws under which they must live.

The promise satisfied no one, and the agitation for a constitution became more concertedly organized. In May, representatives of fourteen professional unions (unions of lawyers, doctors, university professors, teachers, engineers, journalists, and the like) established a central committee, the Union of Unions, and put forth demands for a constituent assembly elected by universal suffrage. In July, a Peasants' Union was organized, largely by the Socialist Revolutionaries, and it too adopted a plank calling for a constituent assembly, while also demanding equal civil rights for the peasants and distribution of the land. The Social Democrats stepped up their organizational campaign among the workers, supporting the demand for a constituent assembly along with more radical measures.

Meanwhile, the war with Japan had turned into an utter rout of the Russians. Mukden was captured, and the Japanese Navy under Admiral Heihachiro Togo easily demolished the Russian fleet in the straits of Tsushima. The Russians, defeated in war and confronted with virtual revolution at home, had no choice but to ask for peace. They sent word that they were willing to accept the good offices of the President of the United States, Theodore Roosevelt, who had offered at the very beginning of the war to mediate.

So far, the military had remained loyal. The troops in the Far East had fought with their usual resigned gallantry, and despite pleas from the strikers, the soldiers assigned to domestic duty had fired upon them. As long as the troops could be relied upon, the government was safe. But the military defeat inevitably tended to demoralize the armed forces. This was especially true in the navy, where there had long been serious discontent because of the wretched conditions of shipboard life and where, also, the Social Democrats had managed to win a great deal of influence. When the crew of the battleship *Potyomkin*, which was stationed in the Black Sea, staged a demonstration in protest against the serving of foul meat, the officers, quite in accord with naval custom, threatened to hang the ringleaders. The crew mutinied.

Odessa, Wednesday [*June 28, 1905*]. The red flag of revolution is hoisted at the masthead of the Kniaz Potemkine, Russia's most powerful battleship in the Black Sea, which now lies in the harbor in the hands of mutineers.

The captain and most of the officers were murdered and thrown overboard in the open sea, and the ship is completely in possession of the crew and a few officers who have thrown in their lot with the mutineers.

From the harbor at Odessa, the mutinous crew of the *Potyomkin* bombarded the city in support of the revolutionaries. On the steps leading to the waterfront Cossacks fired upon unarmed demonstrators during the uprising. (*Keystone View Co.*)

The guns of the Kniaz Potemkine command the city and in the streets masses of striking workmen who yesterday fled before the volleys of the troops are now inflamed by the spectacle of open revolt on board an imperial warship, and are making a bold front against the military.

Although the mutineers succeeded in inducing only one other battleship of the Black Sea Fleet to join them, and the *Potyomkin*, after frantically steaming to Rumania, surrendered, the episode made it evident that disaffection was spreading to the armed forces. The revolutionaries took heart, but the liberals, particularly the more moderate among them, were afraid that the situation was getting out of hand, and pleaded with Nicholas for generous concessions. The reactionaries urged him to stand firm, to suppress the dissidents now while he still could.

Czar Grants Assembly

A Meagre Measure
of Popular Government Conceded

St. Petersburg, Aug. 8 [1905]. The Russian National Assembly, the first gathering of the representatives of the Muscovite people since Emperor Alexei Michaelovitch summoned the last zemsky sobor in the seventeenth century, will be proclaimed on Saturday next [August 19].

The National Assembly will be a consultative organization in connection with the Council of the Empire, and not a legislative body. The powers of the Emperor remain theoretically absolute. As the Emperor is the supreme law giver and autocrat, the decisions of the Douma [the National Assembly—Duma] have only a recommendatory and not a binding force, though the rejection of any legislative measure by a two-thirds majority of both houses is sufficient to prevent that measure from becoming law.

The suffrage, though wide, is not extended to the entire nation. It is based on property qualification, the peasantry having a vote through membership in communal organizations. A considerable number of the residents of the cities, possessing no lands, together with women, soldiers, civil officials, etc., are without suffrage.

Douma Coldly Received

St. Petersburg, Aug. 21 [*1905*]. The "Novoe Vremya" and the "Slovo" unreservedly praise the Douma scheme. The other two St. Petersburg newspapers, however, fail to show much enthusiasm. While half-heartedly admitting that the project makes for improvement, these latter papers freely criticize the limitation of the powers of the Douma and ask for an extension of the freedom of the press, freedom of meeting and political amnesty.

Prince Ouktomsky, Editor of the "Vedomosti," says,

"The project dissipates the illusion that the government would meet the hopes of the liberal majority. The Douma question has been settled by admitting only loyal subjects, cultivating ideals of autocratic authority."

The principal objection to the project is the high qualification necessary to city voters, ranging from $675 annually in St. Petersburg and Moscow, to $400 in the smaller towns. This, it is held, will exclude the vast majority of educated persons from suffrage. Peasant representation, however, is fully assured everywhere.

Representation was bestowed upon the peasants because the government assumed that, despite Socialist Revolutionary agitation and sporadic outbursts of violence, their political instincts were essentially conservative, that they were in the final analysis loyal to the "Little Father."

The zemstvo leaders and other moderate liberals decided to accept the Duma prescribed by Nicholas as a means of pressing for greater reform. Inadequate though the grant was, it was at least a beginning. Moreover, they were leary about inciting further disorders. But the people in general —particularly the workers, who were disenfranchised, but also a good many of the members of the professional unions who had pledged themselves to the demands for a constituent assembly, as well as the students— were not so acquiescent.

Moscow in Rebellion

Moscow, Oct. 10 [*1905*]. The majority of the factory workmen here, especially in the great industrial quarter of Zamoskvoretch across the river, joined the strike of printers and bakers to-day. The movement threatens to become general, though it is opposed by a strong minority of the workmen.

The workmen generally are demanding an eight-hour day and a large increase in wages. Among their demands is one for the abolition of religious lectures by priests in the factories and the substitution of lectures on economic and political subjects. . . .

Political questions have been forced to the front in the demands of the men. Agitators are openly preaching a revolution and inciting the workmen, many of whom are well armed with revolvers, to attack the Cossacks.

Strike Sweeps Nation

St. Petersburg, Oct. 18 [*1905*].   The strike at Moscow has given an impetus to the new wave of strikes and disorders which is sweeping over the country and promises a repetition of the period of stress that prevailed in January and February last, though, it is hoped, on a less serious scale. Besides the tumult in St. Petersburg and Moscow, strikes and disorders are reported from Saratoff, Kieff, Kazan, Kharkoff and other cities, while the strike movement has again broken out in Warsaw.

A large part of the working population seems to be inspired by a spirit of unrest. The movement is largely political and is engineered by the Social Democratic and Social Revolutionary parties, many of the leaders of which deplore the outbreak at this time, as it will interfere with the projected campaign of the parties in the elections in the Douma. They say, however, that it was necessary to take advantage of the outbreak at Moscow, even though they were not fully prepared for the movement.

The men in the Nevsky Works on the Schlüsselburg road, dissatisfied with the exclusion of the working classes from the Douma, struck to-day and forced the men in the Pahl Cotton Mill and other concerns to join them.

A regiment of Cossacks and sappers and infantry were called and were fired on by the strikers and stoned. The troops had been instructed not to fire on the strikers, and retired after firing in the air.

A railroad strike beginning in St. Petersburg and Moscow within a few days turned into a general strike.

All Russia Rising in a Mighty Revolt

Professional Men and Workers Unite to Paralyze Every Branch of Social Activity

Raise Red Flag, Demand Republic

Disorder Stayed and Troops Stand Ready to Put Down Riots

Train Tie-Up Absolute

Freight Blockade at Frontier

Warsaw Station Is Burned

Incendiaries at Work in Polish Capital Where Troops and Police Are Virtually Helpless

Virtually all work stopped. Lawyers would not take cases. Juries refused to sit. Officials stayed away from their offices, teachers from their classrooms. University students, who had been permitted by a reform decreed in August to use their lecture halls for discussion, conducted public meetings thinly disguised as student assemblies.

St. Petersburg, Saturday [*Oct. 28, 1905*]. At the meeting last night at the university, which was attended by thousands of striking workingmen and their sympathizers, the scene beggared description. In the great open-air court, with no light except a few flickering candles on a hastily constructed tribune, from four thousand to five thousand workmen, students and professional men stood wedged together in the cold and wet snow fall listening to revolutionary harangues.

Another great meeting was held in the central hall of the university, and scores of smaller meetings of the separate trades and professions were held in the other rooms of the building. Halls were set aside for teachers, physicians, bank clerks, journalists, printers, chinovniks, pharmacists, women, engineers, lawyers, tailors and persons of other callings and trades, and a room was even set aside for noncommissioned officers of the army, but only a half dozen of these were present.

One such meeting, held in the Technological Institute, on the night of October 26, consisted of about eighty delegates from the various factories in St. Petersburg. They constituted the first elected body of the striking

workers, and this Soviet (the Russian word for council) of Workers'
Deputies, as it called itself, promptly assumed the administration of the
strike.

> The strike committee which is at the helm of the movement here
> is well organized, and sits constantly. Its directions are obeyed un-
> hesitatingly by the workers. One of the members to-day advocated
> attacking the arsenal, but his comrades opposed violence. The com-
> mittee consists of representatives of the Social Democrats, the two factions
> of which have settled their differences and are working in harmony.

The formation of the Soviet was inspired by the Mensheviks, the Bolsheviks joining only reluctantly, but once it got started the two factions,
as well as the Socialist Revolutionaries and persons not members of any
party, worked in utter accord. Its guiding spirit was the zealous young
Menshevik, Leon Trotsky. Soviets began to spring up throughout the
country.

Nicholas wavered, again. His inclination was to follow the advice of
the governor general of St. Petersburg, D. F. Trepov, and put an end to
the hateful business with a crushing display of force. Indeed, he gave
orders more or less to that effect, but only whispered them hesitatingly in
Trepov's ear, then complained to his wife that the governor general himself hesitated. He considered establishing a military dictatorship and
asked his uncle, the Grand Duke Nicholas, to become dictator. However,
the old man, amidst a flood of tears, threatened to shoot himself then and
there if the Czar foisted the job on him. On the other hand, some of
Nicholas's ministers were vigorously insisting that he give in to the liberals
before the country was torn apart by the raging mobs. Most important of
these ministers was Count Sergey Witte, who had just returned from
Portsmouth, New Hampshire, something of a national hero after winning
from the Japanese (with President Theodore Roosevelt's help) a much
better peace treaty than Russia expected. Witte, with his usual self-
assurance, which Nicholas both envied and despised, laid the question
before his monarch in cold terms: Nicholas must either go all out in an
attempt to crush the rebellion or he must make concessions.

Czar Bows to Nation's Will

Russian Autocracy Forced to Grant the Demand of the People for Freedom

Premier's Message to America

Count Witte Heads Cabinet—Signs of Cessation of Disorders in the Empire

St. Petersburg, October 30 [1905], *midnight.* "I am sure the American people, who understand what freedom is, and the American press, which voices the wishes of the people, will rejoice with the friendly Russian nation at this moment, when the Russian people have received from his imperial majesty the promises and the guarantees of freedom, and will join in the hope that the Russian people will wisely aid in the realization of these liberties by co-operating with the government for their peaceful introduction. Only thus will it be possible to secure the full benefits of the freedom conferred upon the people."

Count Witte, Russia's first Premier, to-night sent the above message to the American people through the Associated Press. He had just arrived at his residence . . . from Peterhof, where, at the Alexander Palace, the Emperor two hours before had given his final approval to a manifesto and to a Programme which will forever end the rule of absolutism exercised by him and his Romanoff ancestors for three hundred years.

St. Petersburg, Oct. 30 [1905]. The text of the Imperial manifesto, granting a real measure of self-government to the people, is as follows:

"We, Nicholas the Second, by the Grace of God Emperor and Autocrat of All the Russias, Grand Duke of Finland, etc., declare to all our faithful subjects that the troubles and agitation in our capitals and in numerous other places fill our heart with excessive pain and sorrow.

"The happiness of the Russian sovereign is indissolubly bound up with the happiness of our people and the sorrow of our people is the sorrow of the sovereign.

"From the present disorders may arise great national disruption. They menace the integrity and unity of our empire.

"The supreme duty imposed upon us by our sovereign office requires us to efface ourself and to use all the force and reason at our command to hasten in securing the unity and co-ordination of the power of the central government, and to assure the success of measures for pacification in all circles of public life, which are essential to the well being of our people.

"We therefore direct our government to carry out our inflexible will in the following manner:

"First—To extend to the population the immutable foundations of civic liberty, based on the real inviolability of person, freedom of conscience, speech, union and association.

"Second—Without suspending the already ordered elections to the state duma, to invite to participation in the duma, so far as the limited time before the convocation of the duma will permit, those classes of the population now completely deprived of electoral rights, leaving the ultimate development of the principle of electoral right in general to the newly established legislative order of things.

"Third—To establish as an unchangeable rule that no law shall be enforceable without the approval of the state duma, and that it shall be possible for the elected of the people to exercise real participation in the supervision of the legality of the acts of the authorities appointed by us.

"We appeal to all faithful sons of Russia to remember their duty toward the Fatherland to aid in terminating these unprecedented troubles and to apply all their forces in co-operation with us in the restoration of calm and peace upon our natal soil.

"Given at Peterhof, October 30, in the eleventh year of our reign.

NICHOLAS."

A perusal of the manifesto shows how complete is the Emperor's abdication of his autocratic power. The style of the document is clear and direct and devoid of the verbose, vague and bombastic phraseology which heretofore has characterized his majesty's manifestoes. It not only betrays real authorship, but shows that the Emperor at last has bowed to the inevitable. He does not even conceal the fact that the discontent and agitation of his subjects have driven him to take this step, and practically yields everything—civil liberty, the inviolability of person, and liberty of conscience, speech and assembly. He not only converts the farcical imperial duma, with only consultative power into a true legislative assembly, without the assent of which no measure shall become law and before which all government authorities must answer, but promises, eventually, general suffrage.

The title, "Autocrat of All the Russias," with which the manifesto begins, now takes its place with the title of the "King of Jerusalem," borne by the King of Spain and the Emperor of Austria, and with other obsolete titles of European sovereigns.

The popular response was ambivalent.

St. Petersburg, Oct. 31 [*1905*]. The strike committee this afternoon decided to continue the strike, joining the students in their demand for the deposition of General Trepoff, general amnesty, the removal of the troops twenty miles from the city and the creation of a national militia.

All Russia to-day celebrated enthusiastically the Emperor's gift of freedom, which the greater part of the people received with deepest joy, though in St. Petersburg, Moscow and other cities Socialists and revolutionists organized anti-government demonstrations and red flag parades, which, with the patriotic manifestations, led to a number of conflicts between the "reds" and "whites" as the anti-government and royalist factions are respectively termed. On the whole, the day passed more quietly in Russia than had been expected, though a number of collisions between the people and the troops were reported.

However, the major political demands of the workers had been met. Despite the prodding of the revolutionaries, the workers were not interested in turning the strike into a socialist revolution. A spontaneous back-to-work movement began, and the strike was called off. Another call for a general strike a few weeks later was largely ignored. In November, serious mutinies broke out in the armed forces, but these were eventually suppressed by the government. The workers, the liberal intellectuals and professionals, and the soldiers now settled down to Russia's first experience in representative government.

Chapter Four

Czarism's Last Chance

FORCE TO RULE IN TSAR'S REFORMS IN HIS EMPIRE

New Premier Announces Policy of Progress as One of the Strong Hand.

DENOUNCES DOUMA AS INCAPABLE

Says It Was Not Representative and That the Tsar Does Not Favor Reaction.

WOULD GIVE PEASANTS LAND

Imperial Funds Advance on All Continental Bourses, Making Good Gains for the Day.

Even before the Duma convened, storm clouds appeared in the political sky. Once the worst disorders were brought to an end, the government felt perfectly free to tighten the reins. Limitations were imposed upon the freedom of the press. The right of assembly was restricted, and the structure and powers of the new legislature as defined in the Fundamental Laws promulgated shortly before the Duma opened belied the promise implicit in the October Manifesto. An upper chamber of the Duma was established, half of whose members were appointed by the Czar and the other half elected indirectly. The Czar could veto all legislation, ministers were to be responsible to him, not to the Duma, and the people's representatives in the assembly were denied effective control over the national purse. When the Duma was not in session the government had the power to enact laws, although these were supposed to be subject to approval by the Duma when it reconvened. Count Witte, at whose urging the October Manifesto was issued, now completely lost the confidence of the liberals, who wrongly held him responsible for the Fundamental Laws. The Czar, who deeply resented Witte for giving him unpleasant advice, gladly accepted the premier's resignation, replacing him with the more congenial I. L. Goremykin. Yet many people believed that the Duma was a first step toward a parliamentary government for Russia.

Another alarming development was a wave of pogroms against the Jews. These attacks had been increasing in number and ferocity since 1903, and murder and arson now swept through the pales of settlement (the areas in which Jews were legally compelled to live). The government made no serious attempt to protect the victims.

A New Russian Peril

Bureaucracy Rampant

Massacres of Jews and Death
Of Count Witte Advocated

St. Petersburg, March 11 [1906]. Some of the reactionary organizations are pushing the agitation against the radical elements to a dangerous point. At the Horse Guard Riding school, the fighting society of the "League of the Russian People" held a meeting and listened to inflammatory speeches by Dr. Doubrovin and Professor Nickolsky, two extremist leaders, in which the orators openly summoned their followers, the Black Hundreds, to kill the Jews and hang Count Witte.

Prince Mestchersky, Editor of the "Grashdanin," who supported [Count Witte], charges the bureaucracy with support of the court clique which is opposing the plans of the Cabinet and with inciting class hatred and strikes in order to make the National Assembly a failure. As proof of the complicity of the bureaucracy, Prince Mestchersky prints [in the "Grashdanin"] a proclamation against the Jews which, he asserts, was printed in the office of the police with the approval of the censor and widely distributed. The proclamation, which is addressed to workmen and peasants, says that the authors of Russia's misfortunes are the Jews, who throughout the world hate Russia and want to rob the peasants of their land and make them slaves, "unfrock the priests and turn the churches into Jewish stables and pigsties." The proclamation also asserts that the Armenians, English and Germans want to destroy Russia and divide the country among its enemies. The proclamation calls Count Witte a supporter of the Jews and the chief enemy of the country, and summons the faithful, wherever they find Jews, to "tear the Christ sellers to pieces."

A few months earlier, the radical left had launched an attack on the forthcoming Duma.

St. Petersburg, Nov. 11 [1905]. Perhaps the most interesting phase of the confused situation in Russia caused by the sudden loosing of all the political forces is the attitude of the Social Democrats, who claim all the credit for the overthrow of absolutism and who are determined that they shall not be cheated of the fruits of victory by bogus Liberal leaders who took no part in the real contest.

Not only a democratic republic, but a universal socialistic Utopia is their dream. Their far-reaching programme as announced in two newspapers which have just been launched, the "Novaia Zhizn" ("New Life") and "Nashalo" ("The Beginning"), in which their aims and views are set forth, will repay careful consideration on the part of foreign students of the present political struggle in Russia. The staffs of the papers are composed of forty of the most brilliant writers in Russia, including Maxim Gorky and Kieff, author of "The Red Laugh."

Political visionaries those men may be, but they have embraced the doctrine of international socialism with their whole hearts, and are bound to exercise great influence on Russian thought in the present chaotic conditions. They openly scorn the teachings of history, claiming the world is entering on a new stage of social and political evolution. After the complete overthrow of the present regime in Russia, they propose to erect upon the ruins a new politico-social edifice which will form the nucleus of the future utopian system of international democracy and the achievement of political equality.

Gorky makes a scathing characterization of the attitude of the bourgeoisie, in which he classes the Zemstvoists and other Constitutionalists who now, he says, would like to play the part of "the progenitors of Mark Twain," adding: "While the workmen's army marched to battle they hung in the rear, but when the army returned after destroying the outer bulwarks of the autocracy, they were at the head singing songs of triumph."

The Social Democrats and the Socialist Revolutionaries decided to boycott the elections to the "bourgeois" legislature and to intensify their agitation for a socialist revolution, with the result that the liberals won a disproportionate number of seats. Of the 486 representatives elected, 179 belonged to the Constitutional Democratic party (the Kadets, as they were called), which consisted mostly of the progressive liberals, such as members of the professional unions and militant zemstvo representatives, who were determined to press for the extension of democracy and the enactment of social reform. They were led by the liberal historian Paul Milyukov. The second largest group, with 94 representatives, was the Trudoviki (Toilers), which was more a caucus than a party and quite close to the moderate Socialist Revolutionaries in outlook; indeed, it included some S.R.'s who defied the party's boycott of the elections. In addition, there were 101 nonpartisans, most of whom were liberal or radical in their sympathies, 18 Social Democrats, who like the S.R.'s in the Trudoviki defied the boycott; and 12 Octobrists, who advocated strict compliance with the

October Manifesto and Fundamental Laws. The rest belonged to relatively conservative or national groups. Thus the Duma was overwhelmingly Left-oriented. Nevertheless, because of the attacks on it by the Social Democrats and Socialist Revolutionaries, it had little real support among the workers and peasants, many of whom voted for Kadets and Trudoviki simply because there was no one of more revolutionary persuasion running.

The tone set at the opening session was distinctly hostile.

Emperor Opens Russian Douma In Great Pomp

Tsar Promises to Keep Inviolate Institutions He Has Granted and Reminds Deputies That Order and Justice Are Necessary

Parliament Hears In Sullen Silence

M. Petrunkevitch in Fiery Speech. Calls Upon the Members to Demand Amnesty for Political Prisoners, That the Jails May Be Emptied

St. Petersburg, Thursday [*May 10, 1906*]. . . . The ceremony at the palace was set for one o'clock. . . . Accepting papers from the Chamberlain, the Emperor proceeded to read the speech from the throne.

The message in reality was less a throne speech than a greeting and required only three minutes for its delivery. Emperor Nicholas read slowly. The admirable and even cordial tone of the sovereign in renew-

Nicholas II addressing the Duma. (*The Bettmann Archive*)

ing his pledges and asking the co-operation of parliament for the regeneration of the country was only negatively satisfactory.

Courtiers and spectators other than members of the national parliament, led the cheering, but the members were ominously silent, expressing neither approval nor disapproval. What rankled most was the failure of the Emperor to mention amnesty [for political prisoners], and later, when the members assembled in the Tauride Palace, away from the spell of the throne room, many of them were with difficulty restrained from precipitating matters by offering resolutions on the subject.

Weakened as it was by the attacks from both the right and the left, the Duma at the very beginning of its shaky existence had to tackle the most difficult and complicated problem facing Russia. Revolts had been frequent in the agricultural areas, and finally late in 1905 there began a large-scale convulsion that got decidedly worse over the winter.

The Peasants Arming

At least one meeting of the First Duma was held in the woods. (*The Bettmann Archive*)

During its brief history the First Duma was little more than a debating society whose decisions the government heeded or not as it chose. (*Photo from European*)

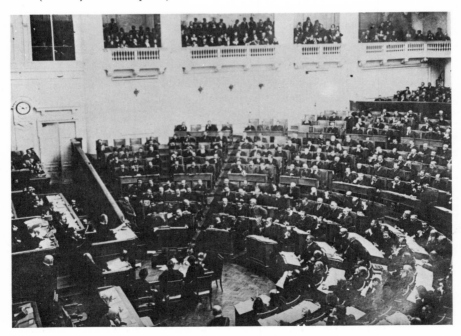

St. Petersburg, March 24 [1906]. A great change seems to have come over the spirit of the peasants during the winter. Whatever troubles are reported the peasants invariably are shown to be resisting the rural guards, and troops are sent to restore order. At Kolpino, almost at the gates of St. Petersburg, peasants who were cutting trees in the forest put to flight a number of guards sent against them.

Near Pskoff, the peasants who decided not to pay taxes, arranged a system of trumpet signals and on the appearance of the guards escorting the tax collectors the peasants from the whole countryside were summoned, armed with scythes, pitchforks and clubs.

The Council of the Empire, by a vote of 49 to 15, has adopted [a] measure to grant a loan of $5,000,000 to landlords who suffered from the agrarian troubles.

The October Manifesto had little meaning for the peasants. Constitutional government was all well and good, but their overwhelming desire was for land, free land, land of their own. If parliamentary democracy were to find a strong popular base to sustain it against both the reactionaries and the extreme socialists, the Duma would have to proceed quickly to agrarian reform.

[May 16, 1904.] Careful examination of the needs of the peasantry and the measures called for by them will form parliament's next task. The rural population is impatiently awaiting the satisfaction of agrarian needs. Parliament would not be doing its duty if it did not make a law for the satisfaction of these needs by the aid of the crown domains [and] monastic lands and the expropriation of land belonging to the owners of the estates.

A plan was drawn up by the Kadets in cooperation with the Trudoviki and presented to Nicholas. The Czar's reply was a firm no.

Russia Facing Revolution

A General Strike on Monday Threatened— Movement Spreads Along the Black Sea— The Peasants Deeply Stirred

St. Petersburg, May 26 [1906]. The lower house of parliament to-day indignantly rejected the government's policy as presented by Premier

Goremykin, and, with only seven members dissenting, voted a lack of confidence in the ministry, practically throwing down the gauntlet to the bureaucracy with a demand for the retirement of the present Cabinet and its supersession by a ministry approved by the majority of the house.

The spirit of revolution is in the air and a conflict between the crown and the nation now appears to be inevitable.

While the Premier's statement promised cooperation with the lower house "in so far as the latter does not transgress the limits of the fundamental laws," it recognized the agrarian question as paramount, proposing to remedy the deficiency in land through the operation of an agrarian bank and migration to Siberia. The expropriation of appanages of the crown and Church and private lands was held to be inadmissible. The right of investigation of administrative acts, the statement added, belonged to the crown, the house having only the power of interpolation. Amnesty, Premier Goremykin said, was solely the prerogative of the Emperor.

The Premier's words seemed to arouse all the latent resentment in the hearts of the members. The Constitutional Democratic leaders for the first time gave free range to their passion. With biting words, speaker after speaker declared the government's programme inadmissible and said that the ministry must give way to a cabinet in which the people have confidence.

The Czar did not even consider the demand to dismiss his ministers and establish a cabinet responsible to the parliament, and he refused to cede the other points made by the Duma, particularly the unthinkable proposal to expropriate lands.

Russia Ready to Rise

St. Petersburg, June 17 [*1906*]. The general situation is hourly growing more disquieting, and the country seems to be on the verge of another upheaval. In St. Petersburg and Moscow the populace is greatly excited, and nothing is talked of except a general political strike to bring the government to its knees. The proletariat leaders, who have been preparing for months for a blow, believe the moment has come. The agrarian troubles now are sufficiently widespread and disorders in the army are rife. The government has openly refused to accede to the demands of parliament, and a rupture is imminent there. The ultimate plans of the leaders depend upon the success achieved, but there are reports that if the government is brought down they are determined that they and not parliament shall take the reins of government.

The government appears to be waiting for the blow to fall before raising its hand, and it is reported that the attempt of several ministers to raise the question at the Cabinet meeting yesterday was apparently fruitless. Heavy patrols have been placed in the streets, but no action has been taken to stop the agitation. The Emperor is reported to be spending most of his time playing tennis at Peterhof.

The Spread of Revolt

More Mutinies in the Caucasus— Peasants Attack Troops

St. Petersburg, July 4 [*1906*]. The military situation in the Caucasus is exceedingly grave. Disaffection has appeared among practically all the troops, including Cossacks. Murder, robbery and general lawlessness are increasing through the mountains. Thirty-five newspapers have been suppressed in Transcaucasia in the last five months.

The agrarian movement in several sections has resulted in conflicts between landowning peasants and peasants who hold no land.

A detachment of Cossacks that had been sent to make retaliations for attacks by striking peasants on rural guards and for the wounding of the commandant met a desperate resistance at the village of Uman, near Kieff.

The Duma obstinately went ahead with the framing of the agrarian law, the very first section of which contained the forbidden provision for expropriaton of Crown and Church lands. This was a challenge that the government had to meet head on.

Douma Dissolved by Czar

The Russian Emperor Takes Action to Maintain the System of Autocracy

St. Petersburg, July 22 [*1906*]. Russia's first experiment in parliamentary government came to an ignominious end this morning with the promulgation of two imperial ukases, the first dissolving the present parliament and providing for the convocation of its successor on March 5, 1907, more than six months hence, and the second proclaiming the capital of Russia and the surrounding province to be in a state of extraordinary security, which is only infinitesimally different from full martial law. Bloodshed [is] anticipated throughout [the] Empire.

Army the Last Hope of Czar

Government and People Arrayed for Struggle Which May Decide Fate of Empire

St. Petersburg, July 22 [*1906*]. With the imperial ukase dissolving parliament . . . the curtain rose upon possibly the last act in the great drama of the Russian revolution. The people and the government now stand face to face, and upon the loyalty of the army depends the immediate issue.

An imperial ukase removes M. Goremykin from the Premiership and appoints M. [Pyotr Arkadyevich] Stolypin Premier. He also retains his present post of Minister of the Interior.

The work of gathering in revolutionary agitators began immediately after the ukase placing St. Petersburg in "a state of extraordinary security" was promulgated, and hundreds of arrests were made before daylight.

The proletariat organizations have been preparing for months for just such provocation to declare open war. A council of workmen's deputies already has been elected at Moscow, and with a similar council here, in conjunction with the Group of Toil of parliament, a rising of the people will be engineered.

Douma Members Flee to Finland

After a hurried secret conference this morning, it was decided, on account of the possibility of . . . the members of the Douma being arrested, that they go immediately to Finland and decide upon the future course to be pursued. Small groups left this city this afternoon and evening by train. It is the plan of the members of parliament to assemble at Viborg. They have drawn up a proclamation to the people, saying that if the authorities prevent them from assembling there, it is their intention to take a steamer and go into the gulf of Finland, and, if pursued by warships, to go to Sweden.

The two hundred Duma representatives who gathered at Viborg issued a manifesto calling upon the populace to follow a course of "passive resistance" by refusing to pay taxes or to obey the military conscription laws until the Duma was convened again. But the appeal, which was essentially for restraint, was ignored. Once again rebellion flared, and this time detachments of the military forces joined in.

Mutineers Hold Sveaborg

Helsingfors, Aug. 1 [*1906*],*1:40 a.m.* Sveaborg is entirely in the hands of the mutineers, who now have in their possession every kind of armament.

Mutiny on Mutiny

St. Petersburg, Aug. 3 [*1906*]. The crews of two Russian cruisers— the Asia and the Pamyat Azova—mutinied and raised the red flag.
Military disorders have broken out at Reval, the capital of Esthonia.

Great Strike Begins

The Censorship, Strict

Nearly 70,000 Men Quit Work in Capital—Firing at Cronstadt

25,000 Armed Miners Join Russian Strike

Thirty Workmen Reported Blown to Pieces by Premature Explosion in Moscow

Bomb Kills Two at Railway Station

Bomb Kills Twenty-Seven

Russian Premier Escapes with Slight Injuries—His Daughter, Secretary and Chief of Guard Dead

Attempt to Kill Him at Home

Was Holding Public Reception—Son Hurt—Two of Conspirators Perish, Two Prisoners— Twenty-Four Persons Injured

General Min Killed

Murdered at Peterhof

Wife Seizes Girl Assassin—Thirty- Two Dead from Bomb

More than 4,000 people were assassinated in 1906 and 1907, most of them officials.

This time, the government, led by Premier Stolypin, acted decisively and effectively. On the one hand, harsh measures were taken to suppress disorders. Trial by military court was instituted for political crimes and every radical leader and terrorist the government could get its hands on was imprisoned, sent to Siberia, or, in the case of proved murderers (of whom there were surprisingly few) executed. The mutinies were stamped out before they had a chance to spread very far. Recalcitrant strikers were made subject to criminal prosecution. On the other hand, Stolypin, who unlike his ministerial predecessors enjoyed the Czar's full confidence, induced Nicholas to divest the state of some 10,000,000 acres of land, sell a portion of his own, and enact an extensive program of agrarian reform.

Equality in Russia

Offices Open to All—Communal System and Poll Tax Abolished

St. Petersburg, Oct. 19 [*1906*].   The government has issued a ukase regarding employment by the state, making all equal before the law and releasing the peasants from the vexatious communal system. It prescribes also that the peasants are now free to choose their place of residence, and abolishes the poll tax from January 1, 1907.

The new proclamation of the Czar relieves the peasant of all the restrictions laid upon him by the communal system, allows him to travel wherever he wishes and to live where he sees fit, abolishes the special courts of law instituted for dealing with mujik offenses, and establishes the fact that henceforth peasants shall have the same civic rights and liberties as all other citizens of the Empire, excepting the Jews and Poles, who are specifically excluded from the benefits of the decree. It is the most sweeping measure and most radical reform that has taken place in Russia since the liberation of the serfs; more important, indeed, and more wide reaching in its effects than the grant by the Czar of a parliamentary form of government to his people a couple of years ago.

Other decrees promoted the transfer of communal land to private ownership and, in general, the transformation of the Russian seignorial system into a system of small private farms.

All the Stolypin laws, both the repressive measures and the reforms, were enacted under Article 87 of the Fundamental Laws, which permitted the government to legislate during the adjournment of the Duma. Despite a change in the franchise greatly restricting the suffrage, the new parliament, to Stolypin's chagrin, was much more radical than the first, primarily because the Social Democrats and Socialist Revolutionaries decided to enter the elections in order to use the Duma as a forum. When the legislature met in March 1907 a fight with the government broke out almost immediately over the Stolypin laws, especially over the agrarian reforms, which were much less radical than those proposed by the First Duma. Again Stolypin acted promptly. He dissolved the Duma and promulgated a new, even more restrictive electoral law.

Apprehensions that these actions by the Czar and his tough-minded prime minister would lead to new uprisings proved unfounded. Many of the revolutionary and even liberal leaders had been arrested or forced to flee into exile. Discipline had been restored in the armed forces. The agrarian reforms, though inadequate, took the edge off the peasants' fury. But most important, perhaps, was the inertia that overcame the people— as if they had been exhausted by the great expenditure of energy during the past few years or enervated by disappointment at the modest results. The number of strikes dropped to a comparative handful. Whereas in 1905, 1,424,328 people took part in political strikes, in 1910 there were only 3,777. During the same period the number of participants in economic strikes dropped from 1,438,841 to 42,846. The Social Democrats were almost completely occupied with internecine political fights between the Mensheviks and Bolsheviks. The Socialist Revolutionaries similarly disintegrated, especially after it was revealed that Evno Azef, the long-time head of the Terrorist Organization, was in fact a spy for the Secret Police even at the time when he had organized the execution of his superior, the Minister of the Interior, V. K. Plehve. Both radical parties resorted to armed robbery of banks and government funds to replenish their diminished treasuries. A certain amount of revolutionary activity, especially terrorism, continued, but it excited little popular response and seemed to have no definite purpose. Finally, the elections to the Third Duma, held according to Stolypin's new electoral law, returned a safe majority of government supporters.

Czar Autocrat Still

Declaration of the Government Read in the Duma

St. Petersburg, Nov. 29 [*1907*]. The keynote of the declaration of the government, read by Premier Stolypin before the Duma to-day, was a reiteration of the idea of the autocratic power of the Emperor as the sole guarantee of security and welfare in an era of disorder. The announcement was made also that the Duma is expected to take its cue from the administration in the matter of legislation, and the Premier outlined what future legislation was expected. He excoriated the radical parties as fosterers of crime and sedition, and said their excesses would be tolerated no longer.

Among these prisoners beginning the long journey into exile in Siberia was the seasoned revolutionary Josif Vissarionovich Dzhugashvili, who used the name Stalin (second from the left, front, indicated by an X). (*Sovfoto*)

The Premier attacked university autonomy, and said that nothing would be permitted to stop the government from taking an active course in introducing order and discipline in the schools. The government was convinced of the necessity of the speediest possible abandonment of martial law and a return to normal conditions, but had decided to make use of all measures possible to strengthen judicial procedure and hasten its operations, and he counted on the help of the representatives of the people in uncovering illegal acts of government officials. The government was inclined, the Premier said, to punish the arbitrary use of power as severely as slackness of administration.

Once order had been restored, the government would be able to devote all its attention to the internal development of the empire, and the settlement of the agrarian problem was first condition to this end. The Premier recommended the inviolability of private property and the allotment of certain lands to small proprietors. On these principles he based his hopes for a solution to the agrarian problem, and he said he hoped the Douma would assist the government by enacting the agrarian laws proposed by it.

Premier Stolypin's utterances marked the turning point in the attitude of the ministry toward the country, and his reiteration of the terms of the autocracy, as well as his appeal to the patriotic imaginations of the Russians, in marked contrast to all former utterances, indicate that the government has taken the offensive and does not intend to allow the Douma's work to proceed on the Douma's initiative, but is determined to take the reins into its own hands. . . . That the domineering tone of Stolypin met with undoubted success in the Right half of the Douma was shown by almost uninterrupted applause and the great ovation to him at the close of the session.

Chapter Five

War and
Revolution

Czar of Russia Abandons Throne; Army Revolts and Joins People

Duma Leaders in Complete Control After Fierce Battles; Protopopoff Reported Killed

New Cabinet Is Formed; Prince Lvoff Now Premier

One effect of the crushing of the Duma was to remove a potential check to the influence of individual ministers, at a time when international relations were growing ominously brittle.

The foreign minister, A. P. Izvolsky, although a skilled and by no means stupid diplomat, was given to grandiose and dangerous schemes to enhance Russia's prestige—and incidentally his own. In pursuit of one of these he arranged, without consultation, a secret meeting with the Austrian foreign minister in September 1908, during which an agreement was reached permitting Austria to annex Bosnia and Herzogovina, two Serbian provinces already controlled by the Dual Monarchy, in return for Austrian support of Russian demands for the opening of the Dardanelles and the Bosporus to the passage of warships. The closure of these straits, agreed to by the major powers in a convention signed in 1841 and many times renewed, prevented the Russian navy from direct year-round access to the western seas, since the northern ports were frozen in during much of the winter. England was absolutely determined to maintain the convention in order to protect her rapidly expanding interests in the Middle East.

Austria acted swiftly, annexing Bosnia and Herzogovina on October 6. The international response was explosive. Serbia prepared for war. Russian opinion—including that of the Czar, who was only vaguely, if at all, aware of what Izvolsky had done—rallied passionately to the Serb cause, and a shrill cry for war was raised. Germany, which, with Italy, was bound to Austria by a defense treaty, the Triple Alliance, signified her support for her Teutonic ally. France, which hated Germany because of the occupation of Paris and the annexation of Alsace-Lorraine after the War of 1870, was steadfast—indeed, eager—in her alliance with Russia. Relations between France and Italy were badly strained by conflicting colonial ambitions in North Africa. England, antagonized by the German naval construction program which threatened her supremacy on the seas, and by German truculence in various recent episodes, had formed an entente—a loose alliance—with France in 1904 and another with Russia in 1907. And all of them—Russia, Austria, Germany, France, Italy, England, and the Balkan states—were engaged in machinations in the decadent Turkish Empire. An agreement to open the straits would require the negotiation of a new treaty concerning Turkey, which could very well precipitate a war.

The crisis passed. Austria was allowed to keep Bosnia and Herzogovina, although the straits remained closed to warships. But Pandora's box had been opened. Italy seized Tripoli from Turkey in September 1912. A month later Bulgaria, Serbia, Greece, and Montenegro, taking advantage of Turkey's preoccupation with Italy, declared war on the Ottoman Empire. In this adventure they were greatly encouraged by the Russian ministers to Sofia and Belgrade, intense Pan-Slavs who acted contrary to the instructions of the new Russian foreign minister, S. D. Sazonov. The Balkan states were victorious and then immediately fell to fighting among themselves. Bulgaria attacked Serbia and Greece, which were now joined by Turkey and Rumania. Serbia, emerging from this conflict relatively well off, then invaded Albania in September 1913. Austria forced the Serbs to withdraw and set up an independent Albanian state, thus blocking Serbia's access to the sea. This did nothing to lessen Serbian hatred for the Austrians, and the Serbs found ready support in Russia. Anti-Austrian propaganda and agitation in Serbia became increasingly bellicose, while Austria-Hungary watched for an opportunity to crush the Serbs and extend control in the Balkans.

Heir to Austrian Throne Assassinated; Wife by His Side Also Shot to Death

Sarajevo, Bosnia, June 28 [*1914*]. The Archduke Francis Ferdinand, heir to the dual monarchy of Austria-Hungary, and his morganatic wife, the Duchess of Hohenburg, were shot to death to-day in the main street of this, the Bosnian capital. Bullets from a magazine revolver in the hands of an eighteen-year-old youth riddled the heir apparent and his wife, and thus completed the grim task a madman had unsuccessfully attempted only a few hours before by hurling a bomb at the royal automobile.

Another terrible chapter has thus been written into the tragic and romantic history of the House of Hapsburg, and to-night the aged Emperor lies prostrated by the news in his summer palace at Ischl.

The assassination had been carefully planned. It was while the heir to the Austrian throne and the woman he had loved so well were on their way to the town hall that Nedeljo Gabrinovics, a journeyman printer, slung a smoking bomb at the royal automobile. The Archduke himself warded it off with his arm and it fell at the back of the car and, rebounding on the road, exploded.

After the bomb exploded the Archduke and the Duchess proceeded to the City Hall. The automobiles were fleet and the news had not yet filtered through the crowd in waiting. Indeed, there had hardly been time to telephone. So the burgomaster was astonished when he met his royal guests at the door to have his customary address of greeting interrupted by the snapping words of Francis Ferdinand:

"Herr burgomaster, we come to pay you a visit and bombs are thrown at us. It is an insult!"

Then his princely dignity overcame his indignation, and he paused and said:

"Now you may speak."

After the ceremonies the Archduke and his wife announced that they would visit the wounded members of their suite in the hospitals on their way to the palace. They set out in their car, this time protected by a cordon of police. They drove rapidly down the Franz Josefstrasse and were nearing the Rudolfstrasse when Gavrio Prinzip, a pale-faced boy—indeed, a mere stripling, but with all the zeal of a fanatic shining in his countenance—popped out of the front rank of the crowd like a seed from an orange. No one seemed exactly to realize what he meant to do. It was as real and unreal as a moving picture.

Just as the automobile slowed up on the turn into the Franz Josefstrasse the boy raised his arm from his side. The sunlight struck on the dull steel of the magazine revolver and soldiers leaped to grab the youth, but before they reached him he had accomplished his deed.

The statesmen of the Dual Monarchy started collecting and manufacturing evidence to prove Serbian responsibility for the assassination, and on July 23 Austria made known the price it intended to exact for the Archduke's life.

Belgrade, July 23 [*1914*].   The Servian [Serbian] government received to-night a note from the Austro-Hungarian government bearing on the relations between the two countries and dealing directly with the assassination at Sarajevo on June 28 of Archduke Francis Ferdinand, heir to the Austrian throne.

The note reviews the relations with Servia since 1909 and complains that although the Servian government promised loyalty to the Austro-Hungarian government it has failed to suppress subversive movements and agitations by the newspapers, and that this tolerance has incited the Servian people to hatred of the Austro-Hungarian monarchy and contempt for its institutions.

This, says the note, culminated in the Sarajevo assassinations, which are proved by depositions and confessions of the perpetrators to have been hatched in Belgrade, the arms and explosives having been supplied by the connivance of Servian officers and functionaries.

"The Austro-Hungarian government," continued the note, "is unable longer to pursue an attitude of forebearance and sees the duty imposed upon it to put an end to the intrigues which form a perpetual menace to the monarchy's tranquility."

There followed a list of demands, including the suppression of publications propagandizing against Austria-Hungary, the dismissal of certain Serbian officials, the arrest of all those involved in the assassinations, and the participation of representatives of Austria-Hungary in a judicial investigation into the affair. Serbia was given forty-eight hours in which to reply. The humiliating ultimatum was calculated to be refused.

Russia was now faced with the consequences of her long-time ambitions and machinations in the Balkans. To permit an attack on another Slavic nation would entail the utmost humiliation for Russia and would be a betrayal of Russia's loudly proclaimed national interests in the Balkans. It was obvious that the dynamics of the alliance system threatened a general war between the Triple Alliance countries—Austria, Germany, and Italy—and the Triple Entente nations—Russia, France, and Great Britain.

Europe at Point of War;
Russia Back of Servia in Resisting Austria

Dual Monarchy's Ultimatum
Sent to Belgrade
Expires at 6 P.M.

Czar Asks Delay; Vienna Refuses It

Threat from St. Petersburg
to Take "Extreme Meas-
ures" Disdained

Germany Ready to Aid Her Ally

Great Britain and France Striving
to Find Modus Vivendi—
Mediation Idea Scouted

Terrified, Serbia acceded to every demand except that for participation by representatives of Austria-Hungary in the investigations. Austria refused to accept the reply.

Austrian Envoy Quits;
Russia Mobilizes Troops;
Germany Eager for War

Vienna, July 25 [*1914*]. Shortly before 6 o'clock the Austro-Hungarian Minister at Belgrade presented a note to the Servian Foreign Office saying the Servian reply was unsatisfactory. The Austro-Hungarian Minister and the staff of the legation then left Belgrade.

Diplomatic relations between Austria-Hungary and Servia were thus formally broken off. War is regarded by the public as almost a certainty.

The Servian government waited until the last moment left it by the terms of the note, and only ten minutes before the hour of six, when the Austro-Hungarian ultimatum expired, did the Servian Premier appear at the legation and present his government's reply to the Austrian Minister, Baron Gicsl von Gieslingen.

St. Petersburg, July 25 [1914]. The mobilization of the Russian army will proceed immediately. The Emperor has fully approved the decision of his ministers to this effect.

The Austrian ultimatum is unanimously regarded here as an indirect challenge to Russia.

There was an all-round tumbling of prices on the Bourse to a point of panic to-day. Banking and mining shares were the heaviest sufferers.

The prompt mobilization of the Russian army was anticipated as a result of the Council of Ministers presided over by the Emperor held at the Palace of Peterhof to-day. Russia thus appears prepared to go to any extremes rather than tolerate the downfall of Servia.

Austria's Declaration of War on Servia Plunges Europe into Gloom All Listening for Word from Russia Which Will Mean Peace or Chaos

[*July 31, 1914.*] Austria-Hungary, in a brief but significant proclamation, has declared war on Servia, and all Europe waits now on the decision of St. Petersburg, where late last night a momentous conference was being held between the Russian Foreign Minister and the Austrian Ambassador with a view to localizing the conflict.

London, while admitting that the situation was one of extreme peril, still was inclined to place some hope in the success of the efforts at localization that were in progress in St. Petersburg.

Vienna expressed delight over the declaration of war.

Berlin's answer to Sir Edward Grey's proposal for a mediation conference was a refusal to take part, and in this Austria, of course, acquiesced, following immediately with the declaration of war.

World Peace Hangs on Russia's Decision, While Kaiser's Envoy Seeks Czar in Last Effort for Peace

Cossacks mobilizing in St. Petersburg on the eve of the First World War. (*Photo from European*)

Soldiers of the Russian army march to war. (*The Bettmann Archive*)

St. Petersburg, July 30 [*1914*]. The following official statement is authorized:

"Russia desires no war. Our partial mobilization is a precautionary measure to preserve the independence of Servia."

London, July 31. To-day the word will be said that means war or peace, according to the dispatches from Berlin. The Kaiser and his Cabinet, after practically an all-day conference, determined on wording a new question to Russia asking why she was arming so long as neither Germany nor Austria was threatening her.

Everything will depend upon Russia's answer, for it is understood that the least evasion will cause the Kaiser to mobilize his army and fleet overnight.

Foreign Minister Sazonov and General N. N. Ianushkevich, Chief of the General Staff, prevailed upon Nicholas to order general mobilization as a necessary military measure in the circumstances. Nicholas was reluctant, still half hoping that the mess could somehow be avoided, but they pointed out that failure to act promptly would mean a serious initial setback if the decision was for war.

Russia Declines to Answer Germany; All Europe Sees Clash Inevitable

Germany Declares War on Russia; France Prepares to Join Her Ally; Italy Quits the Triple Alliance

Double German Invasion of France Reported Repulsed Near Nancy; Russian Army Invades East Prussia

England Hesitates, But Moves Troops Toward Seaports

Luxemburg Overrun by Kaiser's Forces in Rush on France Before War Is Declared

Namur, Belgium, Aug. 2 [*1914*].   The invasion of France by the German army has begun, although no declaration of war has been made as yet by either of the two countries against the other.

The formal declaration of war came on August 3.

England Declares War on Germany; Battles Begin on Land and Sea; Kaiser Loses Warships Off Algiers

London, Aug. 5 [*1914*].   Great Britain declared war on Germany at 7 o'clock p.m. yesterday, "as from 11 o'clock p.m."

The following official statement was issued by the Foreign Office at 12:15 o'clock this morning:

"Owing to the summary rejection by the German government of the request made by his Britannic majesty's government for assurances that the neutrality of Belgium be respected, his majesty's ambassador at Berlin has received his passports and his majesty's government has declared to the German government that a state of war exists between Great Britain and Germany as from 11 p.m., August 4."

Paradoxically, Austria did not declare war on Russia until August 6.

In Russia, as in all the other belligerent nations, there was a great surge of patriotism. The city of St. Petersburg changed its name from the German form to the good Russian Petrograd. The Duma—it was the Fourth, which first met in 1912—voted overwhelmingly to support the war. Only the Bolsheviks were steadfast in their opposition, and as a result the five Bolshevik deputies were arrested in November and sentenced to Siberian exile for sedition. The industrial strikes, which in June and July 1914 had showed signs of leading to another large-scale upheaval, practically ceased. For the moment at least the deep breach between the government and the people seemed to have been spanned by a common purpose. Just after the outbreak of the war, representatives of the zemstvos organized the All-Russian Union of Zemstvos for the Relief of Sick and Wounded Soldiers, and a few weeks later the municipalities formed the Union of Towns to perform similar relief work. In the summer of 1915 a number of war industries committees consisting of representatives of the government, the Unions of Zemstvos and Towns, business, and labor, were established to expedite the production of war materiel. As in 1904, there was a vague feeling that once victory had been won, many of the old problems would disappear, that the evils of the past would be purged by the war and Russia would emerge as a democracy.

But, just as in 1904, the Russian military machine early began to creak and strain. After an initial successful thrust into Poland, the army bogged down. Then in the spring of 1915 the Germans launched an offensive.

Russian Army In South Poland Starts Retreat

Germans Retake Przemysl; Crushing Blow to Russians Crowns Month of Victories

Teutons Retake Lemberg, Storming Fort After Fort; Russians in Full Flight

Germans Capture Warsaw;
Russian Defenders Escape
Leaving Nothing of Value

---◆---

Brest-Litovsk Falls as Czar's Armies Retreat

Russians Make No Effort to Defend Main Fortress

And, as in 1904, the blithe illusion of a patriotic union between the government and the people was quickly dispelled.

In August 1915, Nicholas, without consulting his ministers or any other responsible official, dismissed the Grand Duke Nicholas Nikolayevich as

Without consulting his ministers, the Czar peremptorily dismissed the Grand Duke Nicholas (right) as commander-in-chief of the Russian armies and assumed command himself. (*Keystone View Co.*)

chief of the army and assumed command himself. The peremptory decision infuriated the cabinet. With Nicholas away at the front, Russia would in effect be ruled by the Czarina, and the Czarina had become the puppet of the Siberian religious fanatic Gregory Rasputin.

This uncanny peasant, who had won renown as a *starets*, or unordained preacher, had been summoned to the court in November 1905 because of his reputed powers as a healer. The infant Czarevich was suffering from an incurable and inevitably fatal blood disease, hemophilia. Rasputin, chanting hypnotically in his resonant peasant's voice, on a few occasions actually appeared to stop the flow of blood. The Czarina's gratitude and her faith in his divine inspiration were boundless. Nicholas also came to believe in him. Herman Bernstein, Russian correspondent of the *Herald*, later uncovered the story.

> The evil influence of Rasputin over the Tsar and the Tsaritsa kept growing. The uncouth, illiterate, unclean, licentious peasant became the popular "saint" of the Russian court—the actual ruler of Russia. The Tsaritsa, carried away by superstition and the peculiar doctrines preached by Rasputin under the guise of religion, which made him popular among women close to the Russian court, worshipped and regarded him as a "saint."
>
> The scandal at the Russian court was becoming known beyond the walls of the Tsar's palace. The escapades of the "saint" and his strange grip on the royal family were discussed, at first secretly, in exclusive social circles in Russia. Then, from time to time, members of the Duma made indirect references to the Rasputin scandal. They dared not speak of it openly. Rasputin was a powerful man. Ignorant, unable to write correctly, he nevertheless could appoint members of the Cabinet and remove them; he appointed the head of the Synod and removed dignitaries of the Church. His will and authority were more powerful than that of the Russian Premier.

Alexandra Fyodorovna would transmit the religious man's cunning advice to her adoring husband, and more often than not he would act directly upon it. It was at her (which meant Rasputin's) urging that Nicholas decided to take charge of the army. Ten members of the cabinet appealed to the Czar to reverse his decision. Nicholas paid no attention. During the next few months the Czarina had seven of the audacious ministers dismissed.

Gregory Rasputin, the peasant *starets* whose sinister influence on the Czarina and hence the Czar contributed to the undermining of confidence in the regime. (*The Bettmann Archive*)

The Czarevich Alexis inherited through his mother the incurable blood disease hemophilia; Rasputin's supposed success in stopping the boy's bleeding enabled the *starets* to become the Czarina's trusted adviser. (*The Bettmann Archive*)

Russian losses during the first year and a half of the war were appalling—more than three million dead, wounded, and captured by the end of 1915—a tragedy due as much to economic and administrative failures as to purely military ones. A war correspondent reported:

[*June 21, 1915.*] I went along the 500-mile front within the Russian lines and saw men driven into the trenches without guns or ammunition. They had to do the best they could, picking up rifles and cartridges from dead or wounded comrades.

Russia's fledgling industry was simply not able to meet the needs of modern warfare. The breakdown of railway equipment under the strain of heavy wartime demands was attributable to economies of maintenance and capital outlay made in the pre-war years. Inflation inevitably resulted from the curtailed production of consumer goods. The bureaucracy was incapable of acting imaginatively and quickly, and it was not until the summer of 1915 that a modicum of public involvement in the organization of the war effort was permitted with the establishment of the War Industries Committee. But at precisely that point Nicholas left for the front.

In the fall of 1915 and throughout 1916, the situation grew worse in every respect. Prices soared as industry now devoted itself exclusively to the production of war materiel. A rash of strikes broke out. The railway system began to crumble. Severe food shortages occurred. The large estates, which supplied Moscow, Petrograd, and other large cities with food, were desperately short of labor because so many farmers were conscripted into the army. Consequently, less than a third of the acreage that had been planted in grain on the large estates in European Russia before the war was growing cereal in 1916. In addition, many of the small peasant farmers refused to market the grain they produced because there was nothing to buy with the money they received.

Morale in the armed forces was extremely low. Retreats easily turned into routs. The high Russian losses were felt most keenly in the agricultural areas, where the war was bitterly resented anyway because it was used as an excuse for halting the Stolypin agrarian reforms, which on the eve of the war had just begun to show results. In the cities, revolution began to be urged again. There were 243 political strikes in 1916, as compared to only 7 between August and December 1914.

And in this desperate state of affairs, Russia, incredibly, was being governed by a vicious, perhaps mad, Siberian peasant. Rumors spread that the German-born Empress and her intimate adviser were actually German agents, or at least were deliberately impeding Russia's war effort. When the Duma convened in November 1916 after a five-month recess, heated speeches were delivered by Paul Milyukov, leader of the Kadets, and by others, warning of the "dark forces" dominating the government and demanding that the Czar rid himself and Russia of them. The latest prime minister, B. V. Sturmer, a corrupt old bureaucrat in his dotage and a friend of Rasputin, was dismissed by the Czar, but Rasputin remained in power. Sometime later the *Tribune* learned the story of the behind-the-scene entreaties and their reception by the Czar.

Late in November Grand Duke Nicholas Michaelovitch [Nikolaye-vich] took to the palace a letter which he had written and read it aloud to the Emperor and Empress. It expressed in most blunt fashion the danger the country was in and showed how only the promptest action by the Emperor could save the Empire from complete collapse. The grand duke took no pains to conceal the Rasputin scandal, but when the name of the Empress was mentioned the latter snatched the letter from Nicholas Michaelovitch's hand and tore it up.

When the Emperor received in silence the statement that Protopopoff (Minister of the Interior) had been foisted upon him by Rasputin and listened to the other accusations without denying or showing the signs of being the least confused by them, the grand duke lost all patience and shouted at his majesty: "Do none of these things move you? You make me think of Alexander I."

An appeal to the Emperor signed by seventeen grand dukes made no greater impression, and Vladimir Purishkevich, Vice-President of the Union of True Russians [a right-wing organization] and a prominent member of the Duma, paid a fruitless visit to the palace on the same mission. All spoke freely to Nicholas of the growing danger to the dynasty and the necessity of his protecting himself against the influence of the Empress. To all of these the Emperor replied:

"What has Alexandra to do with politics? I refuse to believe that she is unpopular among the people."

There was only one solution possible.

Rasputin Lured
To Death in Palace,
London Hears

London, Jan. 3 [1917]. The morning newspapers in their Petrograd dispatches to-day feature stories of the reported death of Gregory Rasputin, the Russian monk who exercised such influence over Emperor Nicholas. The reports of the death of Rasputin evidently are making a stir in Russia, not only on account of his personality, but owing to allegations that two persons of exalted rank and a well known . . . member of the Duma were concerned in his taking off.

The assassins were the most unlikely people: the Grand Duke Dmitry Pavlovich, a nephew of the Czar; Prince Felix Yusupov, also a relative of Nicholas; and V. M. Purishkevich, a rightist Duma member. Prince Yusupov invited the hated *starets* to a late supper to be held for a few intimates at his palace on the night of December 29. Ignoring warnings, Rasputin accepted. The table was set in the cellar, and while the other conspirators waited upstairs, straining to hear, Yusupov sat down with Rasputin for a tête-à-tête. A bottle of poisoned Madeira had been prepared, but the wily Rasputin first refused to eat or drink. Finally, however, he accepted a glass of wine. While the trembling Yusupov watched, he drank thirstily. Nothing happened. Yusupov ran upstairs to report to his fellow conspirators. Bewildered and half-believing that Rasputin's reputed powers really existed, they decided to shoot him, and again the task fell to the unhappy Yusupov. He shot Rasputin in the heart. With a roar like a wounded animal, Rasputin fell back. But he was still not dead. Finally, they dragged his bleeding body to the Grand Duke Dmitry's car, drove to the Neva River, and drowned him beneath the ice. No attempt was made to apprehend the murderers, though their identity was known.

No change in the Czar's or the Czarina's attitude followed the assassination. Two of Rasputin's friends were kept in high office, the latest premier, Prince N. D. Golitsyn, and the minister of the interior, A. D. Protopopov.

Protopopoff Rules Czar, Defies Duma, Worries Allies

By Isaac Don Levine

[*Jan. 21, 1917.*] A cloth manufacturer is to-day the real power behind the Russian throne. At his will the Czar issues ukases and promulgates decrees. The membership of the Cabinet is entirely changed [and] . . . the Duma prorogued and threatened with dissolution, all because of the activities of a political adventurer who knows how to make use of the sinister forces pervading Russian life. His name is Alexander Dmitrovitch Protopopoff.

A few years ago Protopopoff's only distinction was the fact that he was the owner of one of Russia's largest cloth manufacturing establishments. To-day he holds in his hands the fate of ministers; the Duma fears him, and the Allies are uneasy over his moves. The fortunes of humanity and civilization, to a certain extent, depend on the way he will carve Russia's future policy.

SERVED AS CAVALRY OFFICER

Who is this Protopopoff? Born in 1865, he received a military education and served in the cavalry up to 1890, when he resigned. He settled on his large estate in the province of Simbirsk, where he devoted himself to business and social work. National politics were foreign to Protopopoff till 1908, in which year he was elected to the Duma by the Octobrists—the party of the Centre.

Shrewd, persistent, ambitious, Protopopoff was unlike the standard type of Russian politician. His qualities, to be sure, could never win him popular admiration and respect in Russia. But opportunity never found Protopopoff asleep or slow. When the junior vice-president of the Duma resigned some years ago, Protopopoff was suddenly advanced to fill the vacancy. There was no powerful support and no strong opposition to Protopopoff's candidacy, and he became vice-president of the Duma.

BECOMES EXTREME REACTIONARY

From a Duma progressive he turned into an extreme reactionary. And he affiliated himself with the dark forces in Russian high circles. This added to his security and prestige with the Czar.

The depth of feeling aroused by Protopopoff in Russia can be measured from the fact that Rodzianko, the president of the Duma, turned away from the Minister of Interior when the latter offered his hand to him during the New Year's reception at the court. This will undoubtedly increase Protopopoff's bitterness against the Duma, at the same time broadening the breach between the government and the people.

Protopopoff's Treachery Stirring Revolt in Russia

By Isaac Don Levine

[*Jan. 29, 1917.*]   Not since the days of the revolution in 1905 has the tension in Russia been so strained as it is to-day. The latest act of Protopopoff, Minister of the Interior, provoked the nation's feelings almost to the bursting point of revolt. The situation in Russia was never so dangerous and critical as at the present moment.

Protopopoff has just struck the ugliest blow yet at the popular forces and the Allied cause. He prevented by force the executive meetings of the great national organizations [the Union of Zemstvos and the Union of Municipalities], engaged in helping the War Ministry to supply the army with munitions and food. No more revolting and provoking act on the part of the government could have been possible.

Enraged protests, in which even the Imperial Council—the conservative upper house of the legislature—joined, were ignored. Indeed, they seemed only to drive Protopopov and his protectress, the Czarina, to acts that under the circumstances verged on madness.

Russian Arrests A Blow at Allies

By Isaac Don Levine

The arrest in Petrograd of eleven members of the workmen's group of the Central War Industries Committee is a sinister government move intended to discredit the activities of social Russia. The arrest of these men by Minister of the Interior Protopopoff, on the charge of engaging in revolutionary activities, is another stab in the back to the Allies and Russian democracy.

The Central War Industries Committee is one of the leading public organizations the activities of which are devoted to the rehabilitation of the army and the mobilization of the country's industrial resources. Headed by some eminent Duma leaders, this committee has achieved phenomenal successes. The British and French generals who have visited Russia during the last year expressed their admiration for the efficiency of the organization. The Russian War Minister, General Shuvaieff, praised the committee repeatedly.

The workers employed by the War Industries Committee have shown themselves to be patriotic and intelligent. It is eleven of these patriotic workers whom the government of Protopopoff now has placed under arrest. The Minister of Interior has scored another point against the popular organizations, which stand for fighting Germany to the end. The Russian government is now doing its best to paralyse their intensive activities. And there is no better way of achieving this than by casting on these organizations the shadow of revolutionism.

Members of the Duma and officials of the various organizations began talking quite openly about the necessity of removing the Czar, of a quiet and hopefully bloodless *coup d'état*, before it was too late. The disintegration of the economy was getting more desperate by the day. Transportation was almost at a standstill, so that raw materials were not getting to the factories and food could not be brought to the cities or to the men at the front. Fuel was so short in some cities that almost no one had heat. Inflation raged. There were reports from the front of mutinies, and in January and February 1917 violent food riots broke out in Petrograd, Moscow, and other cities.

On Thursday, March 8, the annual socialist celebration of Women's Day took place in Petrograd. When the oratory was over thousands of women marched out of the factories and began a spontaneous demonstration for bread, in which a number of male workers joined.

Friday and Saturday the demonstration continued, its size greatly augmented. Then suddenly, as if someone had put a match to gasoline-drenched shavings—

Flame of Revolt Spreads Swiftly Through Streets of Petrograd

Petrograd, March 15 [*1917*].   For several days Petrograd has been the scene of one of the most remarkable uprisings in history. Small manifestations of hungry factory workers crying for bread [have] changed . . . into a revolution which [has] swept the whole city.

The early period of the uprising, beginning a week ago, bore the character rather of a mock revolution staged for an immense audience. Cossacks charging down the street did so in a half-hearted fashion, plainly without malice or intent to harm the crowds which they playfully dispersed. The troops exchanged good-natured raillery with the working men and women, and as they rode were cheered by the populace.

MACHINE GUNS FIRE BLANKS

Long lines of soldiers stationed in dramatic attitudes across Nevsky Prospect, with their guns pointed at an imaginary foe, appeared to be taking part in a realistic tableau. Machine guns, firing roulades of blank cartridges, seemed only to add another realistic touch to a tremendous theatric production, which was using the whole city as a stage.

Until Sunday night this pageant continued without serious interruption. Then in a flash the whole scene lost its theatric quality; it became a genuine revolution.

The regiments had received an order from the commandant to fire upon people assembled in the street. This caused immediate dissension among the troops, who did not understand why they should be compelled to take violent measures against fellow citizens, whose chief offense was that they were hungry and were asking the government for bread. The Volynski regiment shot its officers and deserted. Several others followed, and a pitched battle began between the troops who stood with the government, and those who, refusing to obey orders, had mutinied. The police joined with the "loyal" troops.

BATTLE THROUGH THE NIGHT

A long night battle occurred between the mutinous regiments and the police at the end of St. Catherine Canal, immediately in front of the historic church built over the spot where Alexander II was killed by a bomb. The police finally fled to rooftops all over the city, and were seen no more in the streets during the entire term of the fighting.

Still, on Monday morning the reactionary government troops appeared to control all the principal squares of the city. Then came a period when it was impossible to distinguish one side from the other. There was no definite line between the factions. The turning point appeared to come about 3 o'clock in the afternoon. For two hours the opposing regiments passively confronted each other along the wide Liteiny Prospect in almost complete silence.

From time to time emissaries from the revolutionary side rode to the opposing ranks and exhorted them to join the side of the people. For a while the result seemed to hang in the balance. The troops appeared irresolute, awaiting the commands of their officers, who themselves were in doubt as to what they should do.

FORT AND ARSENALS SEIZED

Desultory firing continued along the side streets between groups of government troops and revolutionists. But the regiments upon whose decision the outcome rested still confronted each other, with machine guns and rifles in readiness.

Suddenly a few volleys were exchanged, there was another period of

The soldiers who built this barricade on the Litany Prospekt near the arsenal in Petrograd were among the first to go over to the side of the demonstrators as the March revolution began. (*Photo from European*)

silent suspense, and the government regiments finally marched over to join the revolutionists. A few hours after the first clash, this entire section of Petrograd, in which are located the Duma building, artillery headquarters and the chief military barracks, passed into the hands of the revolutionary forces, and the warfare swept like a tornado to other parts of the city, where the scene was duplicated. In the arsenals and fortress of St. Peter and St. Paul arms and ammunition enough were seized to supply the civil revolutionaries. At the same time the political prisons were opened and the prisoners joined the revolt.

At first it seemed a miracle that the revolutionists, without prearranged plan, without leadership or organization, could in such a short time, with comparative ease, achieve a complete victory over the government. But the explanation lay in the reluctance of the troops to take sides against the people and their prompt desertion to the ranks of those who opposed the government.

STUDENTS JOIN SOLDIERS

The scenes in the streets were by this time remarkable. The wide streets, where the troops were stationed, were completely deserted by civilians, except for a few daring individuals, who, creeping along walls and ducking into courtyards, sped from one side to the other. But the side streets were choked with people.

Groups of students, easily distinguished by their blue caps and dark uniforms, fell into step with rough units of rebel soldiers, and were joined by other heterogeneous elements united for the time being by a cause greater than partisan differences. Unkempt workingmen, with ragged sheepskin coats covering the conventional peasants' costume of dark blouse and topboots, strode side by side with well-groomed city clerks and shopkeepers.

The strange army of people, mustered on the street corners, shouldered their newly acquired rifles and marched out to join the ranks of the deserting regiments.

At nightfall only one small district of the city, containing the War Office, the Admiralty buildings, St. Isaac's Cathedral and the Astoria military hotel, still resisted the onslaught of the revolutionary forces and the battle for the possession of Petrograd came to a dramatic conclusion. In the Admiralty building the Council of Ministers secretly gathered for a conference and the last regiments loyal to the old government were drawn up as a guard.

The Moscow District police station in Petrograd was destroyed by the revolutionaries when the police resisted them. (*Photo from European*)

The police, in general the most despised officials of the Czarist regime, were not permitted by the populace to go over to the side of the revolution even if they wanted to. The more fortunate—those not shot on sight—were arrested. (*Photo from European*)

Marchers with red flags—the symbol of the revolution. (*Photo from European*)

After the overthrow of the Czar, crowds packed the Duma, as well as every available meeting place, in order to debate politics and revel in the newly won freedom. (*Photo from European*)

BUILDING IS BESIEGED

While the council sat . . . the building was surrounded and the be-
siegers poured rifle and machine gun fire on the defenders. For a few
hours the fiercest battle of the day continued. The streets were swept by
a steady fusilade and the crowds scattered for the nearest shelter, some
of the people being compelled to spend the night in courtyards or cor-
ridors of office buildings, or wherever they first found refuge.

Toward morning there was a sudden lull, broken by exultant shouts,
which deepened into a roar and was succeeded by the "Russian Revolutionary Marseillaise." The regiments defending the Admiralty had surrendered and gone over to the side of the revolutionists.

The ministers in the Admiralty building were then arrested, and the
Russian national colors were replaced by the red flag of the revolutionists.

Although sporadic fighting continued between small groups until
Wednesday, the "cause of the people" had triumphed.

Events had tumbled one upon another with dizzy rapidity. The
Volinsky regiment had mutinied in the early morning hours of Monday,
March 12; on the same day Golitsyn ordered the suspension of the legislature, believing that this would help quell the disturbances by dispersing
the Duma representatives who had been attacking him and his government. The members of the Duma, while not ready to defy the government
by staying in their seats, were also not willing to dissolve. They moved
to another room in the Taurida Palace and established a Temporary
Committee to help restore order and proceed with negotiations with the
government. That afternoon deputies of the radical parties in the Duma
and representatives of the workers met to reconstitute the St. Petersburg
Soviet, which had played such an important role in the rebellion of 1905.
A general session of delegates from the factories and from the mutinous
regiments was held the same evening in the Taurida Palace and the
Soviet, under the new name Soviet of Workers' and Soldiers' Deputies,
in effect assumed governmental functions by establishing a militia,
making plans to deal with the food situation, and otherwise taking charge.
The next day, March 13, the Temporary Committee of the Duma also
donned the mantle of government by appointing commissars to direct the
various ministries. The members of Nicholas's cabinet were formally
placed under arrest.

That same morning, Nicholas, who was at army headquarters in

Moghiliev, boarded a train for Tsarskoye Selo, his residence near Petrograd. But because word was received that the stations between Malaya Vishera and Petrograd had been occupied by mutinous troops, he went instead to Pskov, arriving there late on the 14th.

Czar Dethroned on Way to Petrograd

Petrograd, March 15 [*1917*]. The Emperor of Russia has abdicated, and Grand Duke Michael Alexandrovitch, his younger brother, has been named as regent. After his abdication, Emperor Nicholas returned to General Staff Headquarters.

The abdication . . . was signed at the town of Pskoff, where the train on which he was travelling toward Petrograd was halted early in the week.

REBELS DEMANDED ABDICATION

From Pskoff . . . the Emperor communicated with members of the Executive Committee of the Duma, who informed him that they were sending emissaries to meet him there. Accordingly, a member of the Duma committee and one of the ministers of the new cabinet proceeded to Pskoff, and had an interview with the Emperor in the presence of General Nicholas V. Ruzsky, a member of the Council of the Empire and of the Supreme Military Council; Baron W. Fredericks, Minister of the Court, Count Narishkin and others.

After relating to the Emperor the latest developments in the revolution the emissaries advised him not to send any troops from the front to Petrograd, since all the troops were going over to the revolutionists as fast as they arrived.

"What is it desired that I should do?" the Emperor inquired.

"Abdicate the throne," was the reply.

After devoting some time to deliberation Emperor Nicholas said:

"It would be very hard to be separated from my son. Therefore I will abdicate in favor of my brother, in behalf of myself and my son."

Though the emissaries from the Duma did not know it, Nicholas had actually made the decision earlier in the day.

The Grand Duke, after failing to receive a guarantee of his safety, declined to serve as regent.

Romanoff Dynasty Is Ended with the Formal Abdication of Tsar Nicholas And of His Brother, Regent for a Day

Petrograd, March 16 [1917], 6 p.m. (via London, March 17, 3:14 a.m.). Emperor Nicholas abdicated at midnight last night on behalf of himself and the heir apparent, Grand Duke Alexis, in favor of Grand Duke Michael Alexanderovitch.

At 2:30 o'clock this afternoon Grand Duke Michael himself abdicated, thus bringing the Romanoff dynasty to an end.

The government, pending a meeting of the Constitutional Assembly, is vested in the executive committee of the Duma and the newly chosen Council of Ministers. The members of the new national Cabinet [announced yesterday are] as follows:

Premier, President of the Council and Minister of the Interior—Prince GEORGES E. LVOFF.

Foreign Minister—Professor PAUL N. MILUKOFF.

Minister of Public Instruction—Professor MANUILOFF, of Moscow University.

Minister of War and Navy, ad interim—A. J. GUCHKOFF, formerly President of the Duma.

Minister of Agriculture—M. SHINGAREFF, Deputy from Petrograd.

Minister of Finance—M. TERESCHENKO, Deputy from Kiev.

Minister of Justice—Deputy KERENSKI of Saratoff.

Minister of Communications—N. V. NEKRASOFF, Vice-President of the Duma.

Controller of State—M. GODNEFF, Deputy from Kazan.

The executive committee of the Duma and the representatives of the soldiers and working classes, it is reported, have reached a full agreement to waive all minor differences until the meeting of the constitutional assembly, which will decide just what form the new government of Russia will take.

Thus four centuries of Russian autocracy fizzled to an end.

Chapter Six

The Government or the Soviets?

Coalition
Is Voted
in Petrograd

Socialists' Committee
Decides to Enter
Government

Collapse of New
Republic Averted

Workmen's Body Calls
on Soldiers to
Fight On

The revolution came as a surprise to everyone. In barely one week—in just a few days, if one counts from the events of March 12—the Russian autocracy had been swept away, and with very little bloodshed, considering the enormousness of the achievement. That a confrontation with the Czar was imminent, few people either in the opposition or in the government itself doubted. But the assumption was that it would take the form of a parliamentary coup, in which the lower house of the Duma, supported by the Imperial Council, prominent nobles, gentry, and businessmen, would force Nicholas—or if Nicholas refused, his successor—to appoint ministers responsible to the government. They envisaged no more than the establishment of the British cabinet system. Simply to exorcize the "dark forces" and secure a little more democracy would constitute a great victory for the people in autocratic Russia.

True, there had been portents of an explosion: mutinies in the armed forces, an acceleration in the number of strikes, bread riots, talk of revolution, a thickening atmosphere of discontent and resentment. The mood of the populace had been getting ugly. But in March 1917, the situation was not yet revolutionary. There had been no campaign to win popular support for a revolution or certainly for a parliamentary coup. Indeed, when the demonstrations began the liberals begged the people to be calm. There was no incitement by the radicals, since virtually all the leaders were in exile or prison and the revolutionary parties were empty shells. There was no organization, no planning, not even a period of terror and violence such as preceded the 1905 uprising. The countryside was relatively quiet. The actual revolution itself was less tumultuous than many of the industrial strikes. In Moscow there was some desultory fighting, and that was the end of it. Other cities were advised by telegram that a successful revolution had taken place.

What actually toppled the regime, what transformed peaceful food demonstrations into a revolution, was the decision of the Petrograd garrison and then of other units of the armed forces not to fire upon the demonstrators. The turning point occurred during the night of March 11–12, when the soldiers of the Volinsky Regiment, stricken with remorse at having shot some strikers, agreed among themselves not to obey any more such orders. Early next morning they sent representatives to the barracks of other regiments, where their plea for an agreed policy of disobedience was given a very receptive hearing. Their comrades, many of them peasant draftees, had no taste for the war, despised their upper-class officers, and were in complete sympathy with the demonstrations. The government had no one it could rely upon. All that was necessary was to take advantage of the opportunity, which the liberal leaders of the Duma did by establishing a cabinet and proclaiming the existence of a new regime. They encountered no opposition.

Czar's Chair Cast Out By Holy Russian Synod

Church Breaks with Its 'Little Father' and Adopts the Revolution

Army and Navy Also Support the People

Generals in the Field Telegraph Assurances of Loyalty to New Government

Petrograd, March 18 [1917]. The first meeting of the Holy Synod since the revolution was held to-day under the presidency of the Metropolitan of Kiev. The new Procurator General of the Holy Synod, M. Lvoff, in opening the sitting, said he rejoiced at the advent of freedom of the Orthodox Church. He ordered the removal of the imperial chair from the conference room, symbolizing termination of interference by the Emperor in the affairs of the Church.

The armies in the field report that the abdication of the Emperor has been enthusiastically acquiesced in, according to a Foreign Office official. Telegrams from virtually all the commanders have been received, assuring the support of the government guaranteed in advance by General Michael Alexieff, chief of staff.

Meanwhile the last vestiges of the empire are disappearing. Portraits of the erstwhile members of the imperial family—ones seen upon the walls of almost every government office—have been removed. While the correspondent waited in the anteroom of the Foreign Minister's office a liveried attendant mounted a chair and quietly took down portraits of the former Emperor and Empress. The national colors, with their eagles, have given place to plain red flags, one of which floats over the famous Winter Palace, where the Duma will now meet.

WHILE WE ARE LOOKING FOR AN OPPORTUNITY TO HELP

America First
To Recognize
Freed Russia

Quick Action Taken as Hint
To German People to
Demand Liberty

Washington, March 22 [*1917*].   Secretary of State Lansing announced late to-day that Ambassador Francis at Petrograd had to-day extended formal recognition to the new Russian government, on instructions sent by the State Department.

The United States is the first nation to recognize formally the new government of Russia.

George Calls Revolt
Russia's Greatest
Service to Allies

London, March 22 [*1917*].   Premier David Lloyd George to-day telegraphed to the Russian Premier, saying he believed the revolution in Russia was the greatest service the Russians had yet rendered to the Allied cause, and that it was a sure promise that the Prussian military autocracy, the only barrier to peace, would soon be overthrown.

"It is with sentiments of the most profound satisfaction that the peoples of Great Britain and the British dominions have learned that their great ally, Russia, now stands with the nations which base their institutions upon responsible government" [the telegram said].

Two days after the United States acted, official recognition was extended by Great Britain and by France.

Even the Petrograd Soviet of Workers' and Soldiers' Deputies, dominated though it was by Mensheviks and Socialist Revolutionaries, gave its consent to the establishment of the distinctly middle-class government (while, however, refusing to dissolve itself).

Prince G. E. Lvov, president of the Provisional Government from March to July 1917. (*Keystone View Co.*)

John Reed, writing in the *Tribune* (*Mar. 25, 1917*), about a week after the Czar's abdication, pointed out:

[The revolution] is not, as many Americans believe, a successful repetition of the revolution of 1905; it is not a peasant uprising; it is not a revolt against war. Its prime movers and dominating figures are liberal-minded provincial nobles, business men, professors, editors and army officers. Its purpose first of all is to unite Russia against Germany. This means at bottom to provide Russia with a Constitution like that of France and England, and a government, like theirs, responsible to the representatives of the people assembled in the Duma. In short, to put Russia's government on a par with that of the nations of Western Europe. As an official of the National City Bank said in an interview: "It was apparent that the influences back of it were the solid, respectable and conservative element in the community."

Look for a moment at the Ministry. Prince George Lvov, Premier and

Minister of the Interior, is an idealist of royal blood, with an income of 5,000 rubles a year, and president of the Union of Zemstvos. . . . Michael V. Rodzianko, president of the Duma, is a rich landlord. M. Terrestchenko, Minister of Finance, is a millionaire of the type of Lvov. Paul N. Miliukoff and M. Manuilov, respectively Minister of Foreign Affairs and Minister of Public Instruction, are both professors in the University of Moscow, and are now both editors of newspapers. A. J. Guchkov, Minister of War and Navy, is a wealthy merchant of Moscow, long a preacher of preparedness against Germany, a former president of the Duma and the leader of the Octobrist party. M. Shingarev, Minister of Agriculture, is a prominent physician.

The Soviet of Workers' and Soldiers' Deputies agreed to the establishment of the Provisional Government (as the new regime called itself), but without relinquishing any of its own authority. On March 14 it had

Alexander Kerensky (center), whose first post in the Provisional Government was as Minister of Justice, is shown here with two aides and the commandant (right) of the palace of Tsarskoye Selo, where the Czar was confined after his arrest. (*Photo from European*)

issued an order to the armed forces providing for the establishment of soviets of soldiers and sailors in every unit of the army and navy and putting the troops on an equal basis with the officers—indeed in effect giving them control, although they were admonished to maintain discipline. Paragraph four of the proclamation stipulated: "The orders of the military commission of the State Duma are to be fulfilled only in those cases which do not contradict the orders and decisions of the Soviet of Workers' and Soldiers' Deputies." The Duma leaders had no choice but to accede to the edict, since they were not willing to risk a conflict with the Soviet, which commanded the allegiance of the vast majority of the workers and probably of the soldiers in Petrograd. Paragraph four, extended to everything in Russia, military and otherwise, became the explicit proviso in the Soviet's grant of permission to the liberal Duma leaders to establish a government.

As far as the people were concerned, the true government of Russia was the Soviet, not the Provisional Government. For one thing, it had, as the Duma had not, a broad electoral base: one delegate was elected for every 2,000 workers and soldiers in Petrograd. But more important, it executed the will of its constituents expeditiously and faithfully. There were no legal procedures to bind it, and it did not have the liberal ministers' scruples about observing formal democratic processes. Since the hundreds of soviets that sprang up throughout the country within a few weeks after the revolution looked to the Petrograd Soviet for leadership, its edicts had the effect of law and were for the most part obeyed. The halls of the Taurida Palace where the executive met were packed day and night with vociferous men and women offering suggestions, making demands, or simply pressing near to the seat of authority in order to feel the surge of their own strength as orders affecting the entire nation were issued.

Russian Cabinet Powerless In Face of Labor Hostility

By Isaac Don Levine

[*April 18, 1917.*] There is no danger of a separate peace between the new Russia and the Central Powers. There is danger of internal strife in Russia which may well lead to disaster.

This summarizes the present situation in Russia. There are two governments in the Slavic country to-day. One is called the Provisional Government of Russia. The other is called the Council of Workmen's and Soldiers' Deputies. The former is the recognized government, representing the Duma and the nation's progressive forces. The other is a de facto government, instituted of its own authority, and represents the radical elements of the country.

The latter has recognized the former. It has voted by an overwhelming majority to continue its struggle against Prussianism. There is no possibility of its ever favoring a separate peace, as no Russian radical would ever desert France, England or America. The official and unofficial Russian governments are, therefore, fully united against a separate peace.

DIVIDED ON REFORMS

But there is division between the two on internal questions. The extremists aim at the widest and most radical immediate reforms. The moderate liberals insist on gradual reformation. It is this latter attitude on the part of the Provisional Government which provokes suspicion in the hearts of the radical masses. They fear that the government is too conservative and reactionary.

This is the meaning of the resolution adopted by the Congress of Workmen's and Soldiers' Deputies early in the week calling upon the people to see that the Provisional Government maintain the "conquests of the revolution."

It is the vague term "the conquests of the revolution," which provides the basis for the differences between the Council and the Provisional Government.

HOLD DIFFERENT VIEW

To the Council the term may mean the abolition of private property or some similar measures. To the Provisional Government it means sound reforms and political freedom.

In other words, extreme socialism and capitalism are now battling in the politically freed Russia. This battle, considering the raw state of the Russian democracy, may well lead to bitter strife and disastrous consequences.

With this division of power—"dual power," as it came to be called—neither the government nor the Soviet could tackle any of the major problems facing the country. A number of reforms were enacted: the

political prisoners were all freed; trade unions and strikes were legalized
and a system of factory committees of workers to negotiate with management was instituted; the disabilities against the Jews were lifted; the death
penalty was abolished. (Restrictions on freedom of speech, assembly, and
the press simply disappeared with the autocratic regime.) But the land
problem, extensive economic reorganization, codification of the law, civil
service reform, and other major matters were left until the convening of
the Constituent Assembly. And for that neither side was anxious to set a
date for fear of the strife that would almost certainly arise over these
fundamental questions.

The economic situation continued to deteriorate, and the surge of enthusiasm following the revolution began to give way to restiveness and
despondency. There was a good deal of pressure brought on the Soviet
to assume full power—to get rid of the Provisional Government and carry
the revolution to its socialistic conclusion. The reason given for its refusal
was a Marxist historical dogma which the Mensheviks, the Socialist Revolutionaries (whose philosophy contained many Marxian elements), and
also many Bolsheviks had propounded since the early days of the revolution. Russia, they insisted, had to pass through a capitalist stage before it
could become socialist. The revolution, therefore, was bourgeois in character, and it was historically necessary that the regime be middle class.
The Soviet was supposed to be merely acting as a watchdog against
counterrevolution, a guardian of the people's liberties, a vigilant opposition representing the most advanced tendencies of the historical period,
the crystallizing antithesis in the dialectical process.

However, there was also a political consideration. Russia was exhausted
from the war, and the desire for peace had been a chief cause of the
revolution. Both the Mensheviks and the Socialist Revolutionaries were
committed to the struggle against Germany, although a handful in each
of these parties had denounced it from the very beginning, as had Lenin's
followers. It was expedient, therefore, that the decision to continue the
war should appear to be the responsibility of the Provisional Government.

Miliukoff Pledges New Russia
To Fight Until Allies Triumph

Will Correct Errors Which Paralyze People In Struggle Against "Predatory Race Aiming to Subject Europe to Prussian Militarism"

It was this assurance, given by the Provisional Government immediately upon its assumption of office and often and clearly repeated, that secured such speedy recognition from the Allies and from the United States, which was just about ready to enter the war.

The Soviet, however, under considerable popular pressure, interpolated a condition.

Russian Radicals Oppose Indemnity And Annexations

Congress of Workmen and Soldiers Demands Peace on Basis of World Freedom

Whereas the Provisional Government was presumably pursuing the war with the same commitments and intentions as the government of the old regime, the Soviet took the position that it would support only a "revolutionary defensive" war, that Russia would not countenance a re-shuffling of territory either to its own advantage or anybody elses's. This pledge was without collateral, but the effect was to isolate the Provisional Government even further from the people, without the Soviet's actually taking a forthright position in opposition. A no man's land was created in which the more radical socialists—the left Mensheviks and Socialist Revolutionaries, and especially the Bolsheviks—began to thrive.

Russia Prepares to Meet Peace Drive by Socialists

Police photographs of Stalin, taken about 1910. (*Sovfoto*)

London, March 27 [*1917*]. Russia's provisional government is arming itself against two enemies—the expected German attack near Riga and a strong peace drive by the Socialists at home. The latter will probably come first, and it is viewed with fully as much concern as the offensive which it is expected Hindenburg will launch about the end of April in the hope of capturing Petrograd.

An odd situation exists in Russia. A month ago the autocrats were trying to end the war by disorganizing the country, and now the extreme Socialists have the same aim. They are organizing disorders, promoting social unrest and furthering a wild-eyed propaganda. Through misguided patriotism they are attempting to swing the country from one extreme to the other.

Now the exiles, the most obdurate of the revolutionaries who had been arrested or forced to flee during the Stolypin repression, were returning home. From Siberia came Josif Vissarionovich Dzhugashvili (Stalin), a young member of the Bolshevik Party's central committee; Lev Borisovich Rosenfeld (Kamenev), an editor of the Bolshevik newspaper *Pravda*; and others. In New York on March 27, Leon Trotsky and his family, along with a number of other Russian émigrés, boarded the Norwegian ship *Christianiafjord*. From Switzerland, by a devious route through Germany, came another group.

Russian Peace Agitators Allowed to Cross Germany

Stockholm, April 14 [*1917*].   Reports concerning a meeting of Russian and German Socialists in Stockholm to further the agitation for peace now appear to have been anticipatory. Such a meeting, however, may be held soon.

The fact that Russian peace agitators have been permitted to cross Germany from Switzerland seems also to indicate that the German government at least does not desire to throw any obstacles in the way of such a movement.

The party which arrived here Friday included thirty Russians, who came through Germany in a sealed coach. Among the principal members of the party were Nickolai * Lenin, the Russian Radical Socialist Leader, and Zinovyof [G. Y. Zinoviev], another Radical and peace advocate.

While in Stockholm the Russians issued a statement attacking England, accusing it of trying to "destroy one of the Russian revolution's results—political amnesty," and of refusing to permit Russian revolutionists abroad, who oppose the war, to return to Russia. The statement reviewed the negotiations with Germany for permission to cross that country and declared that the Germans had loyally kept their agreement. It was disclosed in the statement that the Russians had been in communication with German Radical Socialists.

The Russian party is now on its way to Petrograd.

Lenin arrived in Petrograd, at the Finland Station, shortly before midnight April 16. An immense triumphal demonstration had been arranged by the Bolsheviks. The square outside the station was thronged with people holding aloft bright red flags. Radical soldiers of the Petrograd garrison ensconced themselves on armored cars, and a mounted searchlight blessed the noisy assemblage with great sweeps of ghostly white.

---

* Many foreigners, including editors of American newspapers, assumed that the "N." in "N. Lenin" stood for Nickolai. Actually, it was merely an initial in a pseudonym.

Inside the station it was a breathless, sweating crush. On the platform, honor guards of Petrograd troops and sailors from the Kronstadt naval base stiffly lined the track. When the train arrived at the station a military band roared out the "Marseillaise."

A delegation from the Soviet, which was by no means overjoyed to see the man who fulminated against the Mensheviks and Socialist Revolutionaries, greeted Lenin with a bouquet and a very pointed speech, delivered by N. S. Chkheidze, president of the Soviet:

"Comrade Lenin, in the name of the Petersburg Soviet and of the whole revolution we welcome you to Russia. . . . But—we think that the principal task of the revolutionary democracy is now the defense of the revolution from any encroachments either from within or from without. We consider that what this goal requires is not disunion, but the closing of the democratic ranks. We hope you will pursue these goals together with us."

Lenin disinterestedly clutched the bouquet and studied the ceiling of the waiting room. As soon as Chkheidze had finished he abruptly turned away and addressed the crowd.

"Dear Comrades, soldiers, sailors, and workers! I am happy to greet in your persons the victorious Russian revolution, and greet you as the vanguard of the worldwide proletarian army. . . . The piratical imperialist war is the beginning of civil war throughout Europe. . . . The hour is not far distant when . . . the peoples will turn their arms against their own capitalist exploiters. . . . The worldwide socialist revolution has already dawned . . . Germany is seething. . . . Any day now the whole of European capitalism may crash. The Russian revolution accomplished by you has prepared the way and opened a new epoch. Long live the worldwide socialist revolution!"

If there were any doubts about his meaning, Lenin made it unmistakably clear that night at a meeting of the Bolshevik Central Committee and again the next day at a caucus of Bolsheviks attending the All-Russian Conference of Soviets. The war, he said, was no less "predatory imperialist" now than it had been under the Czar, and its continuation would be tenable only if "power be transferred to the proletariat and its ally, the poorest section of the peasantry" and if "all annexations be renounced in deeds, not merely in words . . . without the overthrow of capital it is *impossible* to conclude the war with a really democratic, non-oppressive

Lenin expounding his program to a meeting of Bolsheviks in the Taurida Palace, April 17, 1917.

peace." There should be "no support to the Provisional Government." The Bolshevik party must explain "to the masses that the Soviet of Workers' Deputies is the only possible form of revolutionary government and that, therefore, our task is, while this government is submitting to the influence of the bourgeoisie, to present a patient, systematic, and persistent analysis of its errors and tactics. . . . While we are in the minority, we carry on the work of criticism and of exposing errors, advocating all along the necessity of transferring the entire power of state to the Soviet of Workers' Deputies. . . . There must be established "not a parliamentary republic—a return to it from the Soviet of Workers' Deputies would be a step backward—but a republic of Soviets of Workers', Agricultural Labourers' and Peasants' Deputies throughout the land, from top to bottom."

Lenin's demands also included:

"Abolition of the police, the army, the bureaucracy.

"All officers to be elected and to be subject to recall at any time, their salaries not to exceed the average wage of a competent worker.

"Confiscation of all private lands.

"Nationalization of all lands in the country, and management of such lands by local Soviets of Agricultural Labourers' and Peasants' Deputies.

"Immediate merger of all the banks in the country into one general national bank, over which the Soviet of Workers' Deputies should have control.

"Not the 'introduction' of Socialism as an immediate task, but the immediate placing of the Soviet of Workers' Deputies in control of social production and distribution of goods."

Here was raised the cry with which Lenin proposed to rally the people to further revolution: "All Power to the Soviets!"

The program, which also included changing the party's name to "Communist," was published in *Pravda* on April 20; it was later known as the *April Theses*. It displayed Lenin's incomparable political acumen, particularly in the sections dealing with the war. While not actually advocating immediate peace at any price (there was not yet wide enough support for that extreme view), he sensed that anti-war sentiment would grow, and he wanted to channelize it into revolutionary activity. Without revolution, there could not be peace; hence the first task was to prepare the people by education and agitation for the seizure of power. Since the Mensheviks and the Socialist Revolutionaries were unwilling to take power, it would be up to the Bolsheviks.

Russian Pacifist Fails

Socialists Reject Lenin's Proposal To Overthrow Government

The Jewish "Forward" received yesterday [April 24, 1917] the following special cable message from its Petrograd correspondent:

"Representatives of the various Socialist groups of Petrograd, Moscow and other cities met in conference this week. The conference was called for the purpose of conciliating the opposing factions. The speech of Lenin, the ultrapacifist, however, only deepened the existing differences.

"Lenin demanded the overthrow of the Provisional Government and the setting up in its place of the Council of Workmen's and Soldiers' Deputies. The country should be governed, he said, by a labor dictatorship in conjunction with a democratic army.

"The majority, however, opposed these demands, voicing its support of the present government. The Social Democratic press is very wrought up by the extremist paper 'Pravda' for agitating against the new government."

Socialist Causes
Riot in Petrograd
By Urging Peace

Petrograd, April 26 [1917] (*via London, April 27*). A small riot was precipitated last night when a crowd drove the audience of the Socialist Lenine into the street as a protest against his exhortations for a cessation of the war and his attacks on the Provisional Government. A score of Lenine's followers were arrested, but the agitator remains at liberty.

Lenine, who recently returned from exile through Germany, has become the leader of a faction of Socialists who seemingly desire a cessation of the war, regardless of the consequences to Russia. He is living in the palace of the famous dancer Kshesinska, a former favorite of the Emperor, from the balconies of which he daily and nightly harangues his followers.

It is generally assumed that he is in the pay of Germany, and at any rate his return, facilitated by the German government, leaves little doubt in the minds of the great majority of Russians that he is working in the interests of a separate peace at the instigation of Germany.

LESS HARMFUL AT LIBERTY

His activity is permitted by the government, which fears that his arrest would make him a martyr and that he is less harmful at liberty.

With the new freedom of speech in the press and assembly, there is a deluge of new dailies and periodicals and numberless conferences and conventions of peoples of all trades, professions and callings. The separate-peace elements seem to be concentrated in the group under Lenine's domination. Their views are quite generally repudiated by the rank and file of the Socialists and working classes and even by the Socialist Peace party, which is working for the unanimous cessation of the war. On the question of peace the newly established "Workingmen's Gazette" says:

"Every day the bourgeois newspapers repeat the same thing, namely, that peace without annexation means a separate peace and that those opposed to a separate peace must continue the war to a full victory and the ruin of German militarism and imperialism. That is an error. We do not want a separate peace, because Belgium, Servia and France would be the victims of such a peace."

The paper then outlines the peace conditions which it advocates and which are based on a restoration of the previous map of Europe and full freedom for all nations.

SHUNNED EVEN BY ANARCHISTS

The press and public opinion have not been slow in arriving at the conclusion that the activity of Lenine and his group is a species of provocation not far removed from the efforts of the extreme reactionary clique. Commenting on the isolation of Lenine from other socialistic elements in the country and the fact that he represents no decent element, the "Russkia Volia" says:

"Not only Socialists refuse to recognize Lenine. Communism and 'Leninism' have little political importance, but threaten to cause a breach in the ranks of the Socialists. It is a pity that such a mischievous influence has arisen to blot the greatness of the Russian revolution. Kshesinska's palace, which was formerly the scene of the dancer's scandals, has now become the scene of political scandals and, with the roles changed, Lenine is now performing his anarchistic dance."

This was precisely what Lenin wanted. The forces were becoming polarized. Bolshevism now stood for revolution, while the Mensheviks and S.R.'s were becoming identified in the popular mind with the Provisional Government. That he was accused of being a German agent was of no concern whatsoever to him. His position as an internationalist, as a world revolutionary in the orthodox Marxist tradition was well known, and he took care to advocate revolution in all the belligerent countries, including the United States, which had entered the war against Germany on April 6.

Russia Will Fight To Victory, Pledges New Government

"Strict Regard for Engagement with Allies to Be Maintained"

German Plots Fail

Efforts to Sow Discord Frustrated, Says Note to Foreign Capitals

The note, signed by Foreign Minister Milyukov, pleased the Allies, but it infuriated a great many Russians. Glaringly absent was the Soviet pledge of no annexations and no indemnity.

Petrograd, Thursday, May 3 [*1917*]. The sentiment of the Workmen's and Soldiers' Council in its discussion of Foreign Minister Miliukoff's note promising to stick by the Allies, was to-night apparently against extreme measures, unless they should be absolutely necessary. Still every speaker at the council emphasized the contention that the power in Russia rests in the hands of the representatives of the workmen and soldiers, and that they are determined to enforce their views upon the temporary government or immediately disposses it and construct a government of their own liking.

M. Tcheidse, the president, said that he found the government note quite nullified the effect of the previous declaration of April 9.

"The form of this note and its vague allusions to a victorious end of the war," he said, "are so ambiguous that one can deduce anything he wants to from it, even the ideas of the old government. Steps must be immediately taken to clarify this so that the country will know that the government does not intend to agree to annexations, expropriations and contributions. After this explanation is published and the Allies are informed of its contents the proletariat classes of the Allied countries must take similar steps to make their governments repudiate such intentions."

[An] organized demonstration against Miliukoff and the Provisional Government by workmen and soldiers took place yesterday. . . . They paraded with banners inscribed "Down with Miliukoff!" "Down with Gutchkoff!" (Minister of War) and "Down with the Provisional Government!"

Discontent had been smouldering for some time in the belief that Miliukoff was not in full sympathy with the viewpoint of the workmen and soldiers. Minister Miliukoff . . . has always advocated the acquisition of Constantinople by Russia.

Petrograd, May 4 [1917], 6:50 p.m., via London, May 5 (Saturday), 6:44 a.m. At 3 o'clock this [Friday] afternoon, many hundreds of factory workers—men, women and boys—preceded by double files of soldiers, marched down the Nevsky Prospekt, with a banner inscribed, "Away with the temporary government."

A clash between rival parties followed on the Nevsky Prospekt, in which many shots were fired. The city is in a turmoil of excitement.

A series of demonstrations developed during the afternoon, both for and against the government. Motor trucks crowded with soldiers and civilians traversed the streets in support of the Provisional authorities. Detachments from both camps are appearing in increasing numbers and the agitation is increasing in intensity.

The Council of Workmen's and Soldiers' Delegates to-night accepted the government's explanation of its May Day note by a vote of 34 to 19, and decided that the incident was closed. The anti-government street demonstration was completely swamped by gigantic pro-government demonstrations on Friday evening. There were some clashes, but no serious incidents.

Prince Lvov threw up his hands. The Provisional Government had been made a goat of by the Soviet, which had been acting with deplorable opportunism in forcing the government to take responsibility, then attacking it when popular sentiment was hostile. It was an impossible situation. The theoreticians of the Soviet could not insist upon the establishment of capitalist democracy, yet not give the bourgeois regime the wherewithal to function. This applied, of course, not only to questions of foreign policy but to everything else.

The government was paralyzed. While the members of the Provisional Government were not willing to abdicate to the Soviet—any more than the Soviet itself was willing to assume power—some sort of fusing of authority was necessary. There was only one socialist member of the cabinet, the moderate S.R. Alexander Kerensky, and he had accepted the portfolio of minister of justice in defiance of his party.

In the Soviet there was still stiff resistance to participation in the government, based on principle but also based on very practical considerations. A coalition would deprive the Soviet of some of its popular support, which resulted from its having carefully distinguished itself from the Provisional Government. The Bolshevik influence would be greatly enhanced. On the other hand, the May demonstrations did prove the unworkability of "dual power." As Isaac Don Levine pointed out in the *Tribune (May 5, 1917)*:

> Russia is not through with revolutions yet. The demonstrations against the Provisional Government in Petrograd yesterday may prove the beginning of an attempt at another revolution with the almost certain result of civil war.
>
> The Russian masses, like the masses of any other European country, want peace. Intoxicated with the liberty that came to them through the overthrow of Czarism, these masses expected the proletariat of the rest of the world to follow their example, raise the banner of revolt and stop the world slaughter.
>
> It is clear that the masses that won the Russian freedom intend to run the affairs of the nation. They will force the Provisional Government to exert pressure on the Allies to come out against all annexations. Should the Provisional Government refuse to be controlled by the workers and soldiers Russia would immediately be divided into two hostile camps.
>
> In one camp would be the Provisional Government, the heads of the army and navy, the middle classes, a considerable part of the intellectuals and some soldiers and workers.
>
> Against it would be the Council of Workmen and Soldiers' Deputies, which is supported by most of the labor class and the army. Should an attempt be made to overthrow the Provisional Government a calamitous civil war would develop in the new Russia.

A decision was reached only after long and hard discussion.

Coalition Is Voted in Petrograd

Workmen's Body Calls on Soldiers to Fight On

Petrograd, May 15 [1917]. The radicals who have been disorganizing Russia will join in a coalition government, it was decided to-night when the executive committee of the Council of Workmen's and Soldiers' Deputies voted, 41 to 19, in favor of the plan.

The council also issued an appeal to the army to fight, and joined the Provisional Government in declaring that a separate peace was impossible, and that in permitting Germany to withdraw men to fight France and Britain the Russian army was preparing the way for the overthrow of the new democracy when the other Allies should have been defeated.

The Provisional Government announced that it would permit the Council to determine what places the Socialists would hold in the coalition.

These developments came after it had been learned that Generals Brussiloff and Gurko, two of the great military leaders who had made the revolution possible, had followed Minister of War Guchkoff in resigning because of interference by the Council. The warning yesterday by Minister of Justice Kerensky that the country was on the verge of ruin was also effective.

GENERAL STAFF URGES ACTION

Before the vote of the executive committee was taken representatives of the General Staff visited the committee and spoke most earnestly of the seriousness of the situation. According to their information, the speakers said, several other army commanders purposed to resign, owing to the impossibility of fulfilling their duty to the country under the present conditions.

In so far as it is possible to present any definite picture of the whirling maelstrom of events of which Petrograd is the storm centre, the situation to-day is as follows:

The conflict between the temporary government and the Council of Workmen's and Soldiers' Deputies is nearer solution than it has been since the revolution. But the disorganization, almost anarchy, has reached such proportions that it seems extremely doubtful whether any concentration of power in the government or the belated reconciliation of the two forces which have been pulling in opposite directions can re-create order out of the present chaotic conditions, for a considerable time at least.

URGE TROOPS TO FIGHT ON

The deputies in declaring themselves strongly against a separate peace and in favor of conducting a vigorous offensive war against an army which "is in the grip of German imperialism"—have, in fact, completely indorsed the point of view of the government, which has been attempting since its formation to warn the country against the danger of ceasing active military operations or considering a premature peace, which would sacrifice all the country has gained by the revolution and discredit Russia in the eyes of the world.

But the movement among the masses, soldiers and workmen, who have misunderstood the exhortations of their representatives and have far outstripped the most advanced ideas of their socialistic leaders, has gained such impetus that it will not easily follow the altered course of the Deputies.

The 19 opposing votes in the Soviet executive committee came from Bolsheviks and the more radical Mensheviks and Socialist Revolutionaries. Six socialists—Mensheviks and S.R.'s, the latter including Kerensky—took their places in the cabinet. Milyukov, who had been reassigned to the Ministry of Education without even having been consulted, resigned.

Russia Gets Ready to Fight; "Iron Discipline" for Army

Petrograd, May 19 [*1917*]. The new Russian government to-day began to get ready to fight.

Minister of War Kerensky declared that he would enforce "iron discipline" in the armies and that he would accept no resignations of officers. He warned all deserters to return to the colors by May 28. All generals have gone to the front.

The government issued a declaration that it would devote its attention to reorganizing the army and providing for its needs, both "for defensive and offensive purposes." It declared categorically against a separate peace and said that it would not permit Germany to overwhelm the Western powers and then throw its whole strength against Russia.

The declaration stated also that the new government was working for a general peace and reaffirmed its support of the declaration of the Council of Deputies against annexations and indemnities. It did not, however,

Kerensky urging the Russian soldiers to continue fighting. (*Photo from European*)

further define this phrase, interpretation of which may become the cause of friction with the other allies.

Kerensky now emerged as the propelling spirit of the new government. An extremely emotional man, given to florid outbursts of sentimentality that at times bordered on buffoonery, he had, nevertheless, a personal vitality and a disregard for inconvenient scruples that enabled him to accomplish tasks which people with more delicate sensibilities refused to undertake. Kerensky, more than any other single individual, was responsible for persuading the leaders of the Soviet to enter the government, and now he undertook the equally thankless task of welding an army out of the dispirited men wearing the Russian uniform. He cajoled, he threatened, he negotiated, he inspired—and he succeeded.

London, May 23 [1917]. The executive committee of the Workmen's and Soldiers' Council agreed to dispatch to the front any Petrograd soldiers desiring to leave. The Petrograd garrison consists of 60,000 men, and is considered the main support of the revolutionary elements.

The regiments that started the revolution were the first to announce their willingness to go to the front. The famous Volynsky Regiment, which led the March rebellion, left amid the greatest enthusiasm. Red flags were presented to the soldiers, and big throngs accompanied them with banners bearing such inscriptions as "Long Live the Democratic Republic," "Land and Liberty" and "Make More Shells."

Russian Factions Unite

Petrograd, May 27 [*1917*] (*via London, May 28*). Virtually all the divergent political factions, all class organizations, councils, and even the Socialist leaders, with the exception of the Extreme Lefters, are re-ëchoing the appeal of the Minister of War Kerensky to the troops and applauding the new order of the day, "Advance." It remains to be seen how the army itself will receive the final exhortation to patriotism and the defence of Russia's newly won freedom.

The Mensheviks, the S.R.'s, and the liberals, along with the conservative sections of the military officer corps, the landlord class, and businessmen, were now all identified in a commitment not only to the vigorous prosecution of the war, but to the launching of an offensive. Only the Bolsheviks and a handful of other socialists were in opposition. The polarization envisaged by Lenin in the *April Theses* was taking place. It sharpened rapidly, as the logic of their commitment, the need to maintain stability at home in order not to imperil the offensive, brought the leaders of the Soviet into conflict with the aspirations of many of their most important constituents.

Russia in Labor Crisis
Faces Ruin, Says Minister

Petrograd, May 28 [*1917*]. The industrial crisis in Russia is so acute, according to a recent utterance of the Minister of Finance, M. Shingaroff, that only a miracle can save the country from economic ruin. The demands of the workers were so enormous, he declared, that it seemed impossible to keep the industrial wheels going for any great length of time.

The Socialist ministers at a recent ministerial council said that the only possibility they saw of settling the difficulty was to bring the war to a close.

Neither the coalition Cabinet nor the newly appointed commission to regulate the difficulties between capital and labor has yet found a way to settle the industrial crisis. The commission is composed of the ministers of Finance, Trade and Industry and Labor, but since there is a wide divergence of views between the Minister of Finance and the Socialistic Minister of Labor, it seems probable that this commission will be confronted with the same difficulties that attended previous efforts at reconciliation.

FACTORIES SOON MAY CLOSE

An investigation of the factory conditions in Petrograd leads to the alarming but inevitable conclusion that unless the government soon finds a means of adjusting the present difficulties most of the industrial enterprises working for national defense will be compelled to close within a few months.

The workmen, through their committees, are in virtual command of the factories, and all business has to be submitted to them for approval. Wages in a majority of the factories have already been increased from 100 to 150 per cent, but there yet has been no offset by an advance in prices of the output.

An eight-hour day has become effective in all factories. According to the estimate of a leading manufacturer, the output of these factories has suffered an average decrease of 40 per cent since the revolution. He explained that all these concerns were confronted with an imminent shortage of raw materials and with bankruptcy.

Not only have the prices of products not met the advance in wages, but payment has been so slow that industry is in urgent need of capital. The manufacturers find it difficult to borrow money, as the banks naturally are not eager to extend credit to factories which are in control of temporary workmen's committees.

Strikes Spread in Russia; Ministers Delay Appeal

[*June 3, 1917.*]   Strikes are in progress in all parts of Russia, according to the Petrograd Correspondent of the Jewish daily "Forward." In a dispatch to that newspaper yesterday he states that the government is considering an appeal to the workers, but lack of agreement among the ministers has delayed the proclamation.

The workers, feeling that the revolution was theirs (whatever the theoretical contentions of their leaders in the Soviet), saw no reason to contain their demands within the bounds of what was practical. Having no experience in collective bargaining—and not really interested in it— they made no attempts to reach agreements with their employers, but simply struck when their demands were refused. The employers, of course, resisted making concessions, even when they could perhaps have done so. The Provisional Government was completely unable to do anything about the basic causes: the disastrous state of the transportation system, the insufficiency of consumer goods, and the general economic disorganization, largely because these involved basic economic and political dogma over which the liberals and the socialists were at odds. A solution to such fundamental questions had to wait for the Constituent Assembly, which both sides were now even more reluctant to summon, because of apprehensions about the effects of party strife on the war effort. The Soviet, while passing a resolution that the workers should "create control councils at the enterprises, the control embracing not only the course of work at the enterprise itself, but the entire financial side of the enterprise," at the same time urged the workers to moderate their demands and cooperate with the bourgeoisie.

The situation was made to order for the Bolsheviks. They campaigned tirelessly among the workers and soldiers and by the middle of June had achieved enormous success. The sailors at the Kronstadt naval base and a large number of troops in the Petrograd garrison now wholeheartedly supported them, and on June 13 the Workers' Section of the Petrograd Soviet voted 174 to 144 to endorse the party's demand for the transfer of all power to the Soviet. When, at a session of the First All-Russian Congress of Soviets, which convened on June 16, a delegate stated, "There is not a political party in Russia which at the present time would say, 'Give us power,' " Lenin shouted from his seat, "Yes, there is!"

Chapter Seven

The Emergence of Bolshevik Power

Kerensky Accepts
Dictator's Powers
To Save Russia

All Parties Except Maxi-
malists Vote Their Confi-
dence in Premier

Counter Rebellion
Feared by Leaders

An All-Night Conference
Unites Factions; Strong
Cabinet Promised

The Russian offensive opened on June 30, 1917.

Russian Infantry Begins Violent Attack in Galicia, While Their Big Guns Roar Along 175 Mile Front

Russian Army, Months Dormant, Strikes Heavy Blow at Germans on Eighteen Mile Strip of Front

In a typically extravagant, but not ineffective, gesture Kerensky put himself at the head of the troops.

London, July 2 [1917].   Russia's young Minister of War, Kerensky, led in person the first attacks of the Russian offensive in East Galicia, which already has developed into one of the most sanguinary general engagements of the war, and shows unmistakable signs of extending at once over a front of much greater magnitude.

The example of Kerensky, who is coming to be known as the "Savior of the Revolution," electrified the army, and the troops followed him out of the trenches cheering and singing.

Militarily the offensive began successfully. The Russians thrust into Galicia and on July 12 captured Kalus, headquarters of the Teuton Galician command. But again troops had to be driven into battle by their officers at gunpoint and again there were mutinies. Only now the incidents

147

THE BEAR THAT WALKS LIKE THE MAN WHO CAME BACK

The Russian government having been constrained to yield to the pressure of the leading Entente powers part of the army has been induced to attack.—*Berlin Official Statement.*

were more numerous, running together so that they began to have the appearance of a movement. The demoralization at the front quickly swept back home, accelerating the momentum of opposition to the Provisional

Government and the disaffection with the Mensheviks and Socialist Revolutionaries in the cities. On July 6, representatives of the workers from seventy-three Petrograd factories voted to demand the control of production and the transfer of all power to the Soviet. There was a nasty mood in the working-class sections of the capital and in the barracks.

Four Russian Ministers Quit; Rioting Begins in Petrograd

Petrograd, July 17 [*1917*]. Four members of the Cabinet have resigned and a special session of the Council of Ministers has been convoked in an effort to avert a crisis. Those who gave up their posts are A. I. Shingaroff, Minister of Finance; Professor Manuiloff, Minister of Education; Prince Shakovsky, head of the Department of Public Aid, and M. Stepanoff, acting Minister of Commerce.

The resignation of the four ministers followed a sharp disagreement over questions involving the Ukraine, an extensive region in Russia embracing part of the territories of the old kingdom of Poland.

The split in the ministry occurred last night at a ministerial conference called to consider a report submitted by M. Teresrchenko, Minister of Foreign Affairs, and M. Tseretelli, Minister of Posts and Telegraphs, as a result of their negotiations concerning the Ukrainians.

After the report was read the Cadet [Kadet] ministers promptly took exception to the form of a declaration drawn up by MM. Terestchenko and Tseretelli and objected to the fact that these ministers, without the authorization of the government, took it on themselves to commit the government to a definite policy regarding the Ukraine.

In addition to this cause of complaint, the Cadet ministers criticized the text of the Ukraine declaration—first, because it abolishes all power of the temporary government in the Ukraine; second because it does not specify of what territories the Ukraine consists or make clear how it shall be governed.

[*July 17, 1917*]. Soldiers invaded the printing office of the "Novoe Vremya" to-day and announced that publication of the newspaper should be stopped. They insisted on the compositors setting up a proclamation calling on the people to come to the street with arms in their hands and demand the overthrow of the Provisional Government and the confiscation of the entire bourgeois press.

"Comrades," said the proclamation, "might is on our side. We must immediately seize all factories, land and other sources of production."

The disorder of to-day was a continuation of yesterday's outbreak, when two demonstrations against the government resulted in the firing of shots in the Nevsky Prospect at mid-night.

The demonstrations were organized by the Bolsheviki.

The resignation of the Kadet ministers was not in itself of momentous importance to the soldiers and workers of Petrograd, but it did constitute a break-up of the coalition at the very moment when the demand for the assumption of power by the Soviets was acquiring the emotional tone of a battle cry. The First Machine-Gun Regiment had already voted to hold an armed demonstration to force the Vtsik (Executive Committee of the All-Russian Congress of Soviets) to take over the government and had convinced a number of other regiments to join. In addition, some 20,000 sailors from the Kronstadt naval base swarmed into the city. The resignation of the ministers merely supplied the excuse. The Bolsheviks at first tried to prevent the upheaval, which they believed to be premature. Moreover, the slogan "All Power to the Soviets!" did not provide a realistic rallying cry, since the Soviet was controlled by the Mensheviks and Socialist Revolutionaries. Nevertheless, once the demonstration started, the Bolsheviks assumed leadership, rather than sacrifice their newly won influence. News from the battlefront that the Russians had lost Kalisz and were in retreat undoubtedly fanned the conflagration.

Martial Law Is Declared In Petrograd

Armed Cossacks Patrol the Streets Following Serious Riots

Red guards, a workers' militia organized by the Bolsheviks, in training. (*Sovfoto*)

Bolshevik slogans were prominent in the huge demonstration against the Provisional Government in Petrograd on July 1, 1917. (*Tass from Sovfoto*)

LIBRARY — Allegheny Campus

Street fighting in Petrograd during the "July days." (*The Bettmann Archive*)

Petrograd, July 18 [*1917*]. Petrograd to-night is an armed camp. Martial law has been proclaimed, following a conference between the Cabinet and the Workmen's and Soldiers' Delegates, and loyal soldiers are patrolling the streets.

Serious disturbances recurred to-day following yesterday's disorders, in which eight persons were killed and 238 wounded. The situation passed beyond the point of sporadic shooting and resolved itself in an armed conflict between the Maximalists [Bolsheviks] from Kronstadt, reinforced by sympathizers here, and the government's loyal forces. A group of Maximalists were arrested on their way to take possession of the telegraph and cable offices.

MINISTER SEIZED BY RIOTERS

M. Tchernoff, Minister of Agriculture [and leader of the Socialist Revolutionary Party] was arrested at the Duma by Maximalists, who started to take him away in an automobile as a hostage as he was delivering an address from the steps of the building. The minister was roughly handled by the crowd, but as he was being taken from the ground, he was recognized by Trotzky, one of the agitator Lenine's lieutenants, who protested and harangued the minister's captors and secured his release.

The council [Vtsik] of the new body of Soldiers, Workmen and Peasants of All Russia, the Extremists abstaining from participation, passed a resolution to-day after an all-night session rejecting "with indignation all attempts to influence" the attitude of that body.

As the Bolsheviks had feared, the demonstration was premature. The insurrectionists were really just letting off steam and made no attempt to seize power. Loyal troops easily restored order.

At the same time, the government was presented with a new way to discredit the Bolsheviks.

Russian Revolt Crushed;
Lenine Sought as Spy

Radicals' Leader in Pay of German Staff, Letter Reveals—Government in Control After Bloody Street Battles—Cabinet Reorganization Delayed

Petrograd, July 19 [*1917*]. The Provisional Government controls Petrograd once more. Loyal troops have smothered the uprising of disaffected regiments led by Nicolai Lenine, the Radical Socialist, and the staff of the Petrograd military district believes that all trouble is at an end.

It is probable that Lenine will be arrested as a German spy. A letter from General Brusiloff's Chief of Staff has been received by the government, in which proofs are submitted that the chief trouble maker of the revolution is actually in the employ of the German General Staff.

The discovery of Lenine's dealing with the German General Staff was made, according to the letter from the front, through the confession of a young Russian officer, Lieutenant Ermolenko. He says that Lenine sent him to the front with the Sixth Russian army to spread propaganda in favor of an early peace with Germany.

Lenine's task, for which Germany is paying him, is to compromise the Provisional Government in the eyes of the people in every possible way.

Lenin, in order to escape to Finland after the "July days," disguised himself by shaving off his beard and donning a wig, then procured a false identity card, to which this photograph was affixed. (*Sovfoto*)

Funds have been sent him through an employe of the German legation at Stockholm.

The military authorities Thursday morning searched the office of Nicolai Lenine's newspaper, "Pravda." Among the documents discovered was a letter from a German at Hararanda, Sweden, expressing satisfaction over the activities of the Maximalists and the hope that they would succeed in securing a predominating influence in Petrograd. The writer also expressed the conviction that Germany would be victorious in the war, but maintained that it was indispensable to hasten everything toward the conclusion of peace.

Regardless of the truth or falsity of the accusation, it served its purpose. Lenin and Zinoviev went into hiding, while Trotsky (now aligned with the Bolsheviks), Kamenev, and others allowed themselves to be arrested for the propaganda advantages. But the setback for the Bolsheviks of the "July days" (as the disturbances were called) was not serious. Indeed, the party membership, 80,000 in April, numbered 200,000 in August.

Meanwhile, the cabinet was reorganized.

Lvoff Out; Kerensky Is Premier

Petrograd, July 20 [*1917*]. The "Bourse Gazette" announces that Premier Lvoff has resigned and that Alexander F. Kerensky has been appointed Premier, but will also temporarily retain his portfolio of Minister of War and Marine.

Eleven of the eighteen members of the new cabinet were socialists.

Kerensky Is Made Dictator of Russia; Armies in Flight

Tarnopol Falls; Attack in North Halted by Desertions

London, July 23 [*1917*]. Alexander F. Kerensky, the magnetic young leader of free Russia, is now absolute dictator. He was invested with his extraordinary powers to-day, and henceforth will bear on his shoulders the double burden of stemming defeat in the field and stamping out anarchy behind the battle lines.

The military situation, which Dictator Kerensky is now viewing from the battle front, falls little short of being a debacle. In East Galicia the Russian armies, shattered in morale, impregnated with anarchism and refusing still to obey their commanders, are fleeing over a front thirty miles wide, and already have retreated twenty-five miles.

Tarnopol is reported already in German hands, the Russians are across the Sereth, and on either hand Kerensky's forces are giving way, threatening a complete evacuation of Austrian territory.

The executive committee of the All-Russian Workmen, Soldiers and Peasants to-day issued a stirring proclamation to the soldiers on the front and soldiers at the rear, declaring that the time has come "to act without hesitation" and that the Provincial Government must be supported to the death in its "unlimited power and authority."

"No mercy," it says, "will be shown to cowards and traitors who fail

Among the Bolsheviks attending the Sixth Congress of the party in August 1917 were Y. M. Sverdlov, who acted as a sort of one-man secretariat for the party; Stalin, who was entrusted with delivering the important political report of the Central Committee; V. M. Molotov, the secretary and acting editor of the party newspaper, *Pravda;* and K. Y. Voroshilov, then comparatively unknown. (*Sovfoto*)

to fight against Emperor William's hordes, bringing death and destruction."

The only bright spot in the dark cloud overhanging the nation lies in the fact that the truth is being told and the government seems amply to realize the extent of the danger. As to whether Kerensky in his new position can do more than formerly is a matter of conjecture.

Death Penalty Fails to Check Russian Retreat

London, July 25 [*1917*].   The great Russian retreat continues. To-night comes news from Berlin that the pressure in Galicia has forced a Russian retirement in the Carpathians. The army there already has reached Kirlibaba on the north side of the ridge and is drawing in on Czernowitz, the capital of Bukowina.

Meanwhile the Austro-Germans have taken Bucacz, Tlumacz, Ottynia and Delatyn, all important towns in the evacuated territory, and at the point of their deepest penetration, around Tarnopol, they have stormed the heights west of the Gnizna River as far as the Trembowia-Husiatyn road.

DEATH PENALTY RESTORED

From Petrograd the most drastic orders and appeals are being issued to minimize the catastrophe. The government has unanimously restored the death penalty and appointed courts-martial, consisting of three officers and three soldiers each, to act on all the fronts.

A frantic, almost hysterical, appeal to the committees of the armies and the fleet has been issued by the executives of the Workmen's and Soldiers' Delegates and the Peasants' Congress. It affirms that the panic produced by the "lack of discipline and open treachery" is "preparing the soil for the poisonous seeds of a counter revolution," and that already "the jackals and hyenas of the old regime are howling."

Russia, in Despair, Begs Peace

Workmen's Council Issues Proclamation
That Republic Cannot Fight On

London, Aug. 4 [*1917*].   The executive council of the Workmen's and
Soldiers' Delegates, according to Reuter's Petrograd correspondent, has
resolved to issue a proclamation to the peoples of the whole world, point-
ing out the tragic position in which the continuation of the war would
place them. This was especially true with respect to the Russian revolution, the overthrow of which would involve the wreck of all democracy
and the hopes of a universal and just peace.

The military situation is growing worse with every day of retreat.
Russia no longer holds more than the narrowest strip of Galician territory. Bukowina is being rapidly evacuated and yesterday the Austro-
Hungarian armies crossed the Besserabian frontier northwest of Czernowitz.

The collapse was due in part at least to the utter demoralization of the
Russian troops, which the generals blamed on the weakness and ineptitude of the government, particularly in its failure to suppress "subversive"
influences. With Kerensky's appointment on July 31 of General Lavr
Kornilov as commander-in-chief, the disgruntled military leaders, as well
as other rightist elements, found a spokesman willing and able to throw
down the gauntlet to the regime.

General Korniloff is regarded as the most daring, chivalrous and schol-
arly officer in the army. For a romantic rise from humble origin
Russian history has only one parallel—that of Michel Vassilievitch
Lomonosoff, fisherman's son, poet, philosopher, creator of the modern
Russian language, in the first half of the eighteenth century.

From log cabin to general is the literal text of the chronicle of General
Korniloff's career. Born forty-six years ago, son of a need-stricken Karal-
insk Cossack in Western Siberia, who later reared a large family on a pit-
tance gained as a village clerk, young Korniloff early began rough forest
work.

At the age of nine he received his first instruction. When barely thirteen, he, by his own exertions and all-night studies, qualified to enter the
Siberian Cadet Corps, composed largely of sons of local magnates. Again,
by his own efforts, this indomitable Siberian pioneer gained free training
at the Michaelovsk artillery school, where his amazing mathematical fac-
ulties brought approval from the authorities, even though he was suspected, with reason, of being a secret revolutionary.

Next . . . Korniloff was an officer in the Guards, and, being penniless, was obliged to serve in Turkestan. In the Japanese war he received the rank of colonel and was entrusted with a desperate mission—that of covering the retreat from Moukden of one of General Kuropatkin's shattered armies. It was executed with such resolution and skill that he was given the St. George Cross. Later he travelled all through Turkestan, the Caucasus and Europe studying, observing and writing books on Turkestan and the countries of Central Asia.

Amazing to strangers is his gift for languages, for he speaks not only all European tongues, but also Persian, Chinese and several dialects of Central Asia. At the outbreak of the great war he was in command of the 48th Division, once called Suvoroff's, now Korniloff's. In Galicia in 1915 he was wounded and taken prisoner by the Austrians.

The enemy press related that their generals were so impressed with General Korniloff's accomplishments and noble bearing that the return of his sword showed greater honor to Russia than to them. His restless spirit did not long stand captivity. After a daring escape from an Austrian prison camp and astonishing adventures he reached Russia.

At the outbreak of the revolution he was invited to command the troops of Petrograd, implying full confidence in revolutionary Russia. When the disorders arose [in April] General Korniloff . . . resigned . . . [and] took command of the Eighth Army.

[*Aug. 4, 1917.*]   General L. G. Korniloff in accepting the position of commander in chief of the Russian armies, Petrograd dispatches say, has telegraphed to Premier and War Minister Kerensky the conditions under which he is willing to take the supreme command.

"First, I wish to be responsible only to my conscience and to the people," says the general.

"Second, no one shall intervene in my fighting orders and appointments.

"Third, the measures adopted during the last few days at the front [reintroduction of the death penalty] also shall be applied at the depots in the rear."

The conditions, particularly the first, which would, in effect, relieve him of responsibility to the civilian government, were perforce rejected by Kerensky, and the general conceded without causing too much difficulty. But the issue was not resolved. He began to press publicly for the establishment of a truly dictatorial regime—not a wishy-washy one like Kerensky's, but an iron-fisted one of the military kind. He received a good deal of support, especially but not exclusively from rightists, and he made secret preparations to seize Petrograd. The convening of the Moscow State Conference, a convocation of delegates from various organizations and political groupings summoned by Kerensky as a display of national unity, afforded the General an opportunity to state his views to a wide audience.

Russia Faces
Ruin, Says
Korniloff

Army Chief Tells Council
Only Drastic Measures
Can Save Country

Moscow, Aug. 27 [*1917*]. General Korniloff, the army commander in chief, who on his arrival Sunday was hailed as the "savior of Russia," appeared before the national conference to-day and told the delegates what must be done to save the new democracy from foes within and without.

While the Left, comprising the delegates of the Soldiers' and Workmen's organizations, remained in disapproving silence, the general, wildly cheered by all other groups in the conference, declared that to save Russia the army must be regenerated; anarchy, for which the misapplied democratic zeal of the Soldiers' and Workmen's delegates has been held responsible, stamped out and the country in the rear of the fighting forces organized to produce war material.

A little man, with a Tartar beard and Japanese eyes, General Korniloff appeared before the Assembly, accompanied by Premier Kerensky, with whom he was expected to come in conflict over the means of safeguarding Russia.

Kerensky, faced with disaster at the battlefront and still unnerved by the "July days," was not unwilling to reach an agreement with Kornilov. But Kornilov, whose self-confidence grew in proportion to the ebb of Kerensky's, now demanded that civilian as well as military authority be vested in the commander-in-chief, who, presumably, would continue to be Kornilov. The demand was, of course, completely unacceptable.

'Act of Rebel' Russians Call Demand of General Koriniloff To Hand Government to Him

Deposed Officer Marching on Petrograd as Soldiers and Workmen Denounce Him

The Russian government again is facing a tragedy. General Korniloff, deposed as commander in chief of the army, is marching troops toward Petrograd, the men being moved under the pretext that they are being used to crush the Maximalists in the capital.

The Premier, Mr. Kerensky, is once more adopting his "blood and iron" principles, and already has taken vigorous steps to crush the new outbreak of treason.

General Korniloff, commander in chief of the army, backed by a group of political agitators, demanded for himself dictatorial powers by the surrender of the government into his hands. Mr. Kerensky, although threatened by Korniloff, refused to comply with the demand and incarcerated in the Petropavlovsk Fortress Vladimir Lvoff,* member of the Duma, who acted as Korniloff's mediary, and who under a severe examination had wrung from him the details of the plot to overthrow the government and bring about a return of the despotic regime. The names of the chief conspirators in the plot also have been ascertained, and these men will receive punishment at the hands of the government.

Korniloff was deposed from the chief command of the army, while General Lokomsky was pronounced a traitor for refusing to take up Korniloff's duties.

Meanwhile martial law has been declared in Petrograd and its environs, and the government is taking measures to crush the revolt swiftly and decisively, probably by the creation of a directory composed of a small number of men, tried and true friends of the revolution.

Confronted by a common danger to the revolution, the radical parties drew together. At a meeting on September 9, the leaders of the Vtsik ex-

* Not to be confused with the former premier Prince G. E. Lvov.

tended an invitation to the Bolsheviks to join with them in a united front against Kornilov. Lenin accepted, commenting, "We will fight Kornilov, but will not support Kerensky," and the Bolsheviks, who had gone underground after the July days, now emerged in full panoply. It was they who propelled the organization of the resistance. Working with their usual energy and discipline, they formed a workers' militia, the Red guard (the Vtsik agreed, though with great misgivings), and conducted a vigorous propaganda campaign.

Their success, especially in persuading Kornilov's troops to abandon him, was a chief reason for the quick collapse of the counterrevolution.

Gen. Korniloff To Surrender; Army Deserts

London, Sept. 13 [*1917*]. Without bloodshed, Kerensky has won his battle with Korniloff for the dictatorship of Russia.

Korniloff has communicated to the Provisional Government his intention to surrender on the arrival of General [M. V.] Alexieff, commander in chief of the Russian armies, at Mobitev.

It is good news, the finest Russia has produced for many a day, for it means that after the failure of the leader best qualified to challenge the authority of the government another attempt is not likely for some time.

General Korniloff chiefly depended upon the Mussulman Cossacks, who after approaching within sixteen miles of the capital, failed in their allegiance to the rebel leader and accepted the government's offer to send them back to their homes in the Caucasus. Other rebellious troops took the same attitude, saying they were misled.

ALEXIEFF A BIG FACTOR

The news that General Alexieff joined the forces of Kerensky to become commander in chief showed pretty definitely that Russia was finished with monarchs. Alexieff, who has sound judgement and influential following, would hardly enlist under Kerensky unless he expected the latter to win. With most generals deserting Kerensky, Alexieff had everything to lose and nothing to win if Korniloff succeeded in becoming dictator.

Alexieff's decision followed immediately the resignation of Tchernoff as Minister of Agriculture. He was bitterly opposed by the Cadets because of his extreme views on the land question, Tchernoff proposing the taking of all lands without indemnities. Kerensky accepted his resignation as a concession to the Cadets. By this move, which naturally the Socialists opposed, Kerensky gained his valuable recruit.

The victory, however, belonged to Lenin and the Bolshevik party.

Petrograd, Sept. 14 [*1917*]. The Cabinet crisis continued all day. The evening newspapers assert that Premier Kerensky is in a very difficult position and that his resignation is not excluded from the possibilities.

The situation is complicated by the attitude of the Petrograd Council of Deputies, in which, at last night's meeting, the Bolsheviks for the first time gained an overwhelming majority of 279, against 150, in favor of the extreme radical position, which declared that . . . all the representatives of property-owning classes must be excluded from power.

This programme also demanded an immediate declaration of a democratic republic, the abolition of private property, working class control over production, confiscation of war profits, the "merciless taxation" of capital, an immediate invitation to the warring states to conclude peace, etc.

A few days later the Moscow Soviet also swung over to the Bolsheviks, and within a short time Lenin's followers had gained majorities or sizable minorities in a large number of urban soviets throughout the country. The extent of their influence was indicated by a petition from 126 soviets to the Vtsik, which still supported the Provisional Government, demanding that it assume power. In most of Russia—that is, in rural areas—the Socialist Revolutionaries remained the dominant party, but there was a definite veer to the left, and within that party itself a split developed, a substantial section moving much closer to the Bolsheviks.

The rapid growth of Bolshevik strength in the autumn of 1917 was due to a number of intertwined factors. For the wilting spirit of the battlefront troops, the Kornilov affair was the final blow. Mutinies proliferated, the men not infrequently turning on their officers and shooting them. Desertion became commonplace. The cry for peace, at any price, began to drown out the sullen boom of the cannon. Bolshevik agitators infiltrating the front lines easily enlisted support.

When deserting soldiers reached their homes in the country areas their rebellious mood, whether or not it was conveyed in a political doctrine, incited the already restive peasants. Ever since the March revolution there had been incidents of peasants ferociously ravaging the estates of the landlords, and when the government did nothing about these crimes against private property, the farmers grew bolder, seizing land or using private fields and woods without compunction. As in the cities, soviets were formed. In May and June a Congress of Soviets of Peasants' Deputies was held, during which a "Land Law" was adopted decreeing that "the right of private property in land is abolished forever," and that "all land . . . is taken over without compensation as the property of the whole people and passes over to the use of those who work it." The proclamation, while perhaps not accurately representing the true desire of the peasantry in so far as the abolition of private property was concerned, did reflect the hatred of the landless peasants for the landlords, a passion which was encouraged by some of the richer peasants, the kulaks, who saw the opportunity to obtain more land for themselves. Expropriation and the abolition of private property in land really meant the dispossessing of the estate holders—whether the church, the crown, or the pomyeschiks, that is, country squires who rented out parcels of their holdings. The Provisional Government failed to make any fundamental reforms, insisting that these must wait for the Constituent Assembly. This was the primary cause of the split in the Socialist Revolutionaries, some going along with the government and others, notably those closest to the poor peasants, taking a more drastic position. The revolutionary disposition that was becoming more intense among the peasants helped to stimulate revolutionism among the urban workers, many of whom had been off the land only a few years, and among the soldiers, most of whom were peasants.

Another factor that was both a cause and an effect of the combustible situation in the fall of 1917 was the shortage of food in the cities. It was caused partly by the poor state of the transportation facilities, which hindered the flow of grain from the Black Sea region and Western Siberia; partly by the drain of food to the armed forces; partly by peasant hoarding because of the lack of manufactured goods; partly by the wanton destruction of crop land and harvests by the peasants during their bouts of incendiarism. As a result the bread ration in Petrograd and Moscow dropped from a pound a day per person in the spring to half a pound in October. The deprivation naturally contributed to the discontent. The food shortages aggravated the inflation caused by the shortage of manufactured consumer goods. Real wages dropped from 69.8 rubles a month in 1916 to 38 rubles. Strikes increased. The factory committees became more aggressive, and the workers, in a rebellious mood anyway, asserted control over foremen, engineers, and the productive processes, with the result that production decreased even more, since the workers, who were much less skilled and experienced than, say, their British or American counterparts, often made a muddle of things. Some factory owners simply decided to close down altogether rather than try to contend with the impossible situation. Thus, because of the strikes, the chaos, the closures, as well as the stalled transportation and other factors, the manufacture of arms dwindled, exacerbating the demoralization of the troops; prices rose; and unrest waxed. In a word, a cycle of collapse had set in.

Anarchy Gaining Upper Hand In Russia, Says American Traveller

Stockholm, Sept. 27 [*1917*]. An American who has spent ten years in European capitals and whose position compels him to take the viewpoint of an impartial observer reached here to-day after six weeks in Petrograd and gives a pessimistic report of the fighting spirit in Russia and of political and industrial conditions there. He says:

"There is no fighting spirit except among the Cossacks and Caucasians, and that seems to be waning. The interior cities and villages are filled with Russian troops, who refuse to go to the front. Young Russians of the better class are hunting the streets of Petrograd for men who are willing to become officers. Since the murder of officers by men has become a daily occurrence only the most fervent patriots will assume the risk of taking commissions.

"The reports of open disobedience of the troops at the front and of deeds of violence committed by them are countless. Railway travel in many places, and particularly in Southwestern Russia, is unsafe because soldiers loot trains, steal luggage and maltreat and even murder those who resist.

"The Bolsheviki are gaining the upper hand in Petrograd and are increasing their strength in Moscow. I venture to predict their eventual supremacy. I know this means almost the elimination of Russia as a factor in the war and places new burdens on America.

"A factory near Nizhni-Novgorod manufacturing war materials and employing 15,000 hands has just closed because it was impossible to meet the wage demands. Armed workmen terrorize the owners of factories, workmen's committees spend their whole time drafting wage schedules and nobody may be hired or discharged without their consent."

It was in such circumstances that Kerensky tried to form a new government. In the hope of gaining support for a new coalition, he agreed to a Vtsik demand for a conference of delegates from the soviets, municipalities, cooperatives, trade unions, and other organizations to discuss the situation.

Petrograd, Sept. 27 [*1917*]. Premier Kerensky addressed the Democratic Congress at its first session to-day in the Municipal Theater, receiving applause which came principally from the less radical groups of delegates. The address was largely a defence of the acts of the government under his Premiership.

Nikolai Lenine, the Radical Socialist leader, is reported to have arrived in Petrograd. The police do not deny this report, but say that his present address is not known to the authorities. The Minister of Interior has ordered his arrest.

M. Kerensky was interrupted frequently by shouts from one group and another, which led at times to altercations lasting several minutes.

The conference only made matters worse. Some of the more moderate members of the Menshevik and Socialist Revolutionary parties urged the formation of a strong coalition to deal with the disaster enveloping the nation, but most argued that a more organic solution had to be found, that in any case, a coalition with the bourgeoisie, especially the Kadets, would only increase the estrangement of the workers and soldiers from the two parties. The Bolsheviks, who were in the minority, vociferously demanded the convocation of the Constituent Assembly, not because they really wanted it, but to embarrass the other socialists.

Petrograd, Oct. 3 [*1917*]. The Russian Democratic Congress here, which the Provisional Government has not recognized as an official body, declared to-day its opposition to a coalition government, reversing itself completely.

The congress first voted, 766 to 688, in favor of the coalition idea. Thereupon it offset this vote by adding an amendment excluding the bourgeois elements of the population, especially those concerned in the Korniloff revolt, and the entire Constitutional Democratic party. This move brought on a lively discussion, which terminated in the final vote against coalition by 813 to 180.

Meanwhile serious strikes broke out in Petrograd and Kharkov. Employes of the principal Russian railways, whose recent demands for improved economic conditions had been refused, announced their intention of stopping work to-morrow. Employes of the electric light company at Kharkov arrested the directors and managers and announced they would hold them until higher wages had been granted.

The revolt which broke out Saturday at Tambov, 300 miles southeast of Moscow, has been suppressed, according to an announcement of the government to-day.

In desperation, Kerensky went ahead and formed a cabinet including two Kadets.

Petrograd, Oct. 6 [*1917*]. The Democratic Congress adjourned to-night after having appointed a preliminary parliament of 305 members, who will begin their sittings to-morrow and continue in session until the meeting of the Constituent Assembly.

Simultaneously, the Petrograd Council of Soldiers' and Workmen's Deputies, disappointed with the work of the Democratic Congress, has ordered the convocation of a general council of the Soldiers' and Workmen's Deputies of All Russia to meet in Petrograd.

The adjournment of the Democratic Congress seemed to complicate rather than clarify the Cabinet situation, although the government was still hopeful of reaching a coalition agreement which would satisfy all factions.

While the government and the leaders of the moderate socialists floundered, Bolshevik tactics—and thus the policy of the Petrograd and Moscow soviets—underwent a critical change. Ever since the conclusion of the Kornilov affair, Lenin had been urging that the Bolsheviks prepare to seize power by force. "Having obtained the majority in the Soviet of Workers' and Soldiers' Deputies in both capitals," he wrote, "the Bolsheviki can and must take the state power into their hands. . . . An insurrection must rest on a turning point in the history of the growing revolution, when the activity of the leading ranks of the people is greatest and when the waverings in the ranks of the enemies and of the weak, half-hearted, undecided friends of the revolution are greatest." For the moment the balance of forces was favorable, but this might very well not remain the case. Moreover, the world was on the "threshold of proletarian revolution"; to hesitate "at such a moment, under such propitious conditions," would constitute a betrayal of the principle of world revolutions. And, Lenin maintained, victorious revolution elsewhere would strengthen the Russian proletariat, enabling the transition through state capitalism to socialism and communism to proceed smoothly and rapidly. "History will not forgive us if we do not take power now."

Before the opening of the conference Lenin had proposed to the Bolshevik Party Central Committee that the Bolsheviks walk out after making a declaration of principle and then concentrate all the party's resources on agitation among the workers and soldiers for an armed insurrection. But the Central Committee voted against him. The Bolsheviks, they argued, did not have a majority in the country, and without it a revolution would be doomed. It was better to constitute a powerful opposition, to rally the masses. Insurrection now was too great a gamble; defeat would be a disaster for the party, and defeat was not unlikely, since the Bolsheviks were so isolated both in Russia and in the world.

Characteristically, Lenin, entirely convinced of the correctness of his appraisal of the situation, simply intensified his efforts to win the party over. He wrote article after article, spoke whenever the opportunity arose. Trotsky supported him with all the ardor, stamina, and suppleness of mind of which he was so capable. Substantial weight was added to their exhortations by events in Germany.

Crews in German Fleet Mutiny; Socialists Accused of Aiding Plot

London, Oct. 10 [*1917*].   A serious mutiny has occurred in the German high seas fleet. This was accompanied by rebellious disorders among the soldiers at the front, which were quickly suppressed.

The crews of four, and perhaps five, warships at Wilhelmshaven turned against their officers, and the sailors of the battleship Westfalen threw their captain overboard and drowned him. It is known that mutinies took place on the Westfalen, Nurnberg, Luitpold, and Kaiser.

The fleet uprising had all the elements of a widespread and organized revolt, and was put down only with the greatest difficulty.

German Mutiny Backed by Large Faction in Navy

German Socialists Clamor for "Peace by Understanding"

Gradually, the Bolsheviks were convinced. Trotsky, who had been elected President of the Petrograd Soviet after his release from jail in September, steered the Bolshevik majority there toward a break with the government. At the first session of the Pre-Parliament on October 20, he led the Bolsheviks out. On the same day, a Menshevik proposal in the Executive Committee of the Soviet to establish a Military Revolutionary Committee to take charge of the defense of the capital in case of a German invasion was cunningly seized upon by the Bolsheviks, who immediately saw its possibilities. On the night of the 23rd, Lenin and eleven other members of the Central Committee gathered secretly in the apartment of N. N. Sukhanov, a Menshevik, whose Bolshevik wife had managed to get him out of the house. Once again Lenin presented his arguments. For hours the discussion continued, interrupted only for refreshments consisting of tea and sausages. Finally, the Central Committee resolved, by a vote of 10 to 2, to proceed with the insurrection. Zinoviev and Kamenev, who thought it too risky, cast the dissenting votes.

Russian Workers' Council Decides To Name Its Own Government

Petrograd, Oct. 24 [1917]. The Petrograd Council of Soldiers' and Workmen's Deputies on Monday [October 21] adopted a resolution proposed by Leon Trotsky, president of the Executive Committee and a leading Maximalist, declaring the salvation of the country lies in the conclusion of peace as quickly as possible.

The resolution contains declarations accusing Premier Kerensky of a desire to deliver Petrograd into the hands of the Germans and their "imperialist allies," and also of openly favoring the German Emperor. The resolution demands that all power pass into the hands of the Council of Soldiers' and Workmen's Deputies and instructs the executive committee to propose an armistice to all the nations. As long as peace is not concluded, however, the committee must defend Petrograd and restore the army to the status of a combative force.

TO HAVE OWN GENERAL STAFF

In consequence of this resolution the Petrograd Council of Soldiers' and Workmen's Deputies has decided to form a revolutionary general staff for the defense of Petrograd.

The "Vechernee Vremya" says:

"The Soldiers' and Workmen's Deputies frankly admit that they are planning civil war."

Yesterday's evening newspapers, which publish the programme for the meeting of the Central Council of Soldiers' and Workmen's Deputies on October 20, old style (November 2), are filled with rumors of a Bolsheviki demonstration and an attempt to seize the government on that date.

The programme for the discussions of the council embraces five topics: The revolutionary democracy and its power, the conditions of peace, the constituent assembly, demobilization of the army and the fight against anarchy and pogroms.

WHY BOLSHEVIKI BOLTED

Leon Trotsky, at a meeting of the Council, yesterday explained why the Bolsheviki bolted the first meeting of the Russian Democratic Congress [Pre-Parliament], declaring that that body had not been representative of the people and was not trusted by the soldiers and workmen.

"With the formation of the preliminary parliament," he said, "the independence of the ruling power was confirmed officially. Russia is a republic, but its autocrat is Kerensky."

He urged the Councils of Soldiers' and Workmen's Deputies to be ready to fight to have the power handed over to them. He declared they would be able to save the country and make peace.

The sword had been placed on the forge.

Chapter Eight

The Bolshevik
Revolution

RUSSIAN GOVERNMENT UPSET BY REVOLUTIONISTS, PREMIER FLEES; 'REDS' TO ASK IMMEDIATE PEACE

Winter Palace Capitulates After Night Bombardment from Cruiser and Fortress, Women's Battalion Protecting It Surrenders and Ministers Are Arrested, but Premier Escapes and Orders Are Issued for His Arrest.

ARMISTICE TO BE PROPOSED TO BELLIGERENTS; LAND TO BE HANDED OVER TO THE PEASANTS

Death Penalty at the Front Abolished and Soldiers Are Invited to Send One Delegate from Each 25,000 to Take Part in Governing Country.

The actual task of organizing the revolution fell to Trotsky. Lenin, having laid out the strategy, now withdrew nervously into the background, even though he was not entirely confident in his lieutenant, who had joined the Bolsheviks late and whose broad abilities he felt just barely remained on the safe side of dilettantism. But Lenin was still a fugitive and could not appear openly, and as far as most of the workers and soldiers of Petrograd were concerned, Trotsky represented Bolshevism. Lenin, to be sure, was the acknowledged leader, the towering, if somewhat remote, originator of ideas. Trotsky, however, they knew personally. He often appeared in the factories and barracks and had aroused them with clarion speeches that invariably seemed to articulate their ill-formed thoughts. The Kronstadt sailors, who were more inclined toward anarchism than Bolshevism, adored the fiery revolutionary and obeyed him without hesitation. The workers had more or less the same attitude. Moreover, the insurrection was to take place in the names of the soviets, as well as the Bolshevik Party, and Trotsky was president of the Petrograd Soviet.

Trotsky proved that in addition to his talents as a formulator of doctrine and an orator, he had the instincts of a true commander. The Military Revolutionary Committee was made into an insurrectionary general staff with Trotsky at its head. On November 3, he procured from the Petrograd garrison a resolution "endorsing all political decisions of the Petrograd Soviet" and pledging "to put at the disposal of the All-Russian Congress of Soviets all its forces, to the last man." The commander of the garrison was replaced with commissars appointed by the Committee. Guns were issued to the Red guards, the workers' militia organized at the time of the Kornilov rebellion. Plans were carefully worked out for the occupation of key buildings in Petrograd, such as the telephone exchange. Meanwhile, Trotsky ran from factory to barracks to factory, inspiring, explaining, expounding, crying out for peace, bread, and land.

It was perfectly obvious to everyone what was afoot.

Petrograd, Nov. 2 [*1917*]. The Maximalists continue their preparations for a demonstration, the date of which is being kept secret, but is believed to be set for November 4. It is persistently rumored that they intend to take armed action to seize the supreme power.

The government is receiving offers of help from all quarters and will prevent the proceedings by force, if necessary.

Yet the government and the moderate socialist parties failed to take any precautionary action. They were certainly informed of the Bolshevik intentions early enough, because Kamenev and Zinoviev revealed the decision of the Bolshevik Central Committee in a statement denouncing it, which was published on October 31 in Maxim Gorky's newspaper, *New Life*. But on the day following these revelations Trotsky publicly denied that the Soviet was planning an armed uprising, a slippery statement which was literally true, since only the Bolshevik members of the Soviet were initiated into the plan. This momentarily put the authorities off their guard, a naïve reaction stemming, undoubtedly, from wishful thinking. Even when the thinly camouflaged preparations of the next few days left no room for doubt, however, they let delusions lull them. Without any basis they convinced themselves that the insurrection would be crushed. Kerensky himself sank into a veritable catatonic fatalism. The fact was that the regime and its affiliates had collapsed. By not voting for a coalition at the Democratic Conference, the moderate socialists had completely undermined the Provisional Government, while they had lost the support of the Petrograd workers and soldiers because of their temporizing. Finally, on November 4, Trotsky, looking for an incident he could use as a *casus belli*, goaded Kerensky into action by ordering the Petrograd garrison not to obey any orders unless they were issued by the Military Revolutionary Committee. Also on the 4th a gigantic demonstration of soldiers, Red guards, and other workers was held as a peaceful display of strength in order to give the less fervent workers a sense of confidence and at the same time to discourage opposition. As Trotsky had calculated, Kerensky took action.

At 5:30 A.M. on November 6, troops closed down the Bolshevik newspapers *Workers' Road* and *Soldier,* and orders were issued for the arrest of the Bolshevik leaders. Regiments presumed loyal were called in from outside the city to protect government buildings, especially the Winter

Palace, where they were joined by a battalion of women soldiers. The Bolshevik leaders of the insurrection promptly met and drew up their final plans, assigning tasks to various people. That night the uprising began.

Rebels Seize
4 Buildings
In Petrograd

Madame Bochkareva, leader of the women's battalions. (*Photo from European*)

One of the women's combat battalions organized in June 1917 joined in the defense of the Winter Palace against the Bolsheviks on the night of November 6–7 but was forced to surrender the next morning when the Cossacks and some of the other male troops withdrew. The women reputedly carried potassium cyanide pills to take if their virtue was threatened. (*Sovfoto*)

The strategically critical telephone exchange was captured by the Bolsheviks on the evening of November 6. (*Sovfoto*)

Armed Bolsheviki Break
Up Preliminary Parliament

Petrograd, Nov. 7 [1917]. An armed naval detachment, under orders of the Maximalist (Bolsheviki) revolutionary committee, has occupied the offices of the official Petrograd Telegraph Agency, the Central Telegraph office, the State Bank and the Marie Palace, where the Preliminary Parliament had suspended its proceedings in view of the situation.

No disorders are yet reported, with the exception of some outrages by apaches. The general life of the city remains normal, and street traffic has not been interrupted.

Early in the morning a delegation of Cossacks appeared at the Winter Palace and told Premier Kerensky that they were disposed to carry out the government's orders concerning the guarding of the capital, but they insisted that if hostilities commenced it would be necessary for their forces to be supplemented by infantry units.

They further demanded that the Premier define the government's attitude toward the Bolsheviki, citing the release from custody of some of those who had been arrested for participation in the July disturbances. The Cossacks virtually made a demand that the government proclaim the Bolsheviki outlaws.

KERENSKY'S REFUSAL

Kerensky replied:

"I find it difficult to declare the Bolsheviki outlaws. The attitude of the government toward the present Bolsheviki activities is known."

The Premier explained that those who had been released were on bail and that any of them found participating in new offences against peace would be severely dealt with.

Numerous precautions have been taken by Premier Kerensky to thwart the threatened outbreak of the Bolsheviki. The soldiers guarding the government building have been replaced by men from the officers' training schools. Small guards have been placed at the embassies. The Women's Battalion is drawn up in the square in front of the Winter Palace.

The commander on the northern front has informed the Premier that his troops are against any demonstration and are ready to come to Petrograd to quell a rebellion if necessary.

TROTZKY THREATENS DISTURBERS

Leon Trotzky, president of the Central Executive Committee of the Petrograd Council of Soldiers' and Workmen's Delegates and principal

FOOD FOR THE PACK

Bolsheviki leader, has informed members of the town Duma that he has given strict orders against outlawry, and has threatened with death any persons attempting to carry out pogroms.

Trotzky added that it was not the intention of the Workmen's and

Shortly after the Bolshevik seizure of power, a mass demonstration in support of the new regime was held in front of the Winter Palace. (*Sovfoto*)

During the feverish November days, party workers in trucks and cars sped through the streets of Petrograd and Moscow, distributing newspapers and bulletins, and delivering political diatribes to the populace. This photograph was taken in Moscow's Theater Square. (*Sovfoto*)

Soldiers' Delegates to seize power, but to represent to a congress of Workmen's and Soldiers' Delegates, to be called shortly, that the body should take over control of the capital, for which all necessary arrangements have been perfected.

The government for the present will not resort to armed force against the military committee of the Soldiers' and Workmen's Delegates, but it has ordered the Ministry of Justice to prosecute the members of the committee.

The government hopes for a peaceful settlement of the dispute, on which account it reached the decision not to resort to force. However, the Soldiers' and Workmen's Committee was decreed an illegal organization, and precautionary steps were taken to defeat any attempt at a revolt.

By the morning of November 8 Petrograd had fallen.

Russian Government Upset by Revolutionists, Premier Flees; 'Reds' to Ask Immediate Peace

Petrograd, Nov. 8 [*1917*].   The Bolsheviki, headed by Nikolai Lenine, have overturned the Provisional Government. Petrograd is under their complete control.

Premier Kerensky has fled the capital. Several of his ministers have been placed under arrest, and the Winter Palace, seat of the government, has been seized by the rebels.

A congress of the Workmen's and Soldiers' Delegates of all Russia has convened here to discuss the questions of organization of power, peace and war and the formation of a constituent assembly.

A delegation has been named by the Congress to confer with other revolutionary organizations, with a view to initiating negotiations for an "immediate democratic peace."

WINTER PALACE TAKEN

Government forces holding the Winter Palace were compelled to capitulate early this morning under the fire of the cruiser Aurora and the cannon of St. Peter and St. Paul fortress across the Neva River. At 2 o'clock this morning the Women's Battalion, which had been defending the Winter Palace, surrendered.

The Workmen's and Soldiers' Delegates are in complete control of the city.

Late yesterday evening, after the government forces had been driven into the Winter Palace, the palace was besieged and a lively fire of machine guns and rifles began. The cruiser Aurora, which was moored at the Nicolai Bridge, moved up within range, firing shrapnel. Meanwhile the guns of the St. Peter and St. Paul fortress opened fire.

The palace stood out under the glare of the searchlights of the cruiser and offered a good target for the guns. The defenders held out four hours, replying as best they could with machine guns and rifles.

SPASMODIC FIRING

There was spasmodic firing in other parts of the city, but the Workmen's and Soldiers' troops took every means to protect citizens, who were ordered to their quarters. The bridges and the Nevsky Prospect, which early in the afternoon were in the hands of the government forces, were captured and held during the night by the Workmen's and Soldiers' troops.

The battle at the palace, which began shortly after 6 o'clock, was a spectacular one, armed cars of the revolutionaries swinging into action in front of the palace gates, while flashes from the Neva were followed by the explosion of shells from the guns of the Aurora.

At noon, however, the city had resumed its normal aspect. Even the noonday band accompanying the guard of relief under the previous administration continued its function.

There were the customary lines in front of the provision stores, and children played in the parks and gardens. There was even a notable lessening of the patrols, only a few armed soldiers and sailors moving about the streets.

The Maximalist coup d'etat was carried through without bloodshed, apparently under the leadership of Lenine and Trotzky.

PROCLAMATION TO ARMY

Yesterday the military revolutionary committee of the Central Council of Workmen's and Soldiers' Deputies issued the following proclamation to the army and workmen's committees:

"We have deposed the government of Kerensky which rose against the revolution and the people. The change which resulted in the deposition of the Provisional Government was accomplished without bloodshed.

"The Petrograd Council of Soldiers' and Workmen's Delegates solemnly welcomes the accomplished change and proclaims the authority of the Military Revolutionary Committee until the creation of a government by the Soldiers' and Workmen's Delegates.

"Announcing this to the army at the front, the Revolutionary Committee calls upon the revolutionary soldiers to watch closely the conduct of the men in command. Officers who do not join the accomplished revotion immediately and openly must be arrested at once as enemies.

PROGRAMME OF DELEGATES

"The Petrograd Council of Workmen's and Soldiers' Delegates considers this to be the programme of the authority:

"FIRST—The offer of an immediate democratic peace.

"SECOND—The immediate handing over of large proprietorial lands to the peasants.

"THIRD—The transmission of all authority to the Council of Workmen's and Soldiers' Delegates.

"FOURTH—The honest convocation of a constitutional assembly.

"The national revolutionary army must not permit uncertain military detachments to leave the front for Petrograd. They should use persuasion, but where this fails they should oppose any such action on the part of those detachments by force without mercy.

"The actual order must be read immediately to all military detachments in all arms. The suppression of this order from the rank and file by army organization is equivalent to a great crime against the revolution, and will be punished by all the strength of the revolutionary law.

"Soldiers! For peace, for bread, for land and for the power of the people!

(Signed) "THE MILITARY REVOLUTIONARY COMMITTEE."

ALL RUSSIA CONGRESS OPENS

The General Congress of Workmen's and Soldiers' Delegates of all Russia was convened last night, with 560 delegates in attendance. Of the 560 . . . 250 are Bolsheviki, 150 Socialist Revolutionists, sixty Minimalists [Mensheviks], fourteen of the Minimalist-Internationalist group [anti-war Mensheviks], six of the Nationalist-Socialist group, three non-party Socialists, the others being independent.*

The officers elected comprise fourteen Maximalists, including Nikolai

* Reliable figures were never published; later estimates are that there were 650 delegates, of whom 390 were Bolsheviks. See Donald W. Treadgold, *Twentieth Century Russia* (Chicago: Rand McNally, 1964), p. 149.

Lenine, the radical Socialist leader, and M. Zinovieff, an associate of Lenine, and Leon Trotzky, president of the Central Executive Committee of the Petrograd Council of Workmen's and Soldiers' Delegates. In addition seven revolutionary Socialists [S.R.'s] were appointed.

Nikolai Lenine was introduced by Trotzky as "an old comrade, whom we welcome back."

Lenine said: "Now we have a revolution. The peasants and workmen control the government. This is only a preliminary step toward a revolution everywhere."

The Mensheviks and right-wing Socialist Revolutionaries walked out of the Congress in protest against the coup, leaving it to the unchallenged control of the Bolsheviks and Left Socialist Revolutionaries, who had split off into an independent party.

Petrograd, Nov. 8 [1917]. The congress to-day appealed to the Russian army to stand firm and to protect the revolution against imperialistic attempts until the new government had obtained a democratic peace. Its appeal says:

"The new government will take adquate measures to assure the army of all necessities, and by energetic requisitions from the upper classes it will also ameliorate the economic situation of soldiers' families.

A resolution [was also] passed . . . calling for peace, the proposal declaring that all belligerent governments should enter immediately into negotiations "for a democratic and equitable peace."

"The government considers a peace to be democratic and equitable," says the resolution, "which is aspired to by a majority of the working classes of all the belligerent countries, worn out and ruined by war—the peace which the Russian workmen called for on the fall of the monarchy. It should be an immediate peace, without annexation (that is to say, without usurpation of foreign territory and without violent conquest of nationalities) and without indemnities."

The [resolution] announces [the government's] determination to carry on peace negotiations openly before the whole world, and to make void all secret treaties. It adds that the government is ready to negotiate a peace by written or telegraphic communication, or by pourparlers between representatives of the various countries or by conferences.

It suggests an immediate armistice of three months that the representatives of all the nations in the war, or its victims, may participate in the negotiations, and declares that a conference of all the nations of the world should be convoked to give final approval to the peace terms drafted.

SITS ON PLATFORM

The All-Russian Congress of Workmen's and Soldiers' Delegates, which from its headquarters in the Smolny Institute is endeavoring to collect the reins of authority that it has wrested successfully from the Kerensky Cabinet, is setting about speedily to extend its power over all Russia and bring about an early consultation over its aims. The congress has already selected commissaries to assume control of various departments pending the institution of a permanent government.

Nikolai Lenine, the Maximalist leader, who wears a workingman's garb, sits during the sessions of the congress on a raised platform with Leon Trotzky, M. Kamineff and other Bolsheviki leaders.

There were machine guns and a field piece and a strong guard of infantry protecting the three-story building in which the Workmen's and Soldiers' Congress is meeting. The spacious commencement room of the Smolny Institute was crowded with delegates, with soldiers predominating. There also were a number of sailors seated among the peasant delegates.

The audience wore an expectant, earnest air. On the platform Leon Trotzky was seated, carefully groomed, smiling and triumphant. Nikolai Lenine, quiet, reserved and studious, was beside him. The others of the present controlling government of Petrograd were grouped about them.

At the same session the Congress adopted a Decree on Land, abolishing without compensation the right of landlords to their landed property and placing church, monastery, and privately owned land under the administration of peasants' soviets and land committees. A *nakaz* (a list of instructions), consisting of resolutions passed in August by the All-Russian Soviet of Peasants' Deputies, was appended. Intended as a guideline for action by the peasants' soviets, it recommended the abolition of private property in land; the confiscation of "all land, state, Crown, monastery, Church, which is owned by private persons, by public organizations, by peasants [small peasant holdings excepted], etc.," without compensation; the nationalization of natural resources; the equalization of the use of the land; and other agrarian reforms. In addition, the Congress appointed a cabinet, called the Council of People's Commissars, including Lenin as

President of the Council, Trotsky as Foreign Commissar, and Stalin as Commissar for Nationality Affairs, a new post which was supposed to deal with the problems of the national minorities living in Russia.

However, the formation of the government and the enactment of the decrees on peace and on land were contingent upon the final victory of the Bolsheviks, which was by no means assured.

Kerensky Nears Petrograd; Civil War Is Begun

London, Nov. 11 [1917]. The Bolsheviki revolution in Petrograd is reported to be approaching collapse. Regiments loyal to Premier Kerensky are marching on the capital, and fighting is under way in the city, according to reports reaching here to-day from Petrograd.

The town of Tsarskoe-Selo, fifteen miles south of Petrograd, where former Emperor Nicholas lived much of the time, is said to have been captured by loyal forces after which the rebels retired to Petrograd in disorderly mobs. The chief wireless station is now controlled by loyal troops. The Red Guard has been defeated at Moscow. Premier Kerensky is said to be approaching Petrograd.

Early Friday morning [November 9] a Committee for the Salvation of the Country and the Revolution was formed [in Petrograd]. This consisted of representatives of the city Duma, the original executive committee of the Council of Workmen's and Soldiers' Delegates, the Social Democratic [Menshevik] party, the railway and postal unions, the Provisional Council and war front organizations. The committee issued a proclamation calling upon the people not to recognize the new power and not to obey its orders, but to defend the country and the revolution by supporting the committee.

Rival Russian Forces Battle For Petrograd

Petrograd, Nov. 12 [*1917*]. The feeling in the capital has changed acutely. Early yesterday the Constitutional Democrats sided with the committee for the Salvation of the Revolution. They occupied different institutions, evidently under the the impression that Kerensky's troops were approaching and would arrive in support. In spite of the armored car in front of the telephone station, the Constitutional Democrats, or Cadets, succeeded in occupying the premises.

The same thing occurred at the post-office and at the Michael Riding School, which was used as the headquarters for armored cars. The summer palace of the Emperor Paul, now a military school, also was captured.

RED GUARD RALLIES

Then the soldiers of the Red Guard, greatly infuriated, after a determined effort, succeeded in driving the Constitutional Democrats out of the places, and these were captured with little bloodshed, but in other parts of the town the struggle was more severe, with heavy loss of life.

The incidents of yesterday roused the worst passions of the populace, and excesses were committed.

Stockholm, Nov. 12 [*1917*]. A bloody encounter has taken place near Gatchina between soldiers from the front, headed by Premier Kerensky, and Bolsheviki forces from Petrograd.

Lenine Still Holds Petrograd

[*Nov. 12, 1917.*] The situation in Russia continues obscure, conflicting statements coming in from all sides. The only certain fact seems to be that the Bolsheviki are still in control of Petrograd and are sending forth their own views of the situation to the outside world. What is happening in the rest of the country is not known.

The "Tribune" correspondent reports that forces loyal to the Russian Provisional Government are marching on Petrograd from two sides. Lettish troops are declared to have advanced along the Finland railway to within thirty miles of the capital, while Kerensky, with two army corps, is reported to have reached the southern outskirts of the city.

The Bolsheviki announce officially that the forces under Kerensky and Korniloff were defeated on Monday at Tsarskoe-Selo, fifteen miles south of the capital, and forced to retire. Measures are being taken for the capture of the Premier, the announcement adds.

Stockholm advices say Korniloff has entered Petrograd with his troops and overthrown the Bolsheviki government. Moscow, said to be in control of Cossack forces loyal to Kerensky, will be the new capital, it is added.

Associated Press dispatches from Petrograd, dated Monday, give a remarkable picture of the fighting in the streets of the capital. They report Petrograd still in the hands of the Bolsheviki, following desperate street battles on Sunday, in which a small band of military cadets held off the revolutionists for hours before they were killed or captured.

The Bolsheviki government is declared to be having a difficult time controlling the city.

Reds Report Kerensky Rout In Petrograd

London Hears of Premier's Defeat in Big Battle Near Tsarskoe-Selo

Trotzky Boasts of Offensive Taken

Stockholm Reports Say Kerensky Entered Petrograd in Triumph After Defeating the Bolsheviki

Bolshevik Forces Reported Besieged in Kremlin at Moscow

Rebels Failing
As Kerensky
Enters Capital

**Various Reports Indicate
Complete Overthrow of
Bolsheviki**

**Moscow New Seat
Of the Government**

**Red Guards Believed to
Have Been Defeated
By Cossacks**

Petrograd Is Reported
in Flames; Kerensky's
Army Massed Near City

Then the true situation became clear.

Kerensky Defeated After
Three Days' Hard Fighting

Petrograd (*Wednesday*), *Nov. 14* [1917], *10:20 a.m.* Premier Kerensky's forces which advanced from Gatchina to Tsarskoe-Selo have been defeated by the Workmen's and Soldiers' forces between Tsarskoe-Selo and Pulkova, twelve miles from Petrograd.

The Kerensky contingents have retreated to Gatchina.

The battle in which Premier Kerensky was defeated began last Saturday and continued until Monday night, according to the commander in chief of the Bolsheviki staff.

The correspondent of The Associated Press visited the scene of the fighting to-day and was surprised to find aristocratic officers commanding the Bolsheviki. One of them, who was a colonel, explained that they were disappointed with Kerensky, who first destroyed discipline in the army, and were against him above all.

A colonel of one of the famous Petrograd guard regiments is now commander of the Bolsheviki staff and directs the operations of his army from a house on a hilltop two miles beyond Pulkova. Describing the fight, he said:

"The battle began Saturday and continued until Monday night, Kerensky had only 5,000 Cossacks, several hundred military cadets, a considerable quantity of light and heavy artillery and one armored train. Our forces included four of the famous Petrograd guard regiments together with several battalions of sailors and a large number of the Red Guard."

The correspondent made a tour of the battlefield in a Petrograd drosky, whose driver calmly directed his fat horse over the military road, dodging huge lorries and Red Cross motors homeward bound with wounded. Members of the Red Guard coming from the battlefield walked along the roads singing. Some carried pretzels on their bayonets. These are obtainable in Tsarskoe-Selo, but not in Petrograd, where only black bread is sold.

The drosky passed numerous sentries unquestioned, the soldiers apparently considering the ludicrous conveyance of the correspondent above suspicion. A constant stream of ambulances discharged their cargo of wounded at hospitals along the road just outside the city.

At Pulkova, where the soldiers, sailors and the Red Guard shared their soup and black bread and discussed the victory which had startled the inhabitants of the small village, the correspondent was directed to staff headquarters. There was an extraordinary contrast among the occupants of the bare, lamp-lighted room, which apparently had once been the parlor of a farmhouse. Seated about a pine table were some officers, who, though unshaven and battle worn, showed plain evidences of their aristocratic training. With them were a few common soldiers, plain sailors from the Baltic fleet and one workman wearing the badge of the Red Guard.

The Bolsheviki troops display an anomalous attitude in obeying the officers without question, but at the same time calling them "tavarish" (comrade) and insisting on equal rights elsewhere than on the battle-field.

Petrograd, Nov. 15. Seven thousand military cadets and three thousand troops are besieged in the Kremlin at Moscow by 18,000 Bolsheviki, who are battering the ancient walls and buildings with heavy artillery.

Kerensky in Hiding; Staff Deserts Him

Petrograd, Nov. 16 [1917] (noon). Deserted by most of his officers and virtually ordered to surrender to the Bolsheviki, Premier Kerensky evaded the guards sent for him and has disappeared. General Krasnoff, former commander under Kerensky, who was arrested with other members of the Premier's staff and released on the ground that he was only obeying the orders of his superior, said to-day:

"At 3 o'clock on the afternoon of November 1 (old style; November 14 new style), I called at the quarters of the commander in chief. He appeared nervous and excited.

" 'General,' said he, 'you have betrayed me. Your Cossacks say they will arrest me and give me up to the sailors.'

" 'Yes,' I answered, 'such a discussion is now going on. There appears to be little sympathy for you.'

" 'Do the officers feel the same way?' he asked.

" 'Yes.'

" 'What shall I do? Will I have to commit suicide?'

" 'If you are an honest man you will go to Petrograd under a white flag and appear before the Revolutionary Committee, where you will nego-tiate as head of the government.'

"Kerensky agreed to this, and he was promised a guard. He objected to a guard of sailors on the ground that some enemies were among them. He wanted to wait until night, but finally agreed to make the trip by daylight. I went and called Colonel Kishkoff of the 10th Don Cossacks and ordered him to appoint a guard of eight men. A half an hour later the Cossacks told me that Kerensky could not be found. I raised the alarm, thinking that he could not have left Gatchina."

FLED IN SAILOR'S GARB

M. Bibenko, member of the Committee on War and Marine, has reported to the Workmen's and Soldiers' [Council] that Kerensky fled garbed as a sailor.

The anti-Bolsheviks gathered around the Committee for Salvation in Petrograd were crushed when troops loyal to the Bolsheviks arrived from Minsk on November 15, and that same day the Reds succeeded in storming the Kremlin and capturing Moscow. Although there was still serious opposition elsewhere in the country, the Bolsheviks were now secure enough in the two capitals to pursue the first and most pressing item in the order of business, the negotiation of peace.

A few weeks before the coup, Lenin had summarized his analysis of the war and Bolshevik proposals for ending it in an article which the *Tribune* published on Nov. 9, 1917.

Lenine Denies Bolsheviki Seek Separate Peace

By Nikolai Lenine

(*Translated from the Russian by André Tridon*)

This article by Nikolai Lenine, the head of the Maximalists now in control of Petrograd, was written several weeks ago. It shows exactly what may be expected from the Maximalists.

I cannot protest too energetically against the slanderous statements spread by capitalists against the Bolsheviki party to the effect that we are in favor of a separate peace with Germany. To us the capitalists of Germany are plain pirates, like the capitalists of Russia, England and France. Emperor William is a crowned robber like the rulers of England, Italy, Rumania and other nations.

If we are opposed to the prolongation of the present war it is because it is being waged by two groups of powers for purely imperialistic purposes. It is waged by capitalists anxious to increase their profits by extending their domination over the world, conquering new markets and subjugating small nations. Every day of the war adds to the profits of the financier and merchants, but spells ruin and exhaustion for the industrial and agricultural workers of all nations, belligerent or neutral.

As far as Russia is concerned a prolongation of the war may jeopardize the success of the revolution and prevent it from attaining its ultimate goal.

The assumption of governmental powers by the present administration [the Provisional Government], an administration dominated by landowners and capitalists, could not and does not modify the character and the significance of the war waged by Russia.

GOVERNMENT KEEPS PEOPLE IN IGNORANCE

We might adduce as evidence of it that the present administration not only refused to reveal the secret compacts signed by Nicholas II with the governments of England, France and other nations, but formally confirmed those secret covenants which guarantee Russian capitalists their share in the dismemberment of China, Persia, Turkey, Austria, etc. By failing to reveal the nature of those arrangements, the present government is keeping the nation in ignorance of the actual aims of the present war.

This is why the workers' party cannot agree to continue the present war, nor support the present administration, nor help it in floating war loans, without departing from the spirit of internationalism, which demands brotherly solidarity among the workers of all countries in their struggle against capitalism.

We cannot accept with any measure of faith the statements of the present administration that there will be no annexations—that is, that no part of any foreign country will be seized, and that no foreign nation will be compelled forcibly to remain a part of Russia.

WARNS PEOPLE AGAINST CAPITALISTS

In the first place, capitalists, bound together as they are by the thousand ties of business, could not renounce the idea of annexations, for they could not give up the profits accruing to them from war loans, concessions, war industries, etc. In the second place, the present administration, while committing itself, in order to deceive the people, to a non-annexation policy, has betrayed many a time its annexationist aims. We must warn the nation against the empty promises of the capitalists and draw a clear distinction between words and facts in the question of annexations. We must recognize at once the right of all nationalities to vote freely upon the question as to whether they wish to be independent or to cast their lot with this or that nation.

We intend to exert our energies to the utmost in order to make it clear to the masses of the population that the intimate relations existing between the present government and the capitalists are the most insuperable obstacle to the conclusion of an early peace.

How shall we then secure that early peace without resorting to violent means, but in a purely democratic way?

I must state at first that a mere refusal to fight on the part of the soldiers of one belligerent army or the cessation of hostilities on one side of the line will not put an end to the war.

The war must be fought on by a different military organization, not by an army organized as the present army is, but by a militia whose members shall receive for their services wages equal to those of a first class workman.

The officers of the militia should be elected by the soldiers and subject to recall, and every order of the officers or generals should be approved by a vote of the men. For it is only elected officers whom the men can be expected to obey and respect.

ASKS SOLDIERS TO FRATERNIZE WITH FOE

In order that the soldiers be better fed, a repartition of the lands should be arranged for as soon as possible by the Council of Workmen's and Soldiers' Deputies and the supply of bread and meat thereby increased.

Finally, we must encourage at once every attempt made by the soldiers on both sides of the line to fraternize, in order that these instinctive manifestations of solidarity may ripen into a conscious, organized movement to place the governmental owners of every belligerent nation in the hands of the revolutionary proletariat, which alone can restrain the whiphand of capitalism.

This will be the only democratic way to put an end to this war. That is why our party shall continue patiently, but stubbornly, to make clear to the people that wars are waged by governments and that wars are always waged in the interest of one special class.

However, now that the Bolsheviks were in power—and in power largely because of the platform of immediate peace—more expeditious means than inciting revolution in the enemy camp had to be found to stop the fighting.

Bolsheviki to Ask Armistice For All to Discuss Peace

The Bolshevik tactic was not to conclude a separate peace but to force the Allies to join in the negotiations by bringing pressure on them from the peoples of their own countries.

Bolsheviki Plan to Break 'Imperialism' in France and England

Petrograd, Nov. 23 [*1917*] (*midnight*). At a meeting of the Central Executive Committee of the Workmen's and Soldiers' Deputies to-night the Bolshevik Premier, Lenine . . . declared that Russia did not contemplate a separate peace with Germany, that the belief that an armistice on the Russian front would make it possible for Germany to throw a large force on the French front was groundless, as the Russian government, before signing a treaty for an armistice, would communicate with the Allies and make certain proposals to "the imperialistic governments of France and England, rejection of which would place them in open opposition to the wishes of their own peoples."

But the Allies had made it quite plain that they would have nothing whatsoever to do with the new Russian regime, whose political and social principles they despised and whose declarations in favor of a negotiated peace posed a very real threat to Allied war aims.

Allies Isolate Russia To End Bolshevik Rule

Washington, Nov. 21 [*1917*]. The Allied governments have refused to have any relations whatever with the Bolsheviki administration in Petrograd, refraining from recognizing it even as the de facto authority. Leon Trotzky, Maximalist Foreign Minister, received a rebuff from the British Ambassador to Russia, who declined to receive a visit from the Bolsheviki official.

The lead taken by Britain is understood to have been followed by all other Entente powers, and the application of this treatment, excluding the Bolsheviki government from all intercourse with foreign nations, is expected to hasten the downfall of their power.

It is the determination of all the Allies, it was asserted by a diplomatic authority, to prevent any supplies, either of foodstuffs, clothing or war materials, to be delivered into the hands of the Bolsheviki, and nothing has left the United States for Russia since the rise of the Maximalists that cannot be diverted on the seas.

PORTS ARE UNDER CONTROL

The port of greatest advantage to the Maximalists, Kola [Murmansk] is already controlled by the naval forces of Great Britain, it was learned authoritatively. Kola . . . is the sole entrepôt from the Arctic Sea, as Archangel, on the White Sea, has been ice-locked several weeks.

It was not questioned that arrangements would be made to prevent assistance from reaching the Bolsheviki through Vladivostok, the Pacific port. Russia is already cut off economically from Scandinavia, and there was believed to be every prospect of the starving of the Maximalists into submission.

In an attempt to embarrass the Allies and arouse the ire of the working classes, the Bolsheviks set about publishing the Czarist government's fat dossier of secret treaties. These revealed what everybody had suspected— that the Allied governments had designs on Turkish, Austrian, and German territory. The radical parties in the Allied countries denounced their governments vehemently, but on the whole the popular response was quite cynical. The French certainly expected to recover Alsace-Lorraine and get a little more besides. The British fully intended to expand their interests in the Near and Middle East and in Africa. The Italians anticipated receiving Austrian territory in the Tyrol and elsewhere. The agreement permitting Russia to annex Constantinople had been revealed in 1916, and that Russia would seek other tidbits of Turkey and extend its borders westward was taken for granted. Lenin's fundamental error—

which he made all along—was the assumption that the working classes of the capitalist nations were ready and anxious for revolution, that their proletarian consciousness transcended their nationalist instincts, that the military defeat and economic chaos that brought on the Russian revolution were only incidentals hastening an inevitable historical process.

The Allies simply ignored the Bolshevik demand for negotiations, and the Russians, therefore, went ahead on their own.

Petrograd, Nov. 28 [*1917*]. Representatives sent by Ensign Krylenko, the Bolshevik commander in chief of the Russian armies, have been received in the German lines, and informed by the German commander that the Germans have officially consented to immediate negotiations for an armistice on all the fronts of the belligerent countries.

The Germans have set December 2 for a conference for negotiation of an armistice.

A temporary truce preliminary to actual peace negotiations was concluded on December 5. By then, fighting had already stopped along most of the front as the result of local armistices worked out by the Russian soldiers with officers and men across the line.

In the meantime, it was becoming extremely urgent that the war be brought to an end altogether so that troops could be safely removed from the front.

Don Cossacks Surround Rostov, Where Bolshevik Council Is in Session

Copenhagen, Dec. 1 [*1917*]. A dispatch from . . . Sweden to the "Berlingske Tidende" here says that General Kaledines, hetman of the Don Cossacks, has surrounded Rostov-on-Don with his troops.

Sections of the Bolsheviki Council are still staying in that city. General Kaledines has ten Cossack regiments of cavalry, 10,000 Cossack infantrymen, nine batteries of field cannon and twenty machine guns.

General A. M. Kaledin, the leader of the Don Cossacks, easily took Rostov and established there a headquarters for the Anti-Bolshevik opposition. He was joined by General Kornilov and some of his followers, including General A. I. Denikin, as well as some of the liberal political leaders, such as Professor Milyukov. A "Volunteer Army," which had been organized sometime before by General M. V. Alekseyev, Kornilov's successor as chief of staff under the Provisional Government, now began to take shape as a real fighting force.

Korniloff and Kaledines Lead Cossacks in Revolt Against Bolsheviki Rule

London, Dec. 9 [1917].   A proclamation to the Russian nation has been issued by the Russian government announcing that "Kaledines and Korniloff, assisted by the Imperialists and Constitutional Democrats, have raised a revolt and declared war in the Don region against the people and the revolution."

Cossack Army Is Advancing on Moscow

London, Dec. 10 [1917].   The counter revolt in southeastern Russia, under the leadership of Generals Kaledine, Dutoff and Korniloff, apparently is aimed at seizing the authority in that region and in cutting off food supplied from Siberia. According to the proclamation of the Bolsheviki government, General Kaledines' forces are menacing Ekaterinoslav, Kharkov and Moscow. In the province of Orenburg the Bolsheviki have been overthrown by General Dutoff.

Also in early December the Ukrainian Rada, or Council, which had been installed as a sort of parliament for the Ukraine after the March Revolution, proclaimed the establishment of the autonomous Ukrainian People's Republic. The anti-Bolshevik Rada's dominion extended only over western Little Russia, since a Soviet government had been set up in the industrial city of Kharkov in the east.

London, Dec. 20 [1917].   The Rada, or governing body of the Ukraine, has sent a negative answer to the ultimatum of the Bolshevik government, a dispatch from Petrograd states. This presumably adds the resources of the entire Ukraine to the forces combatting Lenine.

The ultimatum demanded that within forty-eight hours a decision be made whether the Ukraine would cease to assist General Kaledine by sending him troops while forbidding passage to Bolshevik government troops, and also whether it would stop disarming troops in the Ukraine. In case of refusal the Rada would be considered at war with the congress of Workmen's and Soldiers' Delegates.

The Bolshevik agency announced recently that the ultimatum to the Ukrainians was accompanied by a proclamation recognizing without conditions or restrictions the right of the Ukraine to separate from Russia and form its own republican government.

Similar threats were arising elsewhere.

Russia Falling Apart As Many States Arise, Asserting Autonomy

[*Dec. 30, 1917.*] Russia to-day can scarcely be considered a unified country. It is still split into a dozen or more states asserting their independence, which in turn continue to be divided. Present reports identify as many as eleven separate states in this great territory:

The Bolshevik government, ruling territory in and around Petrograd and Moscow.

The Cossack dominion, roughly bounded by Turkestan, Caucasia and the Ukraine.

The Ukraine, including Odessa.

Siberia, which is now said to be splitting into many groups.

White Russia, reported to have declared its independence.

Orenburg, north of Turkestan, reported still loyal to Kerensky and the deposed Provisional Government.

Finland, with an independent rule.

Trans-Caucasia, also with its own Parliament.

Caucasia.

Turkestan, partly controlled by the Cossacks.

Bessarabia.

Even in Petrograd and other Bolshevik strongholds the government was having troubles.

Petrograd, Dec. 19 [1917]. The Executive Council of Workmen's and Soldiers' Deputies has proclaimed a state of siege in Petrograd in an effort to repress disorders due to the looting of wine cellars and shops.

It was probably the greatest drunken spree in all history. The Russian soldiers, whose tippling capacities were unequaled anywhere, had discovered the huge stocks of wine stashed in the cellars of palaces and merchants' homes and acquired them. Lenin took an extremely dim view of the matter. He called in more abstemious troops and to the despair of the revelers ordered the casks split open and their contents spilled into the Neva.

The bacchanal, in itself merely a somewhat excessive victory celebration, nevertheless exemplified the social and economic collapse which had brought on the revolution in the first place and which constituted no less a danger to the Bolsheviks than it had to the Imperial regime or the Provisional Government. Industrial production was almost at a standstill. At the end of 1917 there were fewer than 175,000 railway cars and 9000 engineers—as compared to 540,000 and 220,000, respectively, in 1914. The food shortage was critical. Inflation was getting out of hand, and the government lacked funds to operate with. The civil servants inherited from the old regime were unreliable, yet there were few competent replacements. Political opposition flourished with terribly disruptive effects, even inside the areas controlled by the Bolsheviks.

As far as Lenin was concerned, there was only one real solution to Russia's internal problems: socialism. He began to take measures in that direction. A Supreme Council was established on December 15 and given the authority to nationalize industries and take other steps to put the economy right. Also in December the ownership of large private homes was transferred to the soviets. Banks were nationalized, and private stocks of gold were confiscated. However, any organic reformation of the economic and social structure could not be undertaken until the government was sure that the war was over and the threat of a German invasion removed.

SANTA BOLSHEVIK'S FIRST CALL

London, Dec. 23 [1917]. A dispatch received by way of Amsterdam, from Brest-Litovsk, Russia, dated Saturday [December 22], says:

"To-day at 4 o'clock in the afternoon the peace negotiations were begun at a solemn sitting. The meeting was attended by the following delegates:

"Germany—Dr. Richard von Kuehlmann, Foreign Minister; . . . General [Max] von Hoffmann. . . .

"Austria-Hungary—Count [Ottokar] Czernin, Foreign Minister. . . .

"Bulgaria—Minister Popoff. . . .

"Turkey—Former Minister of Foreign Affairs Nessimy Bey. . . .

"Russia—[A. A.] Joffe, [L. B.] Kameneff, [M. N.] Pokrovsky, [L. B.] Karaghan. . . ."

RUSSIAN STATES TERMS

At von Kuehlmann's suggestion, the chief Russian delegate stated the chief principles of the Russian peace programme in a long speech, which coincided on the whole with the well-known resolutions of the Workmen's and Soldiers' Deputies.

The Russian terms include: First, no compulsory annexation of territory taken during the war and speedy evacuation of such territory; second, that political independence shall be restored to all nations deprived of independence by the fortunes of war; third, the national groups not independent before the war shall decide by a referendum whether they shall become independent, or give their full allegiance to some power; fourth, where mixed nationalities occupy any territory the rights of the minority shall be defended by a separate law assuring educational freedom and administrative autonomy, if possible; fifth, no belligerent country shall be required to pay contributions and private persons shall be compensated for losses incurred through the war from a special fund contributed by all the belligerents on a proportional basis. The same principles shall be applicable to colonies as to parent countries.

The final clause of the terms prohibits the boycotting of one country by another.

Germany Demands Russia Give Up All Kaiser Holds; Treaty Is Partly Drawn

Brest-Litovsk, Dec. 28 [1917] (*via Berlin and London, Dec. 30*). Provisional agreement on many important points was concluded at Brest-

Litovsk by the delegates of Russia and the Central Powers, including:

Restoration of the treaty relations that existed prior to the war.

Reciprocal liberation of war prisoners and interned civilians, and the return of captured merchant vessels.

Speedy resumption of diplomatic and commercial relations.

The chief proposal of the German delegates was:

That Russia take cognizance of the proclaimed independence of Poland, Lithuania, Courland, and portions of Esthonia and Livonia, and that general elections be held in these districts to determine whether they shall be recognized as separate states.

All these areas, which (except for parts of Poland) had belonged to the Russian Empire, were occupied by German or Austrian troops, and the true reasons for Kühlmann's apparent willingness to abide by the principle of national self-determination were obvious. As the *Tribune* pointed out in a series of editorials (Jan. 3 and 4, 1918):

German Peace Terms—A Colossal Fraud

I—The Baltic Provinces

At no time since the World War began has there been any greater peril to the future peace of Europe than that which is inherent in the present peace proposals of the Germans to the Russians. Under cover of Russian formulae, purporting to give small races the right to choose their own political allegiance, the Germans are deliberately undertaking to create a barrier between the Slavs and the Baltic Sea and erect a German-controlled state which shall contain all the Russian Baltic ports from Libau to Reval, including Pernau and Riga.

If the present German proposal be accepted 150,000,000 Russians will be deprived of all outlet upon the open waters, save on the Arctic and Pacific oceans, and Russia will be made industrially and economically a mere slave to Germany. Through her own ports of Danzig and Koenigsberg and through the ports of Libau and Riga, in the new state she is seeking to erect, Germany would control all Russian roads to the sea in the north, and through her mastery of the Turk at Constantinople she would dominate the Russian road to the Mediterranean.

What the Germans are now aiming at is unmistakable. They occupy by force of arms most of this territory; the ruling class in the territory is

German [due to the occupation of the Baltic region by the Teutonic Knights in the thirteenth century] and eager to escape from a Bolshevik Slavdom to a Prussianized Germany, for these Germans of the Baltic Provinces are of the same spirit and hold the same ideas as the other German minorities who rule in East Prussia and Silesia over conquered Slavs. Therefore the Germans, having military control and aided by the ruling class, who are of the Junker tribe, demand that the fate of these provinces shall be determined by a plebiscite and that this plebiscite shall take place before their troops are withdrawn. The result of such a plebiscite would be certain.

II—Poland

The problem of Russian Poland may be simply stated: There are in Russian Poland, so called, some 12,500,000 people, the very great majority of whom are Poles. This territory must be the basis of any Polish state to be created. There are also many Poles in the adjoining Russian governments of Vilna, Grodno and Volhynia. In addition, nearly four millions of Poles inhabit German lands across the frontier in the Prussian provinces of Silesia, Posen and East and West Prussia. Finally, there are more than five million Poles in the Austrian province of Galicia.

Any honest attempt to settle the Polish problem, either by treaty or by plebiscite, would involve permitting the Poles of Prussia, Russia and Austria to determine their allegiance. Were this allowed, they would almost without exception vote to return to a restored Poland. [Poland had been partitioned among Prussia, Russia, and Austria in the late eighteenth century.] Such an arrangement would create a compact state, with a population of over 25,000,000 inhabitants, having its sea gate on the Baltic at Danzig and including very considerable portions of several Prussian provinces and all of the province of Posen.

But the German proposal made at Brest-Litovsk deliberately excludes the Prussian Poles from the question. It similarly excludes the Austrian Poles. . . . Naturally, the Germans are not sincere in their championship of Polish nationality, because they are totally unwilling to surrender their own Polish subjects to a new Poland, and unless such a surrender is made no real Poland can be created. The reason for this the map shows. Seated on the Baltic shore from Memel to Danzig, Germany holds all the seaports and thus the exits of Polish trade. Any Poland created without a seacoast would then, in the nature of things, be an economic dependency of the Germans.

A ten-day recess was called at the peace conference, and the Russian delegation went home for consultation. When they returned, Trotsky was at their head. He proceeded to harangue the Germans, insisting that the withdrawal of German troops must precede a referendum in the areas under discussion if they were to have a truly free choice. Trotsky had no illusions about convincing his opponents, but an outbreak of paralyzing strikes in Germany encouraged the Russians to play for time in the hope that the industrial disorders would turn into revolution. The Germans lost patience and on January 18, 1918, presented an ultimatum. Kühlmann drew a line on the map coinciding with the area held by the Germans. That, he announced, was to be the demarcation of territory; there was to be no more discussion about it. The Russians were either to accept it or pay the consequences. Trotsky called another recess.

When he arrived home the Bolshevik leaders were already debating heatedly. Three distinct positions emerged. Bukharin and others advocated a "revolutionary war" on the grounds that this would weaken the Germans and Austrians further and help prepare the way for revolution. In substantiation of this position, Bukharin pointed to the rash of strikes that had just broken out in Vienna and to the rising clamor of the socialists in Germany against the war and the government, as well as to the naval mutiny and the strikes in that country. Lenin insisted that Russia had to have peace, whatever the cost in territory and sacrifice of principle, and that they could not gamble on a German revolution's saving the situation. If the war were resumed, the Germans would advance farther into Russia, which was too weak to resist. Trotsky proposed a third alternative —that the peace terms not be signed, but that Russia nevertheless lay down its arms. This would be a principled position, encouraging to the revolutionaries in Germany and Austria, and also would bring the fighting to an end, since the Germans would no longer have the excuse that they were waging a defensive war against the Russians. That was nonsense, Lenin snorted. The Germans would simply continue their offensive, but unresisted, and Russia would then be obliged to sign an even worse peace. But in a vote taken by the Bolshevik Central Committee on January 22, Trotsky's formula prevailed.

Negotiations were resumed on January 30. Trotsky, still playing for time, continued the debate. But on February 9, the Germans signed a separate peace with the Ukrainian Rada, which at the invitation of the

Trotsky (center) and other members of the Russian delegation arriving at Brest-Litovsk for the peace negotiations. (*Sovfoto*)

Germans had sent representatives to Brest-Litovsk. The next day Trotsky broke off the negotiations.

Russia Quits the War

Trotzky Sends Home Armies on All Fronts

Decree Signed by Trotzky
Declares Nation Will Not
Fight Brother Workers

The German response was exactly what Lenin had predicted it would be.

Berlin (via London), *Feb. 18 [1918]*. Operations have been resumed on the Russian front. The Germans have crossed the Dvina. This announcement was made by General Headquarters to-night.

Russia, helpless, capitulated the very next day. And, as Lenin had also predicted, the German terms were now much harsher.

Russia Must Lose Baltic Provinces, End Propaganda, Demobilize Army and Navy

GERMANS DEMAND $1,500,000,000 160,000 SQUARE MILES OF LAND, WITH POPULATION OF 18,000,000

Huns Demand Occupation of Esthonia and Livonia, Restoration of Anatolia to Turkey, Demobilization of Russian Army and Disarming of Fleet, Free Navigation of Black Sea and Baltic

Trotsky and others favored putting up some sort of resistance in the hope that aid would be forthcoming from the Allies. This time, though, Lenin put his foot down, threatening to resign unless the peace was accepted. Trotsky gave in, although Bukharin and three other members of the Central Committee voted to fight. The Treaty of Brest-Litovsk was signed March 3. Some modification of the onerous German demands was won, but on the major points the conquerors were unbending. Russia was deprived of the Baltic provinces of Lithuania, Latvia, and Estonia; of Finland (whose independence was recognized), Poland, part of White Russia (Byelorussia), the Ukraine (which was also declared to be independent—under German occupation), and the districts of Kars, Batum, and Ardagan in Transcaucasia, which went to Turkey. Altogether Russia lost about 1,300,000 square miles of territory.

But at least the war was over and the Bolsheviks could concentrate on securing peace at home and consolidating the regime.

Chapter Nine

Civil War

Bolsheviki
Are Alarmed
Over Revolt

Socialist Fatherland Is in
Danger, Their Com-
mittee Warns

Urge Mass Terror
Against Bourgeoisie

Decide Defeat of Czechs
and Obtaining Grain
Are Chief Tasks

Despite the astonishing ease with which the Bolsheviks had established themselves in power, their prospect of holding it long was very dim.

Their following throughout the country was relatively small. In the elections to the Constituent Assembly, which were held in December 1917, they polled barely one-fourth of the votes, while the Socialist Revolutionaries and their various affiliates among the national-minority groups, such as the Ukrainians and Muslims, received more than half. Even in Petrograd and Moscow, the centers of their greatest strength, the Bolsheviks did not win a majority but only a substantial plurality—837,000 votes in the two cities combined, as compared to 515,400 for the Kadets (who campaigned with the disadvantages of having their newspapers suppressed, their meetings broken up, and some of their leaders arrested), 218,000 for the Socialist Revolutionaries, and 194,700 for all the rest, including the Mensheviks.*

An army of counterrevolutionaries under the leadership of some of Russia's most skilled generals was menacing the regime from the south, and much of the Ukraine was ruled by a hostile government. The Bolsheviks had no army to speak of, only the Petrograd and Moscow garrisons, the Red guards, and the sailors of the Baltic fleet. Some of the men straggling home from the front might be enlisted, but the vast majority wanted only to get back to their farms and see what they could do about grabbing land for themselves.

In addition, the Allies had imposed a blockade and were mooting the possibility of armed intervention. The fabric of the economy had unraveled so far that the country was threadbare. National minorities were striking out for independence. Lenin and the other Bolshevik leaders had known from the very beginning that they were taking a prodigious gamble, but now the odds were stacked overwhelmingly against them.

Their advantages, however, were considerable. Small numerically as

* Chamberlin, William H., *The Russian Revolution*, Vol. I, p. 366.

Lenin in his Kremlin office in 1918. (*Sovfoto*)

Lenin speaking in Moscow's Red Square, May 1, 1918. (USSR *magazine from Sovfoto*)

their following was compared to that of the Socialist Revolutionaries, it was nevertheless well disciplined, dedicated, and strategically located in the cities—Petrograd, Moscow, Odessa, Kharkov, Batu, and so on. These were the nerve centers of the nation, and as long as they were held the country could be held. The Volunteer Army would have at least as much trouble as the Bolsheviks in building a fighting machine. The Allies, if they did decide to intervene, could not spare many troops from the raging western front, and their supply lines to Russia would be thin.

But the chief advantage of the Bolsheviks was in their mentality or, to be more precise, the mentality of their leader, Lenin. He had no compunctions about using force, terror, or any other means necessary to win. His conscience was formed by the imperatives of revolution. Rectitude, he taught his followers, was determined solely by the political needs of the struggle. What had to be done to secure the revolution, install socialism, and fulfill the "historic destiny of the proletariat" everywhere would be done. And the Bolshevik Party believed that it had the *obligation* to maintain itself in power. Questions of numerical majorities and minorities were of little consequence, because the people often failed to appreciate their own best class interests. It was a fundamental point of Marxian theory on social psychology that class consciousness often lagged behind political, economic, and social reality, and a primary task of the Bolshevik Party was to articulate political truths and educate the masses. The fact was, Lenin and the other leaders firmly believed, that the party did represent the majority—the laborers, the dispossessed, the oppressed masses, whether they were peasants with little plots of land or urban workers. In any event, this revolutionary perspective, this sense of its own mission and charisma, gave the party a determination, composure, and discipline that none of the opposition had. It was also very much in tune with the Russian historical experience, the messianism, the rigid orthodoxy, the consummate devotion which adores the martyr and the conqueror and never understands the gentler spirits in between. The Socialist Revolutionaries had the tradition from their populist days, but only a soupçon of the quality remained. The Mensheviks had lost it, too. The liberals had never had it; they admired the West too much. They yearned after Western freedom, the sense of personal dignity, and the humanist moderation, and that weakened them, because it was so very alien in a culture where all could be cast with a single throw of the dice, where bound between heaven and hell was a long malaise. The Provisional Government and the moderate socialist leaders of the Soviets had not believed strongly enough to be ruthless. For that spiritlessness they were despised. Nicholas II had tarried. For that he was overthrown.

What this meant in terms of Bolshevik policies was made absolutely clear (if there had been any doubt) when the Constituent Assembly convened on January 18, 1918, in the midst of the peace negotiations with the Germans. Lenin had simply wanted to call off the assembly. The point of the Bolshevik seizure of power was to establish a dictatorship of the proletariat, not parliamentary democracy. But Lenin was outvoted in the Party Central Committee on the grounds that since they had taunted the Provisional Government with not convoking the assembly, it would be impolitic not to let it meet.

Bolsheviki Quit Assembly;
Mob Rule Expected

Defeated by Social Revolutionists, Lenine Delegates Withdraw

Petrograd, Jan. 18 [*1918*] (*delayed*).   The long delayed Constituent Assembly was opened to-day. On the first test of strength the Bolsheviki were defeated by the Social Revolutionists. M. Tchernoff, Minister of Agriculture in the Kerensky government, and the nominee of the Social Revolutionists of the Right for Chairman of the Assembly, was elected by a vote of 244 to [153]. The candidate of the Bolsheviki was Maria Spiridonovo, long a prominent revolutionist, who was released from exile in Siberia after the overthrow of the Romanoffs.

The opening of the Assembly was set for noon, but a controversy over registration caused a delay until 1 o'clock. Slightly more than 400 delegates were in their seats. [703 delegates had been elected.] Of those the Bolsheviki and the Social Revolutionists of the Left, who are working together, have about 150 votes, and the Social Revolutionists of the Centre [i.e., the Mensheviks] and the Right were the remainder. Delegates belonging to the Constitutional Democratic party were absent from the opening session.

London, Jan. 19 [*1918*].   According to a Russian wireless report of the session of the Constituent Assembly at Petrograd, received here to-day, the Bolshevik members and those belonging to the left wing of the Social Revolutionists withdrew.

At 3 o'clock in the morning M. Askokov, a Bolshevik delegate, announced that the Bolsheviki were determined to withdraw permanently from the Constituent Assembly, which, he said, had proved itself not to represent the actual proletariat. "Meanwhile," he declared, "the Workmen's and Soldiers' government will consider what to do with that counter-revolutionary organization."

The withdrawal . . . followed . . . the defeat of the demand made by the Lefts that the Assembly first take up the question of the adoption of the Smolny Institute programme, which proposed recognition of the Bolshevik authority for the approval of all decrees.

The Constituent Delegates, under fear of a permanent dispersal and threatened with treatment as a "counter-revolutionary" organization, hurriedly adopted decrees awarding the lands to the peasants and proposing to send delegates to all the warring nations to arrange a world peace.

Tumult increased toward the end of the session and many members of the Assembly rushed toward Chairman Tchernoff and urged him immediately to put the question of peace. A sailor, who was standing beside M. Tchernoff, raised a hand and addressed him in a loud voice: "We are getting tired. Go home. Good night."

Sailors in the aisles leading to the exits then drew closer while the chairman continued to read the peace resolution.

The spokesman of the sailors then returned to the platform and insisted that all present should go home. M. Tchernoff thereupon calmly put the question of the adoption of the resolution, which was passed instantly. The chairman then announced the adjournment of the Assembly until noon, and the remaining members declared their determination to remain in the city and hold another meeting at that hour.

Bolsheviki Force Closing of Assembly

Sailors Disperse Delegates
to Constituent Body at 4 a.m.

Petrograd, Jan. 20 [1918]. The Constituent Assembly has been dissolved. The decree of dissolution was issued last night by the Council of

National Commissioners and passed early this morning by the Central Executive Committee of the Workmen's and Soldiers' Deputies.

The sailors who dissolved the Assembly [at 4 o'clock this morning] were authorized by the Bolsheviki decree, which, however, at the time of the dissolution had not been proclaimed.

From Moscow it is reported that many persons were wounded and others killed as the result of the Red Guard firing on demonstrators there in favor of the Constituent Assembly.

At about the same time the zemstvos, the Petrograd and Moscow municipal councils, and the All-Russian Soviet Executive Committee (Vtsik) were also dissolved by the Bolsheviks.

Dealing with the Constituent Assembly and other institutional manifestations of "bourgeois democracy" was relatively easy. A far more serious threat came from the Volunteer Army. At the end of January 1918 the government issued a call for volunteers to form a Red Army, the purpose of which was not only to "defend the revolution" in Russia but to abet uprisings anywhere else they might occur.

Bolsheviki Organize "Red" Army to Aid World's Revolts

London, Jan. 31 [*1918*].   An official statement issued to-day by the Bolshevik government at Petrograd says that the "new Workmen's and Peasants' Red Army will serve to support the coming social revolution in Europe."

A Bolshevik decree establishing "an All-Russian Collegium" for guidance in organizing the Workmen's and Peasants' Red Army of the Russian Councils' Republic" is announced in a Russian official wireless statement received here. The committee will be composed of two representatives of the War Commissariat and two representatives of the general staff of the Red Guards.

Some initial successes were achieved. On February 8, Kiev was captured from the Ukrainian Rada, and later that month the Red Army took Rostov from the Volunteer Army. As a result of the defeat, General Kaledin committed suicide. Kornilov, who succeeded to the command, then attempted to take the Kuban capital of Ekaterinodar but was killed in battle in April, and the Volunteer Army retreated further, into the Crimea. The Cossack city of Orenburg also fell to the Bolsheviks. However, on March 3 the Germans occupied Kiev, and on May 8 they took Rostov, establishing their control over the Ukraine, which had in effect been ceded to them in the Treaty of Brest-Litovsk. The Volunteer Army, now led by General Denikin, began to re-form.

Meanwhile, a new threat developed in another area. At the request of the Allies and the Czechoslovak national leader, Thomas G. Masaryk, a Czech brigade that had fought under the Russians against Germany was given permission to escape to France by way of Vladivostok. Naturally, the Bolsheviks did not miss the opportunity to propagandize the Czechs as they traveled across Russia. The Allied officers warned the Czechs that the Russians were only interested in disarming and capturing them. An order to reroute part of the brigade to Archangel aroused the suspicions of the soldiers, who thought the Russians were trying to weaken them by dividing their forces. (Actually the order was given at the request of the French.) Then on May 14, while stopping at a Ural railway station, a group of the Czechs got into a brawl with some Hungarian prisoners of war, and the local soviet instructed the Red guards to arrest them. Infuriated at what appeared to be a confirmation of everything the Allied officers had been saying, others in the brigade overpowered the Red guards and freed their comrades.

Moscow, Thursday, May 30 [*1918*].   As the result of an order by Leon Trotzky to disarm Czecho-Slovak troops who were endeavoring to travel to Vladivostok, and of directions he gave to prevent their movement to that port, a serious outbreak occurred, culminating in violent clashes between Czecho-Slovak and Soviet troops in several places.

After defeating Soviet troops, the Czecho-Slovaks seized the railway station at Penza, in the Volga region, and boarded trains going in the direction of Chelyabinsk, which 12,000 Czecho-Slovaks are holding.

A battle also took place near Zlatoust, where the Czecho-Slovak involved were obliged to abandon their train and force their way forward on foot.

Government reinforcements are flowing in from all sides and great efforts are being made to subdue the Czecho-Slovaks, as they are regarded as a serious menace, being well armed and possessing armored cars. In addition they are obtaining aid from anti-Soviet elements.

The aid came mostly from Socialist Revolutionaries who had fled to Siberia after the dissolution of the Constituent Assembly with the intention of forming an army of their own to fight the new regime. The Czechs in turn helped them, along with some other anti-Bolsheviks, to wrest control of much of Siberia from the Soviets. Early in June two separate governments were set up: one, the so-called West Siberian Commissariat, at Omsk; the other, which called itself the Committee of the Members of the Constituent Assembly, at Samara. Both were originally dominated by the Socialist Revolutionaries, but at the end of the month control of the West Siberian Commissariat was usurped by considerably less democratic elements.

Czech Troops Rout Forces Of Bolsheviki

Slovaks Clear Baikal Region

Russians Presumed to Have Lost Rich Supplies From Irkutsk

Bolshevik Forces Beaten by Czechs; Semenoff Advances

Soviet Ready to Flee

Leaders Alarmed by Vladivostok
Coup, to Seek Refuge in Mongolia

Peking, July 15 [*1918*]. The town of Klutsgevsk, in the southwestern extremity of the Transbaikal region, has been captured by Czecho-Slovak forces, following the capture of Irkutsk. The Bolsheviki are reported concentrating at Verhneudinsk.

A dispatch from Manchuria announces that General Semenoff, [a Siberian] anti-Bolshevik leader, has occupied Sharasun with his forces.

The Russian government in Petrograd was now faced with hostile armies in the east as well as the south.

It had been obvious to the Bolshevik leaders for some time that an army consisting only of volunteers, however dedicated and well disciplined, could not cope with the rapidly growing forces of the Whites (as the anti-Bolsheviks were beginning to be called). But they were extremely wary about introducing general conscription. The peasants on the whole were too unreliable; their hatred for the war and their desire to get on with land reform had been a major precipitating factor in the revolution, and it would be very, very difficult to get them to take up arms again unless it was clearly in their own interests to do so. Moreover, the Bolsheviks had no intention of putting guns in the hands of people who might turn them against the government. An agitational campaign was launched by the Bolsheviks and the Left Socialist Revolutionaries, who told the peasants that if the Whites won, the great land reform introduced by the Soviet Congress in November would certainly be undone. In April the government cautiously introduced compulsory military training (but not service), for workers and those peasants who worked their own land—that is, the groups presumably most reliable. Then, immediately after the outbreak of the war with the Czech brigade, the conscription of workers in Petrograd and Moscow was ordered. The results were satisfactory. There was a hard core of Red guards in the army, many of them Bolshevik party members, and they drummed up the spirits of the indifferent and resentful. Finally,

Moscow, June 28 [*1918*]. The . . . situation of the Russian Soviet republic is such that only a powerful army on the basis of obligatory service can protect it, in the opinion of Leon Trotzky, Commissioner of War and Marine. He has submitted a report advocating universal military service for the bourgeois as well as the workmen and peasants, and hopes that the fifth congress of Soviets will pass such a measure.

Premier Lenine has approved the report and details are being worked out.

In the meantime Trotzky has ordered the registration of all males between the ages of nineteen and forty, and the enlistment simultaneously with the workmen of the bourgeois classes born in 1896 and 1897.

The bourgeois classes will be formed into non-fighting units to dig trenches and clean barracks and camps. Later they may be promoted to service in the ranks, after they have proved "by deeds their loyalty to the laboring class and the poor peasantry."

Trotsky himself undertook to shape this mass of mostly reluctant and weary men into a disciplined army, and he brought to the task the same energy and verve he had displayed in organizing the November revolution. In an open command car, apparently oblivious of stray shells or assassins' bullets, he drove from battalion to battalion, speaking to the troops, explaining, arguing, inspiring, as he had done with the soldiers and workers of Petrograd in October, and wherever he went he aroused enthusiasm for the cause. But this time he did not depend upon the willing cooperation, the revolutionary spirit, of the men. Deserters, of whom there were many, were often peremptorily shot, without trial, without ceremony. Officers who refused to serve the Bolsheviks were threatened with concentration camps, seizure of their property, or execution. Any dereliction of duty, by the officers especially, was ruthlessly punished, frequently with death. A system of political commissars, stalwart party members, was established to keep an eye on the officers and conduct propaganda among the soldiers. By this combination of inspiration and sledgehammering Trotsky succeeded within an astonishingly short time in making the Red Army into a formidable fighting machine.

Meanwhile, the Bolsheviks (who incidentally were now officially calling themselves Communists *, as Lenin had advocated in the *April Theses*) were attempting to deal with another no less serious problem.

* The party's name was changed to Russian Communist Party (Bolshevik); it had been Russian Social Democratic Workers' Party (Bolshevik).

This straggly parade in Red Square was one of the first reviews of the Red Army, which Trotsky began to organize in March 1918 around a nucleus of Red Guards and former imperial officers. (*Sovfoto*)

Commissar of War Trotsky and his staff inspecting the troops during a demonstration of war exercises in Red Square. (*The Bettman Archive*)

Trotsky's exhortations to the troops often succeeded in inspiring enthusiasm even in unwilling conscripts. (*Keystone View Co.*)

Petrograd, June 15 [*1918*] Petrograd is a city of despair and near starvation. For many months a threatening phantom, hunger, has already struck down thousands. A great majority of the two million persons now crowded into the once proud capital of Peter the Great knows what it means to be without food and knows that winter is coming with probably worse in store.

The people talk, dream and—when they can—eat food. Long lines form early in the morning before the shops to buy food. Thousands storm incoming trains in a wild scramble for food brought in by peasants and travelling soldiers. In front of every shop window where foodstuffs are displayed people stand and gaze longingly with their eyes glued to the window panes.

Petrograd is also a city with its pockets full of worthless money. Money presses are working overtime and wages are increasing, but neither can keep up with the rising prices. The Nevsky Prospekt, "the" street of Petrograd, is a picturesque evidence of the city's interest in food. In this season of "white nights" every hour of the twenty daylight sees it lined from one end to the other with street venders selling cakes and chocolate and candles, and queer little pancakes called "bleeneys" and sugar in lumps from carefully guarded little boxes.

ERSTWHILE RICH ARE NOW PEDDLERS

Persons who formerly owned limousines and lived in palace-like homes along the Neva are selling candy and biscuits in the streets to earn their living. The customers are opulent sailors and workmen, who buy biscuits at fabulous prices, because even they, part of the time, cannot get bread.

Some of those on the Nevsky are girls, pretty ones, and they walk the length of the street all the day and into the night, asking for the little postage stamps that now pass for money in Russia—because they are hungry. And then there are other girls, and the number grows larger every day, who do not exactly beg, but look wistfully and hungry and sell themselves, instead of biscuits or chocolates or newspapers, to the rollicking sailors and debonair speculators.

WHERE DO VENDERS GET FOOD?

One of the mysteries of Russia is where the venders of cakes and biscuits get the things they sell. There is absolutely no flour to be had, and the bread allowance per person, which one sometimes gets and sometimes doesn't, is one half of a pound daily for the proletariat and one-eighth of a pound daily for the bourgeoisie. The bread is black and heavy and its ingredients cannot be identified. Sugar cannot be obtained in the shops. In the homes horse meat, dried cabbage and what bread is available is the principal diet for the majority. Eggs, butter and milk are high in price and extremely scarce.

The picture was the same in almost every city.

One reason for the desperate shortage was that the farmers were still refusing to ship their produce to the cities. No consumer goods were being manufactured and the peasants, receiving nothing for what they grew, made liquor out of their precious grain, hoarded imperishables, and destroyed the rest rather than give it away. The situation was aggravated by the German occupation of the Ukraine, which was the largest wheat-growing region in Russia, and by the Czech victories in Siberia which deprived cities under Bolshevik control of grain from that area.

Soviets Pick
Poor Peasants
To Seize Grain

Moscow, June 12 [1918]. The Central Executive Committee to-night voted to create committees of poor peasants for the purpose of taking a census of grain and other food necessaries in villages, confiscating all in excess of that above requirements and distributing food and agricultural machinery among the peasants they decide are needy. The committees, which are permanent, are to be formed by the local Soviets, and only the poor can become members. Their activities are to be directed exclusively against rich peasants, who are declared to be hiding grain, and against the bourgeois opposed to the Soviet government.

To help these committees enforce the measure, armed detachments of workmen have been formed in Petrograd and Moscow, 5,000 in each city, and more are to be formed and will be sent to various villages. Notwithstanding the severe criticism of the measure by the opposition, particularly the Social Revolutionists, who pointed out that it will cause civil war among the peasants and stated that they would oppose its enforcement when passed because they regarded it as injurious, it was adopted by a large Bolshevik majority.

There was a second, political, purpose for the measure. By giving the poor peasants carte blanche to deal as they pleased with the richer peasants—the kulaks, who were often not at all rich—the Bolsheviks hoped to enlist the support of the former for the regime. The results were sanguinary. Poor peasants, encouraged and abetted by the starving workers, slew kulaks mercilessly, and the kulaks responded in kind. The brutal confiscations probably did something to relieve the famine, since at least some food that might have wasted was brought into the cities by the workers, and the political goal, the extension of Bolshevik influence into the countryside, was achieved. But the problem of the food shortages was not solved at all.

The Left Socialist Revolutionaries, who had withdrawn from the government in March in protest against the signing of the Treaty of Brest-Litovsk and whose relations with the government since then had grown steadily cooler, were now enraged. At the V All-Russian Congress of Soviets in July they attacked Lenin's agrarian policy, denounced the Treaty of Brest-Litovsk for surrendering Russian peasants and workers in the Ukraine to the Germans, and announced that they would fight to the death against both. Already they had made plans to deal with the Germans in the traditional manner of their party.

German Ambassador Murdered at Moscow

Paris, July 6. General Count von Mirbach, German Ambassador to Russia, has been assassinated at Moscow, according to a Berlin report received here by the Havas Agency. Two identified persons were involved in the crime.

The two men asked for an audience with the German Ambassador this morning, then attacked him, wounding him with shots from a revolver. They followed this by throwing grenades. Von Mirbach died almost immediately.

The assassins fled and have not been arrested.

The Left S. R.'s proclaimed their responsibility for the assassination, and when the police came to arrest them took up arms.

Revolt in Moscow
Follows Murder of
Germany's Envoy

London, July 8 [1918]. Immediately following the assassination of Count von Mirbach, German Ambassador in Moscow, the [Left] Social Revolutionaries started a revolt against the Bolsheviki and seized the telegraph office in Moscow and a part of the town.

The Bolsheviki have suppressed the revolution, according to a statement by the chief Soviet commissioner. Several hundred leaders of the revolt have been arrested.

The strongest capital will be made of the murder by the German government, advice from many sources indicate. The Bolsheviki have undertaken a complete investigation to placate the German government. The Social Revolutionaries [of the Left] have admitted planning the assassination, according to a German official press dispatch from Moscow.

Coincidentally, on July 6, the day of Mirbach's murder, a rightist group, "The Union for the Defense of the Motherland and Freedom," seized the upper Volga town of Yaroslavl and the next night attacked nearby Rybinsky. On the 8th Murom was taken.

Also on July 6, a crucial decision was made in Washington.

Wilson Agrees to Allied Action in Russia

Washington, July 6 [1918]. America's waiting policy in regard to military action in Russia is understood to have ended to-day at a conference at the White House between President Wilson and Secretaries Lansing, Baker and Daniels, Admiral Benson, chief of naval operations, and General March, Army chief of staff.

For military reasons strictest secrecy is observed concerning the exact nature of steps proposed by the Allies. American and Allied naval forces now are guarding war supplies both at Vladivostok, terminal of the Trans-Siberian Railroad, and Kola [Murmansk], terminal of the railroad on the Arctic Coast, which is reported threatened by German forces in the interior.

The decision to intervene had been long in the making. For the Allies the Treaty of Brest-Litovsk constituted a major military setback. It had enabled the Germans to remove troops from the eastern front and unleash a fearsome offensive in the west. In addition, the Allied governments, especially the British and the French, took very seriously Lenin's repeated declarations that the Russians would instigate and aid revolution wherever they could. The Bolshevik revolution had, in fact, given impetus to radical movements in most European countries, and disturbances had already occurred. An obvious solution to both problems was to intervene. If Allied troops could be sent through Russia, the eastern front could be opened again and the pressure relieved on the Allied forces struggling desperately to hold the line in France. At the same time aid

KEEPING A LIGHT IN THE WINDOW FOR HIM

could be given to the anti-Bolshevik forces, and if the Bolsheviks were
still in power when the war came to an end, an Allied army would be
on hand to crush them. In April some troops actually were landed in
Murmansk to protect Allied stores there against a threat from German

forces regrouping in Finland. (The Murmansk Soviet, against the orders of the government, had acceded to the proviso that the troops were to be under the jurisdiction of the Soviet.) This provided an invaluable foothold, which the British and French were very anxious to take advantage of.

But intervention would have to be a joint undertaking by the Allies, and the President of the United States had withheld his permission. Wilson's attitude toward the Bolshevik regime at first had not been unfriendly. Point six of his famous Fourteen Points for peace, propounded in January 1918, called upon the nations of the world to give Russia "a sincere welcome into the society of free nations under institutions of her own choosing; and, more than a welcome, assistance also of every kind that she may need and may herself desire." To the IV Congress of Soviets, which met in March 1918, he had sent a cordial message.

Washington, March 11 [*1918*]. On the eve of the gathering at Moscow of the Russian Congress of Soviets, which is to pass judgement on the German-made peace accepted by the Bolsheviki at Brest-Litovsk, President Wilson has sent a message of sympathy to the Russian people:

"May I take advantage of the meeting of the Congress of the Soviets to express the sincere sympathy which the people of the United States feel for the Russian people at this moment when the German power has been thrust in to interrupt and turn back the whole struggle for freedom and substitute the wishes of Germany for the purpose of the people of Russia.

"Although the government of the United States is, unhappily, not now in the position to render the direct and effective aid it would wish to render, I beg to assure the people of Russia through the Congress, that it will avail itself of every opportunity to secure for Russia once more complete sovereignty in her own affairs and full restoration of her great role in the life of Europe and the modern world.

"The whole heart of the people of the United States is with the people of Russia in the attempt to free themselves forever from autocratic government and become the masters of their own life.

WOODROW WILSON."

There were undoubtedly diplomatic motives for the note to the Russians. As the *Tribune* pointed out:

President Wilson's message to the Soviet Congress in Moscow discloses his diplomacy with regard to Russia. It is to trust Russia herself to build up a government that will resist Germany's incursion into her territory, and one that will keep at least a part of the German army occupied on the Eastern front.

Moreover, it sees the hope of Russia not in the revolt of the Constitutional Democratic element against the Bolshevik rule, not in such a movement as Prince Lvoff is said to be heading in Siberia [he was trying to organize a White army], but in the peasants' and workers' government of which this Congress of Soviets is the expression. Addressing a message to the congress comes nearer to recognizing it as a government than this country has come to recognizing anything in Russia since the downfall of Kerensky.

It is thought [in Washington] that the President's message will have the effect upon the Soviets' Congress of strengthening those who oppose the acceptance of the peace with Germany, and perhaps of bringing about the overthrow of Lenine. The Bolshevik leader is thought to be now none too strong.

However, Wilson's statement that Russia should be left alone to work out her own destiny was entirely sincere, and he did believe that Allied troops should be sent through Russia to reopen the eastern front only if the Russians gave their permission. Intervention was utterly contrary to the principle of self-determination which he had enunciated so eloquently and which had won for him and the United States applause throughout the world. But the pressures on him were enormous. His former ambassador to Russia, David Francis, urged him to help the anti-Bolshevik forces, who, Francis insisted, were dedicated to restoring democracy in Russia. Kerensky and the Kadet leaders, as well as other *émigré* Russians, presented the same case. Representatives of the Allies argued the urgent need of distracting the Germans, as well as the dangers of Bolshevism.

But Wilson's agreement to intervention was brought about by something quite different. On April 6 the Japanese landed an army contingent in Vladivostok—not because of any special dislike for the Bolsheviks, nor to aid the war against the common German enemy, but to establish themselves in long-coveted territory. It was an eventuality that the United States, which had been attempting to restrain Japanese expansion ever

THE STRANGE CASE OF RUSSIA

since the Russo-Japanese War, could not risk. Then the problems with the Czechs occurred. Considering the dire need for reinforcements on the western front, the Czechs had to be extricated somehow, and the task fell naturally either to Japan or to the United States, since they were the only Allied countries with forces concentrated in the area. But the United States would not let Japan do the job alone (nor, of course, would Japan give way to the Americans). By that time Wilson was more than half convinced anyway, and he had also been completely disabused of the idea that the Bolsheviks could be induced to extend democracy.

Landings of troops on a large scale by the British and the French began at Murmansk on August 1 and at Archangel on August 2.

Washington, Aug. 15 [*1918*]. Allied progress against the foes of Russian freedom made important progress at three points yesterday.

The first regiment of the American Siberian expedition landed at Vladivostok, joining the British, French and Japanese troops already there.

British troops have made a remarkable march across Persia, and appeared at the oil city of Baku, on the Caspian Sea, where, with the Armenian forces, they now face the Turks and Germans on an important road to India.

Japanese occupation forces parading through Vladivostok in 1918. (*Sovfoto*)

A unit of volunteer Red soldiers leaves from Red Square for the front in 1919. (*Sovfoto*)

Allied forces have driven the Bolsheviki 100 miles south from Archangel on the railroad to Vologda and Moscow, and at the same time detachments have landed at Onega Bay, southwest of Archangel, in an effort to cut off the fugitives.

Under the circumstances—with Allied and White armies threatening from the south, east, and north, the establishment of two anti-Bolshevik regimes in Siberia, the Ukraine under German control, famine in the cities, the outbreak of a cholera epidemic in Petrograd—the Bolsheviks were not disposed to deal lightly with disruptive elements.

Moscow, July 31. At a plenary session of the Executive Main Committee, the Moscow Council and the labor organizations, in which two thousand members participated, Premier Lenine and War Minister Trotzky spoke, and the following resolutions were passed.

1. The Socialist fatherland is in danger.

An American soldier stands guard at an outpost near Archangel. (*Photo from European*)

2. The chief tasks at the present moment are the repulse of the Czecho-Slovaks and the obtaining of grain.

3. The most powerful agitation must be started among the laboring classes to explain the gravity of the situation.

4. Vigilance must be increased against the bourgeoisie, who everywhere are joining the counter revolutionists. The Soviet government must protect itself, and to that end the bourgeoisie must be placed under control and mass terror put into practice against them.

5. The general watchword must be death or victory, with mass expeditions for bread, mass military organization, the arming of workmen, and the exertion of all strength to fight against the counter revolutionary bourgeoisie.

The meeting at which these resolutions were passed was held July 30.

F. E. Dzerzhinsky, head of the Cheka. (*Sovfoto*)

The organization made responsible for the terror (which had in fact already begun) was the All-Russian Commission for the Struggle with Counterrevolution and Sabotage—the Cheka. It had been established in December 1917, and although its activities during the first few months of its existence had been confined mostly to the apprehension of criminals, speculators, and overt counterrevolutionaries, it was already widely feared because of its methods. At the head of the Cheka was a long-time revolutionary, F. E. Dzerzhinsky, who had spent many years in Czarist prisons. The selection was not calculated to imbue the secret police with a scrupulous respect for civil liberties. Dzerzhinsky had suffered too much for his dedication to revolution to take a dispassionate attitude toward the party's enemies, whom he indiscriminately labeled "bourgeois counterrevolutionaries."

Hundreds, if not thousands, of Socialist Revolutionaries, both Right and Left, rightists, and others implicated or suspected of implication in antigovernment activities were arrested and shot in July and August. The murderous spirit swept through the country, infecting people on both sides. One notable example occurred about one A.M. on July 16, in the cellar of a house in the Ural city of Ekaterinburg.

Ex-Czar Shot
By Bolsheviki
Without Trial

London, July 20 [*1918*].   Former Emperor Nicholas of Russia has been shot, a Russian wireless statement to-day announces. The former Emperor's correspondence, including letters from the monk Rasputin, who was killed shortly before the revolution, written to the then Emperor and his family, will be published in the near future, the wireless message declares.

The message announces that a counter revolutionary conspiracy was discovered, with the object of wresting the ex-Emperor from the authority of the Soviet Council. In view of this fact the president of the Ural Regional Council decided to execute the former ruler and the decision was carried out on July 16.

After the March revolution, Nicholas and his family had been incarcerated in the Imperial Palace at Tsarskoye Selo, but in August 1917 they were moved, along with a large retinue of servants, to Tobolsk, a small Siberian town, from which they were taken by Red guards in April 1918 to Ekaterinburg. During the period of the Provisional regime, they had been allowed suitable, if not extravagant, luxury and except for their isolation in Siberia led a not unpleasant existence. At Ekaterinburg, though, they were forced to share the deprivations being suffered by the Russian people. Food was short, and their quarters were extremely cramped. It was the government's intention eventually to put the former Czar on trial, with Trotsky as prosecutor, but in July Czech and White forces invaded Ekaterinburg, and the Ural Soviet, afraid that if Nicholas were captured he would become a rallying point for the anti-Bolsheviks,

Nicholas II on his estate at Tsarskoye Selo, where he was confined after the March Revolution. (*Photo from European*)

The house in Ekaterinburg where Nicholas and his family were executed. (*Photo from European*)

Interned with Nicholas were his four children (left to right) Olga, the Czarevich Alexis, Anastasia, and Tatiana. (*The Bettmann Archive*)

Even when the imperial family was sent to the remote Siberian town of Tobolsk in August 1917, they were accompanied by a large retinue of servants. Such tasks as sawing wood were performed by the Czar (in this instance with the Czarevich's tutor, Pierre Gilliard) simply for the sake of exercise and to pass the time. (*The Bettmann Archive*)

decided to dispose of the danger then and there. Along with Nicholas were executed the Czarina, the Czarevich, Nicholas's daughters (although a rumor has persisted that the beautiful Anastasia had earlier managed to escape), the court physician Dr. Botkin, and three servants. All the bodies were destroyed with benzine and sulfuric acid.

In mid-August, Moisey Uritsky, head of the Petrograd Cheka, was assassinated. Then, two weeks later,

Premier Lenine Wounded Twice By Assassin, But Will Recover

Third Attempt on Life of Russian Bolshevik Chief Fails—Reports from Moscow Say Head of Government Did Not Lose Consciousness

London, Aug. 31 [*1918*]. Attempts have been made on the life of Lenine, the Bolshevik Premier, at Moscow, according to a Russian wireless message received here to-day from the Russian capital under date of August 30. Lenine was wounded in two places, but did not lose consciousness.

The attack on Lenine was made Friday evening after a meeting of laborers at the Mochaelson works, where Lenine spoke. As the Premier was leaving two women stopped him and discussed the recent decrees regarding the importation of foodstuffs to Moscow. In the course of the interview three shots were fired.

The Bolshevik response was predictable.

Moscow Now Under Reign of Terror

London, Sept. 3 [*1918*]. The attempted assassination of Nikolai Lenine, the Bolshevik Premier, has been followed by drastic measures on the part of the authorities in Moscow, according to the Helsingfors correspondent of the Hamburg "Fremdenblatt," who reports that, in addition to the removal of thousands of persons from Moscow to Petrograd, the following proclamation has been issued by M. Peters, chief of the extraordinary commission of the Russian capital.

"The criminal adventures of our enemies force us to reply with measures of terror. Every person found with a weapon in his hand will be immediately executed. Every person who agitates against the Soviet government will be arrested and taken into a concentration camp and all his property seized."

The condition of Lenine has so improved that physicians consider all danger passed.

Dora Kaplan, the Russian [Socialist Revolutionary] who attacked Lenine, has refused to disclose the names of her accomplices or give any information regarding the attack. Witnesses stated that a student about fifteen years old stopped the Premier and handed him a paper, and at the same time two women approached him. Dora Kaplan, after the shooting, fled into the street, where she was arrested and taken to the Ministry of War. Poisoned cigarettes were found on her.

Soviets Murder 547
As Reprisals for
Attacks on Leaders

The Reds executed captured Whites. . . . (*Sovfoto*)

And the Whites executed captured Reds. (*Sovfoto*)

Amsterdam, Sept. 9 [*1918*]. According to an official announcement at Petrograd and received here to-day, up to the present 512 so-called counter revolutionaries, including ten members of the Right Social Revolutionary party, have been shot as a reprisal for the murder of Moses Uritsky, chairman of the Petrograd commission for the suppression of counter revolution.

In Smolensk thirty-four large land owners and the former Moscow Archimandrite, Makari, have been shot as a reprisal for the attempt made on the life of Premier Lenine.

The terror spread and deepened. Indeed, it became the ordinary method of dealing with anti-Bolshevik agitators, recalcitrant peasants, army officers derelict in the performance of their duties, and captured personnel of the White forces. There were seldom trials. Executions, when not public, were performed forthwith by agents of the Cheka in the basements of their headquarters or similar shadowy places. The same procedures for eliminating troublesome opposition were employed by the White armies, only not quite as efficiently.

For the Bolsheviks the swift and merciless application of force served its purpose. The numerical weakness of the regime was overcome. An army was created. A valuable ally was made of the poor peasants. Divisiveness and sabotage in areas under Bolshevik control virtually disappeared. By the fall of 1918 the Bolshevik—the Communist—government was firmly entrenched as far as internal threats to its power were concerned.

However, the regime was now faced with a perilous alignment of antagonistic military forces. In the south, the Volunteer Army under General Denikin, who had been greatly encouraged by Czech victories in Siberia and the Volga region, began an offensive. On August 16, Denikin's forces, joined by Kuban Cossacks, captured the Kuban capital of Ekaterinodar, and on August 26 the Black Sea port of Novorossiysk fell. Further north, General P. N. Krasnov, leader of the Don Cossacks, drove the Bolsheviks from the Don territory, despite his inability to take the important city of Tsaritsyn which was held against his siege by Red Army men under the command of Joseph Stalin. Allied forces were ensconced at Vladivostok, Murmansk, Archangel, and Baku. At the end of September representatives of the two Siberian governments and other anti-Bolshevik groups met at Ufa to form a unified government and coordinate the war against the Communist regime.

Russians Join Forces
In War Against Reds

Washington, Sept. 26 [1918]. Out of the chaos which has existed in Russia since the overthrow of the Kerensky government by the Bolsheviki there is emerging a central authority which officials and diplomats here hope will be able to reestablish order and renew the fight against the common enemy.

Official information reached the Russian Embassy to-day that the Pan-Russian conference at Ufa, European Russia, which has been recognized by all the provisional governments opposing the Bolsheviki, including the Siberian government[s], has constituted a committee of five as the lawful authority for all Russia. This committee will be responsible to the constituent assembly of all Russia, which will convene next January 1, provided 250 members attend.

Composing the conference at Ufa were all members of the constituent assembly which have gathered in Samara, except those who belong to the factions of the Bolsheviki and Social Revolutionists of the Left. Attending the conference are also delegates of the [Western] Siberian government, of the Union of Liberty of the People, of the group of the Renaissance and of the Social Revolutionist and Social Democratic [Menshevik] parties.

The outlook for the Bolsheviks was still far from auspicious. Then a crucial change in the situation occurred.

Germany Signs Armistice; Great World War Ended

EXTRA!

Conflict Ended at 6 O'clock This Morning After Germans Had Signed Armistice Terms

State Department Announces Suspension of Hostilities Following the Formal Acceptance by the Envoys of Berlin Government of the Conditions Laid Down by Allies and United States

Midnight the Hour at Which the Great War Was Officially Closed

Guns from Holland to Switzerland Ceased Their Thunder for First Time in More than Four Years at Eleven O'clock Paris Time

Terms Not to Be Made Public until Later

Washington Believes They Will Include Occupation of Enemy Strategic Points, Surrender at Heligoland and Part of Fleet

Chapter Ten

Red Victory

Denikine Faces Disaster

"Reds" Threaten to Cut Anti-Bolshevik Force in Two by Drive on Center in Retreat on Big Front

Richest Mineral Section Near Fall

Kolchak Is No Longer a Factor in Military Affairs, Comes Report

'We Rule,' Soviet Tells the World

With the end of the war came much cheering news for the Bolsheviks.

Rebels Seize Germany's Entire Navy

U-Boat Crews Join Revolution; Control Five Main Harbors

Large Part of Schleswig in Grip of Revolt; Garrisons on South Baltic Desert

20,000 Deserters Parade in Berlin

Reichstag Socialist and People's Council Head Control Kiel; Riots in Hamburg

Wittelsbach Dynasty Deposed By Decree of Diet in Munich

Bremen Capitulates to the Revolutionists And Red Flag Is Hoisted

Kaiser Abdicates, Crown Prince Out; Western Germany Seethes in Revolt

Troops in Berlin Desert to Workers; General Strike On

Only Three Killed as Reds Take Over Public Buildings and Barracks After All Factories Are Closed by Walkout—Rebels Parade Town

Ebert, Proclaiming New Regime, Promises Peace, Urges Restraint

Northern Frontiers Closed to Prevent Escape of Aristocrats; Krupp Heads Arrested; Bavarian Republic Seeks to "Save Germany From Worst"

Berlin, Nov. 9 [*1918*]. (*German Wireless to London*) (*Nov. 10, 12:56 p.m.*). The German people's government has been instituted in the greater part of Berlin. The garrison has gone over to the government.

The Workmen's and Soldiers' Council has declared a general strike.

Troops and machine guns have been placed at the disposal of the council.

Friedrich Ebert (vice-president of the Social-Democratic party) is carrying on the Chancellorship.

Crown Prince Slain; Soviets Now Rule

Reds Seize Helgoland and Grand Fleet

Troops at Front Form Committees; Hindenburg Loyal

Prince Rupprecht Stays With Troops

Grand Duke of Hesse Is Placed Under Preventive Arrest

The long-awaited German revolution had begun, and it ignited disorders in other countries.

Bolshevism Spreads to Neutral States

Reds Active in Sweden and Holland

Radical Doctrines Spread
To Switzerland, Norway and Spain

Street Fighting in Berlin Is Renewed

'Red' Revolts Break Out in 3 Countries

47 Killed and Many Wounded
In Clash with Polish
Troops in Warsaw Streets

Silesia Made a Republic

Bolsheviki Attack Rumanian
Troops in Bucharest;
French March on Kiev

Even in the United States there were rumblings.

Police Bar Red Flag at Big Meeting

Hundreds of Socialists Are
Searched at Webster
Hall by Authorities

Max Eastman Flays "City Hall Autocrat"

Planned "Discussion of Establishment of Soviet of America"

The Russian Communists no longer felt, and in fact no longer were, isolated. Although the flush of revolution at the end of the war quickly paled—a moderate socialist government was installed in Germany and the Rumanians and Poles not unwillingly buckled under to rightist regimes— the Bolsheviks were now more confident than ever of the imminent victory of the world proletariat. Notwithstanding their own preoccupations, they emphatically reiterated their offer of aid to revolutionists everywhere and in return received assurances of support from radical groups throughout the world. In January, Lenin announced the convocation of a "new revolutionary International" at Moscow in March, as a successor to the First International (International Workingmen's Association), established by Marx in 1864, and the Second International, which was founded in 1889 and lasted until the wartime antagonism of its members broke it up.

Moreover, the German defeat enabled the Russians to begin to re-establish control over the formerly German-occupied areas of Lithuania, Latvia, White Russia, and the Ukraine. And as soon as the armistice was signed, the Czech brigade announced its intention of withdrawing from Russia as soon as possible, which threatened to deprive the Siberian government of the only really effective military force they had. The five-man Directory formed at the Ufa Conference in September had proved to be weak and ineffectual. Consisting of two Socialist Revolutionaries and three conservatives, at least two of whom were quite moderate, the Directory was utterly despised by the military and rightist elements gathered at Omsk, where the seat of the new government had been located, and party squabbles, intrigues, and conspiracies rendered it impotent, with catastrophic military consequences. The Red Fifth Army, which had begun an offensive in the middle Volga region in the fall, had been able to advance steadily, taking Samara on October 8 and Izhevsk on November 7 and forcing the Whites and the Czechs to retreat behind the Ural mountains. However, the Czechs, even though hampered by their White allies, had constituted a formidable opposing force; indeed, after the capture of Izhevsk it looked as if the Red Army would be unable to advance farther.

The Czech announcement galvanized the White officers and rightists at Omsk into decisive action.

United Russia
Seen in Coup
Of Kolchak

Admiral Becomes Virtual
Dictator of New Omsk
Government

Vladivostok, Tuesday, Nov. 19 [*1918*]. Through a coup on the part of the Council of Ministers of the new all-Russian government at Omsk, Admiral Alexander Kolchak has become virtual dictator and commander of the all-Russian army and fleet. Two ministers, M. Avksentieff and M. Zensenoff, who opposed Admiral Kolchak's dictatorship, have been arrested. A portion of the directorate of the erstwhile Ufa government, which formed the administrative body of the new government and to which the ministry was responsible, supports Admiral Kolchak.

Telegrams received here from Omsk state that the move was "due to extraordinary circumstances and danger menacing to the state." The Council of Ministers has assumed authority and transferred it to Admiral Kolchak. The latter has accepted the responsibility and, it is announced, has entered upon his duties as "Supreme Governor."

The coup occurred on November 18.

Kolchak and his initial successes were described for the *Tribune* sometime after the coup by John A. Embry, the United States Consul at Omsk.

Admiral Alexander Vasilivitch Kolchak, unquestionably Russia's most popular hero of the war, [is] best known in the United States for his brilliant action in the Black Sea, where upon the very first day of his arrival at Semferopal to take command of the Black Sea fleet, he went out against the two German battleships, Breslau and Göben, and did not return until he had cleared the Black Sea of those two notorious pirates.

This exploit of Admiral Kolchak in the Black Sea parallels in American history that of John Paul Jones, who in command of the wornout French frigate Bon Homme Richard, made short shrift of the British line ship Serapis.

History also relates how the disorders of the Russian revolution of 1917 were stayed in the Black Sea fleet for two months after the Russian army had completely disintegrated[,] due entirely to the influence of Admiral Kolchak's personality on his men. At length, when the sailors of the Black Sea fleet, driven mad by the same pernicious German propaganda which had destroyed the Russian army, mutinied and began killing their officers—first breaking their swords before their eyes and tearing off their epaulettes—their great respect for Admiral Kolchak saved him from a similar fate. Curiously enough, a short time later, these same sailors [helped] elect him a member of the Constituent Assembly, the fate of which is well known to the world.

It was familiarity with these facts in the career of Admiral Kolchak and knowledge of his thorough and uncompromising political and private honesty that decided the agitated [officers] and members of the Council of Ministers to turn to him in their dilemma. Admiral Kolchak was not in Omsk at the time of the coup d'etat but at the Siberian front, whither he had gone in the capacity of minister of war to inspect the Czecho-Slovak battalions there. Accordingly, they dispatched an urgent telegram to him informing him of the events which had transpired and stated that Siberia was doomed unless he could at once return to Omsk, re-form the government and organize an effective resistance to Bolshevism. Admiral Kolchak returned post haste.

With characteristic promptness, Admiral Kolchak set about at once to reorganize the government which is now known as the Siberian government and to create a Russian army which could replace at the Siberian front the Czecho-Slovaks, who since the signing of the armistice had been obsessed with returning to their beloved Bohemia after four years of unremitting toil in Russia and Siberia.

As in the days of the revolution, Admiral Kolchak's genius for leadership again proved a decisive factor. The scattered bands of Russian troops in Western Siberia rallied under that leadership and a few days later resolutely took the place of the Czecho-Slovak soldiers at the Siberian front. From this time onward the Czecho-Slovaks confined their activities entirely to guarding the Transsiberian Railway, their one means of exit from Siberia. Americans and other foreigners at that time in Omsk were amazed at the feat that Admiral Kolchak had accomplished.

The army of the Siberian government steadily increased in numbers, and the improvement in the discipline of its troops as displayed by those we saw daily in Omsk was as rapid as was the army's growth.

THE NEXT CANDIDATE FOR ELIMINATION

That part of Siberia which lies between the Ural mountains and Lake Baikal, a territory as large as European Russia, in November, 1918, recognized the authority of the Kolchak government. Shortly thereafter General Denikin, leader of the patriotic forces in Southern Russia strug-

The Face at the Window

gling against the Bolsheviki, and Tschaikovsky, head of the government of North Russia at Archangel, wirelessed to Admiral Kolchak their recognition of his authority.

Opposition to the new Siberian government was suppressed with measures identical to those employed by the Bolshevik regime. And the effect was the same as that of the Red terror. It secured the Omsk government.

In December, Kolchak's armies began to advance, the northern wing capturing Perm in the Ural mountains and moving toward a junction with the forces of the North Russian Government, which had been established at Archangel by Socialist Revolutionaries under the patronage of the Allied command stationed there. Meanwhile, General Denikin in the south administered severe defeats to the North Caucasian Red Army and by February had begun to turn northward. The prospects of a total White victory seemed increasingly bright. The major worry of the Whites at the moment was the possibility that the Allies would withdraw, now that the war was over. The White forces depended heavily upon the munitions being supplied them by the Americans and Japanese at Vladivostok and the British at Baku and also hoped for more direct military contributions —so far the Allied forces had done comparatively little fighting. In any case, the Allied occupation of major ports and the blockade were of crucial importance. Red Russia was still starving. As long as their chance of importing food, as well as munitions and other necessaries, was cut off, the Bolsheviks would get progressively weaker.

For the Allied governments the situation posed a dilemma. The military reason for intervention no longer existed. Germany was defeated, so there was certainly no need to open a second front. President Wilson was especially disposed to withdraw. Intervention could not in his mind be reconciled with the principle of the self-determination of nations, for which he was struggling desperately against the expansionist designs of some of the Entente statesmen. But considering the revolutionary outbursts scorching central Europe and the suspected complicity of Bolshevik agents in some of them, the political reasons were now even more compelling. The recent successes of the White armies held out promise of a reasonably easy victory over the Communists in Russia, which, as Premier Georges Clemenceau of France argued, would go a long way toward snuffing out the Reds everywhere else.

Largely at Wilson's urging, the Supreme Allied Peace Council proposed to the Reds and Whites that they meet with Allied representatives in a peace conference.

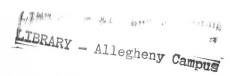
LIBRARY — Allegheny Campus

Bolsheviki Agree to Parley, Allies Select Envoys

'Reds' Agree to Pay Debts of Russia

Paris, Feb. 7 [*1919*]. The second step in the development of official relations between the Entente and the Russian Bolsheviki was taken yesterday, when the Allied Supreme Peace Council received an acceptance from Lenine's government of the invitation to participate in a conference on Prince's [Prinkipo] Island.

The Council at once made arrangements to send two representatives from each Entente nation to the conference.

The commission forming the plan of the society of nations in Paris has completed one-third of its task. The underlying principles of the league have been virtually agreed upon, it is said.

Russians Refuse To Enter Parley With Bolsheviki

Washington, Feb. 19 [*1919*]. Formal rejections of the proposal that they meet with delegates of the Bolsheviki and other Russian governments at Princess' Islands was handed to the peace conference at Paris to-day by representatives of the governments of Siberia, Archangel and Southern Russia, according to a dispatch to the Russian embassy here from Ambassador Bakhmeteff at Paris.

The three governments said they gladly accepted the offer of the Allies to collaborate in the interior pacification of Russia, but there could be no conciliation between them and the Bolsheviki, who were denounced as traitors and fomentors of anarchy.

The White refusal plunged the conferees at Paris into a state of utter consternation. The one course of action on which they had been more or less agreed had been rejected. Since both President Wilson and British

Prime Minister David Lloyd George had gone home and would not return until the middle of March, the question was left in abeyance. But no sooner had those two statesmen resumed their seats at the peace table than the problem was thrust upon them again.

Red Revolt in Hungary
Provokes Near Panic
In Peace Conference

Situation in Rumania Becomes Critical— Poland Is Reported to Be Undermined by Bolshevism, Which Spreads as Conferees Delay Work on Pact by Prolonged Debate

In March also the Third Workingmen's International—Communist International—called by Lenin, convened in Moscow. Only thirty-five delegates were able to attend, but the implications were not lost on Clemenceau, or on the new British Minister of War, Winston Churchill, both of whom argued for an all-out military effort to crush the Reds.

Wilson Blocks War on Lenine;
Bolshevism Divides Council;
France Begins to Act Alone

Clemenceau and Orlando For Force, Wilson and Lloyd George Cling to Policy of Conciliation

The cable message hereunder from the Tribune's *correspondent at Paris describes not merely an impasse in the work of the Peace Conference, but a crisis in the world's affairs.*

Paris, March 30 [*1919*]. It is undeniable that the great majority of Frenchmen consider the daily secret meetings of the Council of Four as a struggle in which the future of the world, and especially that of France, is at stake.

Renewed efforts are being made constantly by the French in the hope of persuading President Wilson to countenance military action against Bolshevism, but they are again being told definitely that America will not assist with men or money. In turn, renewed efforts are being made by the American delegates to persuade the French of the necessity for quickly lifting the blockade maintained against all enemy countries.

These conflicts of opinion as to how to deal with Bolshevism again have been brought into the foreground by the Hungarian action.

Within recent weeks the French evidently have intended to proceed alone against Bolshevism, having sent several divisions to Odessa under the direction of d'Espercy, formerly the Salonica commander. But two regiments have refused to proceed against the Bolshevik forces, which has strengthened the Americans in their belief that their views are correct. That European armies are not in the mood for further fighting seems patent.

Nor were the American armies.

American Draft Troops Mutiny On Archangel Front

'Not at War; Won't Fight,' Say Soldiers

Washington, April 10 [*1919*]. A mutiny among American troops on the North Russian front was described in an official dispatch received by the War Department to-day. A company of infantry refused to obey the orders of their officers to prepare for movement to the front lines and went forward finally only under the urging of their officers and after one enlisted man, placed in confinement for disobedience of orders, had been released, according to advice received by the War Department. The American army contingent on the Russian front is comprised largely of Michigan and Wisconsin troops.

The mutineers, while moving forward, persisted that they would not go to the front lines . . . and predicted general mutiny in the American forces on the Russian front if a statement was not forthcoming from Washington regarding the withdrawal of American troops from Russia.

The French force in Odessa was so mutinous that Clemenceau had no choice but to approve the evacuation of the key Black Sea port, which the Bolsheviks entered triumphantly on April 6. Still he adamantly refused to abandon the intervention. The decision of the Council of Four, consequently, was a compromise—to make no essential change, not to withdraw, but not to extend their commitment, at least for the time being.

At the moment the outlook for the Whites was excellent.

Bolshevik Armies in General Retreat

London, April 19 [*1919*]. Bolshevik troops have suffered severe setbacks on three fronts in Russia, according to advices received to-day from many sources.

The Soviet government admits a retirement along virtually the whole front in Eastern Russia; Russian troops drove the Reds twelve miles to the south in the Murman region, and on the Archangel front Allied forces captured Bolshie Ozerki, and are pursuing the defeated foe southward.

On May 19 Denikin began an offensive in the southeast. The Volunteer Army, which had been renamed the Armed Forces of South Russia after the resignation of General Krasnov in February and the subsequent recognition by the Don Cossacks of Denikin as Supreme Commander, quickly and quite easily expelled the Red Army from the Don territory, taking Kharkov on June 25 and Tsaritsyn on the 30th. Denikin now gave the order to head for Moscow. An attempted offensive against him by the Red Army in August was repulsed, and the Whites, fanned out from the Volga to the Black Sea, continued their advance. Kiev fell to them on August 31 (actually Denikin took it from Ukrainian nationals who had entered the city the day before), Kursk on September 20, Voronezh on October 6, Chernigov on the 12th, and Orel on the 13th. Denikin was now within striking distance of Moscow, with Tula the only large city in the way.

Simultaneously, Petrograd was being seriously threatened by a relatively new White army called the Northwestern Army under General Nikolay Yudenich. The Bolshevik occupation of Latvia in January 1919 had been extremely precarious. Because of the hostility of neighboring Estonia, the Reds had been forced to maintain a broad front in order to protect themselves from a possible attack by Whites based there, thus weakening their forces. Under the circumstances, a nationalist anti-Bolshevik army formed in Latvia, the Iron Division, headed by a junker, Count von der Goltz, gradually forced the Russians back. He took Riga on May 22, then soon drove the Reds out of Latvia altogether. At the same time, the armies of the independent Polish state, which had been established with Allied blessings in November 1919, pushed the Russians out of much of Polish Lithuania, capturing Vilna in April. Out of the disparate collection of anti-Communists, nationalists, and mutinous troops in the Baltic area, including the Latvians of the Iron Division as well as Lithuanians, Estonians, Germans, and Poles, the Northwestern Army was organized in May and June 1919. Its activities remained relatively insignificant until the fall of 1919, when, at Denikin's behest, Yudenich struck northward toward Petrograd.

"Iron Ring" Is Closing In on Bolsheviki

London, Oct. 15 [1919]. Military successes achieved by anti-Bolshevik armies operating on two fronts were reported to-day from various sources, showing that the iron ring established by forces opposed to the Lenine-Trotzky regime are closing still further on Moscow and Petrograd.

Capture of the important city of Orel by General Denikine's army is claimed by General Denikine and is admitted in an official statement of the Russian soviet. Thousands of prisoners and great quantities of materiel are reported captured.

The Northwestern Russian Army of General Yudenich has pushed thirty-five miles beyond Yamburg, which was recently captured, and is within fifty miles of Petrograd, Stockholm reports.

The North Russian government, anticipating the fall of Petrograd, has sent a high official to negotiate with the Finnish government for trade privileges for the relief of the former capital.

On October 16, Yudenich took Gatchina, only thirty miles from Petrograd.

Ironically, when Petrograd and Moscow were almost in the hands of the Whites, the tide of the civil war had already begun to turn. After his successes against the Red Fifth Army's northern flank in March and April, Admiral Kolchak began to suffer serious reverses. At Lenin's insistence every man and piece of equipment that could be spared was thrown into the campaign against the Siberian army. "If we don't conquer the Urals before winter," Lenin warned in May, "I think the destruction of the Revolution is inevitable; strain all forces; look out carefully for reinforcements; mobilize the population in the front territory; take care of the political work." On June 9, Ufa was retaken, and on July 1 Perm fell to the Reds. The capture of the strategically important Ural city of Zlatoust on July 13 and of the railway junction and Ural capital of Ekaterinburg the next day constituted a disaster for Kolchak, whose demoralized troops began now to retreat in confusion. After the Red capture of Cheliabinsk on July 25, the retreat turned into a rout. By September the Communist forces were threatening Kolchak's capital, Omsk.

The reasons for the victory were only partly military. Kolchak was badly weakened behind the lines by peasant uprisings. The poor Siberian farmers, most of them recent arrivals who had managed to obtain only small plots of the less desirable land, had no special love for the Bolsheviks, but they had come to hate the Kolchak regime for its support of the wealthier farmer class and its refusal to consider their demands for redistribution of the estates of the Cossacks and older settlers. When the Omsk government attempted to conscript these peasants, they rebelled. Before long Siberia was in chaos. A veritable partisan movement developed, in which workers from Siberian cities joined, and bands of peasants and workers waged a guerrilla war against the regime. By October, Kolchak was done for. The *coup de grâce* was delivered on November 14.

London, Nov. [*14, 1919*].   Omsk, capital of the All-Russian government, has been occupied by the Russian Bolsheviki, a Moscow official communiqué received here . . . asserts.

The Kolchak forces, the statement adds, are retreating in an easterly direction.

At the end of December, a revolt broke out in Irkutsk, whither the Kolchak cabinet had fled, and the government was replaced by a more liberal but distinctly anti-Bolshevik regime, which adopted the name Political Center. Kolchak abdicated on January 4, 1920. A week and a half later he was imprisoned by the Political Center. Shortly after that, the Communists took over in Irkutsk, and on the bitter cold morning of February 7, Kolchak was taken to a hill and shot.

Meanwhile, the Reds had mounted counterattacks against Yudenich and Denikin. Trotsky himself took charge of the defense of Petrograd. It seemed hopeless, but Trotsky, in opposition to Lenin, who wanted to concentrate on the defense of Moscow, insisted that every effort be made to save the city in which the revolution had begun. In this argument he was joined (it was one of the rare occasions) by Stalin, and Lenin acquiesced. As was so often the case in similar circumstances, Trotsky injected the disheartened population of the city with a fiery esprit and will to win. Detachments of women and workers, organized into a Red guard, reinforced the regular troops. In the factories improvised arms and materiel were hammered out of whatever was at hand.

Petrograd Reds Awaiting Siege

London, Oct. 20 [*1919*]. Assailed by the Russian Northwestern Army under General Yudenitch and isolated from the world, the Bolshevik forces in Petrograd were reported in advices received by the War Office to-day to be preparing for a siege. . . . Supplies of food were being brought into the city and machine guns have been placed to command the principal thoroughfares, the dispatches said.

Tremendous explosions were being heard from Petrograd by the attacking army Sunday night as it closed in on the city. . . . General Yudenitch's troops had then approached to within 8½ miles of the former capital, and the towers of the city could be seen.

Petrograd is virtually isolated, the War Office announced. Anti-Bolshevik cavalry have cut the railroads leading from Petrograd to Vitebsk, Moscow and Vologda. The Petrograd-Vitebsk road is cut at Viritza and the Petrograd-Moscow railroad at Tosna, south and southeast of Petrograd, respectively. The line at Vologda is cut south of Lake Ladoga.

A Bolshevik division, which was being rushed to Petrograd from the

A 1918 photograph of Stalin. (*Sovfoto*)

interior to defend the city against the advance of General Yudenitch, was virtually wiped out at Krasnaie Selo, when General Yudenitch took that outpost in Petrograd, according to the War Office advices.

Reds Line Up in Last Stand to Hold Petrograd

Helsingfors, Finland, Oct. 21 [*1919*]. General Yudenitch has encountered strong Bolshevik resistance beyond Pulkoyo, about seven miles south of Petrograd. He therefore has halted his advance to concentrate his forces while awaiting reinforcements and heavy artillery. One hundred guns reached his army to-day.

Helsingfors, Finland, Oct. 22 [*1919*]. The battle for Petrograd is still continuing, with a heavy engagement 6½ miles south of the city. Bolshevik regiments from Moscow are taking part in the defense of Petrograd, the headquarters report adds.

London, Oct. 24 [*1919*]. A Bolshevik official report, received by wireless, asserts that their troops have recaptured Pavlovsk and Tsarskoe-Selo, south of Petrograd, by a dashing attack. Many prisoners were taken.

Bolshevik Grip
On Petrograd
Grows Tighter

London, Oct. 27 [*1919*]. The chances of General Yudenitch . . . capturing Petrograd before winter puts an end to operations seem again to be fading. The Bolsheviki have brought strong reinforcements from other fronts and have started a successful counter offensive, which already has resulted in recapture of Krasnaie Selo and the withdrawal of the Yudenitch line south of that place.

Yudenitch still holds Gatchina firmly, according to the British War Office review of the situation. . . . The Bolsheviki reinforcements include some of the best Communist troops, led by specially selected commissars from Moscow. They have forced back Yudenitch's troops at several places.

On November 3 Yudenich was driven out of Gatchina and within two weeks he was chased out of Russia altogether, into Estonia, where his army was soon disbanded.

In the meantime, Denikin's advance in the south had been halted. On October 20, the Red Army recaptured Orel, and on the 24th Voronezh was taken. The Communists had won the initiative. Now, with victory achieved both in the east against Kolchak and in the northwest against Yudenich, they could concentrate on Denikin.

Denikine Faces Disaster

London, Jan. 1 [*1920*]. The position of General Denikine, the anti-Bolshevik leader in South Russia, is becoming more critical. Reports received by the War Office show his retreat is continuing along virtually the whole of his 600-mile front, and that the Bolshevik drive against his center, with the purpose of cutting his army in two, has brought about a critical situation.

The Bolshevik advance guards have reached the Donets Coal Basin and are less than one hundred miles from the coast. The basin represents the richest mineral section of Russia, and its acquisition by the "Reds" would be of inestimable value to them.

"REDS" EXPLOIT ADVANTAGES

Further east the "Reds" are imperiling the left flank of the Caucasus army. The Bolsheviki evidently have succeeded in brilliantly concentrating overwhelming forces against Denikine's somewhat thinly held center and are exploiting their advantage to the fullest degree.

Like Kolchak's collapse, Denikin's was due in part to nonmilitary factors. Although he himself tended to be quite moderate, most of his administrative officials were rightists, often monarchists of the most reactionary stripe, and in the areas controlled by his forces they would attempt to restore the prerogatives of the aristocratic landlords and bureaucrats. This earned for Denikin the implacable hostility of the peasants, who forgot their grievances against the Bolsheviks, and constantly harassed him by guerrilla attacks. In addition, Denikin was a Russian imperialist, which aroused the antagonism of the various Cossack groups, who intended, once the Bolsheviks were beaten, to establish independent or autonomous Cossack states. Like Kolchak, Denikin succumbed in part because it appeared to many that the only alternative he offered to Bolshevism was restoration of the sort of regime that had been overthrown in the March revolution. Given a choice, the great majority of the Russian people would take the former.

But the factor that probably tipped the scales against all three White leaders—Kolchak, Yudenich, and Denikin—was the shriveling up of the Allied commitment. The French had withdrawn from Odessa in April. The British had too many troubles in Ireland, India, and Egypt to worry about Russia. Gradually, they too pulled out, evacuating Trans-Caucasia in July 1919, Archangel in September, and Murmansk the following month. By the fall of 1919 the Allied governments were overwhelmed with a multitude of economic and political problems, and, anyway, the danger of Communist expansion now seemed much more remote. The

Reds in Hungary had been beaten; the German government was becoming more conservative rather than more radical; Poland and Rumania were firmly in the grasp of rightist regimes. During the critical fall campaign, the Whites had received hardly any aid from the Allied governments, and after the fall of the Kolchak regime, the annihilation of the Northwestern Army, and the defeat of Denikin, there was no longer any justification, military or political, for continuing intervention.

Allies Partly Lift Blockade Of Russia; League of Nations Formally Launched in Paris

Paris, Jan. 16 [1920]. In an official communication issued this evening the Supreme Council approved of recommendations to relieve the population of the interior of Russia by giving them machinery and other commodities of which they are in sore need, in exchange for grain and flax.

This partial lifting of the blockade is described in the official communication as "an exchange of goods on the basis of reciprocity between the Russian people and Allied and neutral countries," but through cooperative societies.

"These arrangements imply no change in the policy of the Allied governments toward the Soviet government," says the communication of the Supreme Council.

Washington, Jan. 16 [1920]. Reasons which brought about the decision of the United States government to withdraw the Siberian expeditionary force have been set forth in a note to the Japanese government . . . made public to-night.

[In the note] the United States asserts that reinforcements would be impractical and that to maintain the status quo "might involve the government of the United States in an undertaking of such indefinite character as to be inadvisable."

Some Allied contingents remained for a while, particularly naval units and the Japanese, who set up a short-lived puppet state in Manchuria, but the role they played in the civil war was negligible.

Meanwhile, the Bolshevik drive continued.

Odessa Seized by "Reds"; U.S. Aids Refugees

Town in Ciscaucasia, 75 Miles from Novorossisk Reported Taken March 18

"Reds" Take Novorossisk; Claim 112,000 Prisoners

On April 4, General Denikin resigned. He was succeeded by his able subordinate General P. N. Wrangel.

But at the very point when the weary Bolsheviks thought peace might at last be in sight another attack was hurled against them. On April 25, the Polish army marched into the Ukraine. The Poles wanted to recover for their new state all the territory contained within the boundaries of Poland before the partition of the country in the late eighteenth century. The Bolsheviks, disregarding their frequently avowed principles of the right of nationalities to independent statehood, reasserted Russian claims to those areas and in January 1919 invaded them. Attempts by the Russians in the spring of 1920 to negotiate a peace with the Poles were disdainfully rejected by Marshal Josef Pilsudski, the Polish dictator. The attack, in which the Poles were joined by Ukrainian nationalists who hoped to re-establish the government of Rada, was initially successful.

Russians Are Retreating on Various Parts of Front, Losing Important Points

London, May 8 [1920]. Polish and Ukrainian troops captured Kiev on Thursday night [May 6], according to an official statement issued at Moscow yesterday and received here by wireless.

The Polish success, however, was of brief duration.

Bolsheviki in Big Attack on 90-Mile Front

Warsaw, May 24 [1920]. The Bolsheviki are attacking in waves on the northern fighting front in a thrust to break the Polish lines and open communication with East Prussia.

Poles, Cut Off By Bolsheviki, Evacuate Kiev

Warsaw, June 13 [1920]. The evacuation of Kiev has been completed, the Poles withdrawing to the region of Zhitomir.

The Red Army plunged westward, taking Minsk on July 11, Vilna or July 14, Brest-Litovsk on August 1.

France Prepares to Aid Poland; Reds Closing In on Warsaw; Plan to Offer Danzig to Berlin

Paris and London Are Exchanging Views on Adoption of a Policy for Armed Intervention

British Demand Bolsheviki Reply Immediately to Allied Peace Note

London, Aug. 4 [1920].   Acting in coöperation with the French, the British have dispatched another note to Moscow, demanding immediate and unequivocal answer from the Soviet on the question of holding the proposed London conference on Polish peace.

Soviet 20 Miles from Warsaw; British Labor Forbids War on Russia

Warsaw, Aug. 13 [1920].   The Bolshevik armies to-day are within twenty miles of the Polish capital. Martial law has been declared here. Pressing down from the north and northeast with a force which compels the Poles to withdraw slowly upon Warsaw, the Reds at the same time are fighting their way westward from Miawa, fifty miles northwest of the capital, in an effort to cut the last remaining railway line which links the Poles with Danzig, through which their chief supply of munitions is coming.

London, Aug. 13 [1920].   British labor has taken action which may produce the most serious crisis this country has ever faced. Its "Council of Action," well named, to-day pledged the labor of the country to direct action; that is, a general strike, in the event of the government attempting to declare war on Russia. One thousand and forty four delegates stood for a minute in silence to mark their solemn confirmation of this resolve.

This action can cause nothing short of a revolution in England if the government takes action against Russia.

The Bolsheviks were completely convinced that the moment they entered Warsaw they would be greeted by Polish workers hailing the liberation of Poland from Pilsudski and capitalism. But the Poles, the workers as well as the peasants, had no intention of voluntarily submitting to new Russian rulers, whatever their political hue. They rallied to the support of the Polish army, which at the eleventh hour counterattacked.

Soviet Hold on Warsaw Broken

━━━◆━━━

Russians Retreat at Top Speed
To Escape Trap Set by Poles;
Brest-Litovsk Reported Taken

Thereafter, the fighting became inconclusive. Both sides, drained by war and worried about pressing domestic problems, were soon ready for peace.

Riga, Oct. 5 [1920]. An agreement for the signing of an armistice, preliminary to peace, not later than October 8, was reached this evening by M. Joffe and M. Dombski, heads of the Russian and Polish delegations respectively.

Reports of internal dissensions in Warsaw are causing some uneasiness. There are many indications that the speedy signature of an armistice would be a great personal victory for M. Dombski, chief Polish delegate, and possibly make of him such an important political figure in Poland that the peasant party would insist on his elevation to the Premiership.

Paris, Oct. 5 [1920]. Advices reached the French Foreign Office to-day that the advance of General Wrangel, anti-Red leader in South Russia, is continuing.

In interior Russia, the Foreign Office advices showed, it was said, that the situation was desperate owing to the threatened famine, which it was predicted would make the two previous lean winters seem to have been seasons of abundance by comparison.

The Bolsheviki are anxious about General Wrangel's successes in the south, and the latest call of Trotzky is for "liquidation of the southern front before winter."

Eager to be done with the war and wishing to preclude further troubles with the Poles, the Bolsheviks conceded most of the disputed territory to Poland.

Red flags were raised in the Turkestan city of Bukhara on its capture
by Red troops in September 1920. (*Sovfoto*)

The counterattack against Wrangel, who, taking advantage of the
Polish war, had started an offensive northward from the Crimea in
June, began on October 20 and quickly achieved its aim.

London, Nov. 14 [*1920*]. Sebastopol has been captured by the Reds,
according to reports received from Paris to-night. . . . Latest advices
from Constantinople say that General Wrangel, leader of the broken
South Russian armies, was expecting to evacuate Sebastopol to-day.

The greatest activity is reported in the British Mediterranean fleet, but
apparently it consists merely of maneuvers to afford an opportunity to
release certain warships to go to the Crimea and aid the refugees, whose
plight is characterized as terrible.

Wrangel and his fellow Whites in the Crimea escaped in the British
ships, bringing the civil war to an end. Except for a few areas of minor
resistance in the Caucasus and Central Asia, where various national

groups were attempting to retain or establish their independence, Russia was finally at peace after more than six years of war and revolution. Despite the odds against them, the Bolsheviks had prevailed. They now turned to the overwhelming task of repairing their shattered homeland.

Chapter Eleven

The End
of the Revolution

Petrograd a City of Death And Darkness

Red Cross Reports People Are Without Food, Fuel or Lights; Suffering Almost Beyond Belief

Disease Stalks in Homes and Streets

Hospitals Without Heat or Medicine; Epidemics Kill Thousand a Month

At the end of 1920 much of Russia lay in ruins.

Paris, Oct. 6 [1920]. A graphic description by an eyewitness of the fearful conditions existing in Petrograd is given by the Finnish Red Cross in an appeal just issued to the Red Cross societies of the world. It is accompanied by documents prepared by Professor Zeidler, formerly head of the Petrograd Red Cross, but now a refugee in Finland.

The documents which reached the Paris bureau of the American Red Cross to-day tell the story of the agony of a dying city. Petrograd's present population, based on the food cards, is now 500,000 to 600,000, and the capital of the czars is described as having shrunk to one-fourth its pre-war size. The report says:

"Death stalks on every side waiting for winter to aid in the grim work of mowing down the silent, hungry, sick and dying thousands. With streets and houses choked with filth that is already spreading spotted and intermittent typhus, the cold weather will finish the task with pneumonia and abdominal typhus.

HOUSES WRECKED FOR FUEL

"The fuel situation was never so bad. Wooden houses have been torn down for fuel. The material is distributed equally among the population, but during the nights the more energetic citizens steal the quota of wood from the others.

"The woodyards have been nationalized. One of them has been given up entirely to the manufacturers of 30,000 coffins monthly. But even this number is insufficient. People have not time to bury the dead, and the bodies take their turn, waiting several days.

"Only one important tramway line is in operation, and that runs to a suburb. Attempts to repair the streets, which are full of holes owing to bursting water pipes, have failed because the wood blocks for pavement have been stolen for fuel. Lighting is allowed only two half hours each day. Kerosene costs 450 rubles a pound. There are no candles. Most homes are in darkness. There is no means of transporting things by waterway, because the barges were long since demolished for fuel. The railway transportation is devoted almost exclusively to the distribution of flour.

"Only 200 people are permitted to leave Petrograd daily by passenger train. Workmen receive half a pound of bread daily, and sometimes other food is given. The prices of foodstuffs continue to rise to incredible heights. Many products have almost completely disappeared from the markets.

FACES DISFIGURED BY FAMINE

"The mortality has reached a startling rate owing to the lack of food and insanitary conditions of houses and streets. Fat has left the majority of the population long ago. At present, the muscular tissue is consumed. The faces of people have taken on a waxlike color. In order to fill their stomachs with something they drink different substitutes for tea and coffee, or great quantities of plain water, resulting in puffiness and dropsy,

Victims of the Civil War. (*Sovfoto*)

Whites who escaped to hospitable Western cities suffered less physical hardship, but former members of the nobility and officers of the imperial armed forces often had to work for their living in restaurants or shops. (*Keystone View Co.*)

which change the expression of the face so that old acquaintances are unrecognizable.

"The decay of property is aided not only by the colossal prices of materials and wages—the slightest repair work costs not under 100,000 rubles—but also to the fact that house porters are abolished, partly as a bourgeois system and partly because the porters are needed for wood cutting. At present houses are looked after by beggars and committees composed of indigent Communists.

"Indescribable dirt and filth is on every side within the houses. When plumbing gets out of order it remains unrepaired. Whole houses become filthy from top to bottom and it becomes impossible to live in them. These houses are then barred, and tenants move into other houses, which are neglected in the same manner.

"There is no fuel, no hot water or baths, no janitor, doorkeeper or servants for cleaning yards, streets, buildings or for the removal of garbage. The government appointed a special sanitary commission with sweeping authority, but the commission accomplished nothing. The commission is housed in a building where the heating plant is out of order and the water system and toilets are not running.

"Petrograd is facing a dreadful specter of epidemics. Thousands are already dying every month of spotted, abdominal and intermittent typhus, dysentery, Spanish influenza, smallpox, pulmonary diseases, hunger and exhaustion.

"The hospitals are overflowing with dropsy victims, mostly women, elderly men and children.

"The Minister of Health, apparently realizing the gravity of the situation, recently ordered the mobilization of all physicians, regardless of age, to combat epidemic diseases. The infection of soldiers with spotted and intermittent typhus necessitated the reopening of three of the largest military hospitals for exclusive use of the army. The moral breakdown of the population is well illustrated in the hospitals, where there is no discipline and no care of patients.

"Patients are taken in the hospitals without a bath. If they want to be warm while in bed awaiting operation they must bring their own blankets and furs with them. Both the patients and the lower medical personnel are engaged in stealing warm coverings. The medical attendants rob the sick and steal the property of the hospitals. Each physician has 150 to 200 patients.

"In the military hospitals where there are surgical instruments operations are performed in unheated rooms, and almost all the operations result in complications such as pneumonia and ulcers. Medical supplies are very scarce. There are only two thermometers for 150 patients.

NO MILK FOR HOSPITALS

"The hospital food ration is one and a half pounds of black bread, with a mixture of oats, or millet flour, or corn flour. Bread is scarcely baked. For dinner they serve soup with frozen cabbage, or potatoes with herring. Food for the very sick consists of beef soup, made mostly of horse meat. The second meal consists of a limited quantity of gruel. Weak soup is the principal supper. Patients receive no eggs or milk."

To a great extent the tragedy was caused by more than six years of war, revolution, and civil war. Normal production was inevitably upset. Men were pulled from their jobs by both sides to do military service. The factories especially were staffed by older people, women, and children, who lacked both experience and endurance. Most industry was engaged in war work, so almost no consumer goods were manufactured. The rickety railroads could not even begin to meet the needs for transportation. The Whites received some supplies, although not nearly enough, from the Allies, but the Bolsheviks were completely cut off by the blockade, which was not actually lifted until November 1920, despite the relaxations conceded in January.

However, the Bolsheviks themselves were also inadvertently responsible. The measures taken by the government to resuscitate the economy—War Communism, as these came collectively to be known—had to a large degree failed. By the end of 1919 almost every industry and every utility of any importance had been nationalized, from the giant Petrograd metal works to bakeries and public baths. In many instances old managers and engineers were removed and more often than not were replaced by individuals or committees lacking the technical and organizational experience necessary to run complicated modern industries. It was presumed, in accordance with Marxian theory, that the workers, used to the division of labor and the cooperation it required, would be able to determine their own conditions of work rationally and to organize production and distribution along socialist lines. The result was that instead of efficiency and socialist dedication to a common goal, waste, ineptitude, lackadaisicalness, and corruption were the rule. Added to this, of course, was the shortage of manpower.

Early in 1920 the government decided to try a new tack.

Trotzky Tells 'Red' Army to Fight Hunger

London, Feb. 27 [1920]. Leon Trotzky, Minister of War of Soviet Russia, addressing the third Russian congress [of Soviets] held in Moscow January 25, outlined the Bolshevik plan for converting the "Red" army into an army of labor, according to reports of his speech reaching here. Referring to the work of the "Red" army, Trotzky said:

"They [the soldiers] have learned under the very hardest conditions to lead hundreds of thousands of organized masses and have led peasants into battle. They will be trained officers. There is still one way open to the reorganization of national economy—the way of uniting the army and labor and changing the military detachments of the army into detachments of a labor army.

"Many in the army have already accomplished their military task, but they cannot be demobilized as yet. Now that they have been released from their military duties, they must fight against economic ruin and against hunger; they must work to obtain fuel, peat and other heat producing products; they must take part in building, in clearing the lines of snow, in repairing roads, building sheds, grinding flour, etc.

PROJECT ALREADY UNDER WAY

"We have already organized several of these armies, and they have been alloted their tasks. One army must obtain foodstuffs for the workmen of the districts in which it was formerly stationed, and it also will cut wood, cart it to the railways and repair engines. Another army will help in the laying down of railway lines for the transport of crude oil. A third labor army will be used to repair agricultural implements and machines, and in the spring will take part in working the land.

"At the present time among the working masses there must be the greatest exactitude and conscientiousness, together with responsibility to the end, and there must be the utmost strictness and severity, both in small and great matters. If the most advanced workmen of the country will devote their thoughts, all their will and all their revolutionary duty to the cause of regulating economic affairs, then I have no doubt that we shall lead Russia on a new free road, to the confounding of our enemies and the joy of our friends.

"We shall succeed if qualified and trained workers take part in productive labor. Trade unions must register qualified workmen in the villages. Only in those localities where trade union methods are inadequate other methods must be introduced, in particular that of compulsion, because labor conscription gives the state the right to tell the qualified workman who is employed on some unimportant work in his village 'You are obliged to leave your present employment and go to Sormovo or Kolomna, because there your work is required.' "

Russia Is Mobilizing
Its Civilian Man Power

Moscow, March 28 [*1920*]. Mobilization of Russia's working forces is proceeding with giant strides, it is announced here. Newspapers are filled with reports of the activities of the working army on Russian and Siberian railroad systems and in the mining districts of the Urals, and of energetic steps being taken to fully utilize civilian manpower.

Regular mobilization is taking place in many districts, especially in the Caucasus and Ural regions, all males between the ages of sixteen and fifty and all females between sixteen and forty-five being compelled to register for work at Ekaterinburg, Perm, Viatka, Kazan, Vladimir and other places. All former railroad workers are called upon to register, and refusal to obey will be punishable by internment in concentration camps. A number of "industrial slackers" have been arrested at Perm, among them being several technical experts.

Meetings of unions are being held at many places to determine the attitude of labor toward this governmental policy, and opposition was recently evidenced by the Syndicalist element at Viatka. The reports state, however, that this was overruled by the majority of the workers.

A stimulating effect of the activity is declared to have been noticed in several districts. Several bodies of factory employees, according to reports received here, have voted recently to abolish holidays and institute overtime work.

The program started off auspiciously but did not prove very successful. A good many of the soldiers resisted spending their time off between military duties working, and the workers on the whole responded no better to compulsion under a Communist regime than under capitalism. Another difficulty—perhaps more important—was that the workers, and to a lesser degree the soldiers, were simply too hungry to keep up the pace, even with the best of intentions, and food in sufficient quantities was not forthcoming.

Lenin's directive urging the poor peasants to seize the property of the wealthier farmers had had an ironical effect. The class war that he fomented in the countryside tended to equalize the farmers as the estates and larger farms were broken down into individual holdings. Now the poor peasants were landholders themselves, and like the kulaks they would rather let their surpluses rot in the fields than give them up without compensation. Collections of food consequently required the use of force, which only increased the peasants' stubbornness.

Finally, War Communism brought with it the creation of an enormous bureaucracy, an officialdom even more cumbersome and less competent than its Czarist predecessor. Many of the old bureaucrats had fled or been forced out, and their replacements were often entirely unqualified for their jobs.

Petrograd and Moscow in Grip
Of Starvation, Nearly Deserted

Washington, Feb. 5 [1921]. Petrograd is in mourning and almost deserted and no less squalid and desolate are conditions in Moscow, Signor M. Colombino, secretary of the Italian Federation of Metal Workers, declared in his report to the Metal Workers' Federation at Rome upon his return from three months of investigating the Bolshevik regime in Russia, the State Department disclosed to-day in making public extracts from Colombino's report.

Colombino graphically described the terrifying conditions which confronted him while in Petrograd and Moscow. Of Petrograd he said:

"Shops closed, private trade prohibited, shop windows smashed, the shutters hanging in tatters along the streets, contribute to make the city mournful and ugly. Here and there the height of irony is reached when one sees a few shreds of advertisements of Borsalino hats, for China Migonne (an Italian variety of hairwash) and for the latest models of Paris fashions. The trams run at very rare intervals and only for a few hours a day on some of the principal lines, but there are certainly not more than fifty of them.

BARGES LEFT TO ROT

"Along the Neva one may see huge barges left to rot. The roads which were once upon a time paved with wooden blocks are now almost totally destroyed, having been broken up by the citizens themselves for fuel to heat their houses. Thirty-six thousand wooden houses were destroyed last winter to provide fuel. Drinking water is entirely lacking throughout the city because the cold burst the pipes.

"The recent violent epidemic of typhoid, which killed off thousands of victims and left its mark on the population, is to a certain extent the consequence of this state of things, as well as the total lack of hygienic, sanitary and alimentary measures.

"When one notices how the inhabitants are clad and shod one receives a marked sensation of the profound misery which has stricken this heroic and stoic population."

Colombino refers in detail to the scarcity of food, describes the rationing system and tells of the presence of speculators in foodstuffs, who charge exorbitant prices.

WORKMEN ARE INDIFFERENT

The indifference of Russian workmen under the Bolshevik regime is marked, Colombino found. "In the Putiloff works," he said, "there is no longer the feverish pre-war activity. The great chimneys rise skyward without the thread of smoke and a sepulchral silence reigns throughout the buildings. Before the war the Putiloff works furnished employment to 40,000 workmen, and another 10,000 were added during the war. The present roll of workmen numbers 7,000. The management of the works is intrusted to an engineer, but the factory committee, composed of seven workmen, who hold office for six months, has complete supervision of his work. The technical and administrative offices are almost deserted."

Russian Revolts Spread

Riga, Latvia, Feb. 24 [*1921*]. Reports received here from Moscow say that revolts are growing in the Ukraine and in the Tambov and Greburg districts of Russia. In the Tyumen district of Siberia armed peasants are defending foodstuffs against requisition. The Red Army is said to be without discipline.

Peasant Revolt Covers Half of Soviet Russia

General Strike Impending in Petrograd; Distrust of Red Rule Said to Be Growing

Washington, Feb. 26 [*1921*]. Uprisings by numerous small groups of peasants in Russia against the drastic rule of the Soviet regime have broken out in about half the provinces under Bolshevik rule, according to authentic information received by the State Department.

The peasant uprisings are spreading in the Ural, in the Ukraine and in the central provinces of Russia. In the Kronstadt region there have been disorders which required a substantial force of sailors to put down.

Strikes in the vicinity of Petrograd, particularly in the arsenal works and other large plants, have caused considerable uneasiness there, with rumors of an impending general strike in the old Russian capital. More freedom for labor, cessation of the food requisitions . . . and less rigid trade restrictions are among the demands made by the workmen at Petrograd.

Soviet Chiefs
Admit Revolt
Is Widespread

Stockholm, March 2 [*1921*]. The latest dispatches received here from Helsingfors, Finland, assert that the insurrection in Petrograd was crushed after severe fighting and that the city is now quiet with the Soviet master of the situation.

The sailors at Kronstadt remained neutral, supporting neither the workers, nor the government.

The dispatches add that the Soviet has been unable to conceal the fact of the spread of the counter-revolutionary movement throughout the country, and that M. Kalinin, president of the extraordinary commission, has been obliged to admit peasant uprisings everywhere.

LENINE'S LATEST PLEA

Riga, Latvia, March 2 [*1921*]. According to a Moscow report received here the Commissary for Labor and Defense has published a proclamation, signed by Nikolai Lenine, promising that the government will use all the means at its disposal to supply the destitute working population with the necessaries of life. A special fund of 10,000,000 gold rubles will be donated for this purpose and the Commissary of Trade instructed to send abroad a commission for the purchase of required supplies.

The Moscow newspapers also publish a proclamation, issued by the Moscow Soviet, which is addressed to "all workers, peasants and members of the Red army—honest citizens." It accuses the [Socialist Revolutionaries and Mensheviks] of being corrupt agents of the Russian aristocracy, and capitalists and foreign bankers, of trying anew to conquer Russia by hunger in organizing a Cossack revolt in Siberia and disturbances in the Ukraine in order to prevent the transport of supplies to various centers, and of taking advantage of the economic crisis at the moment for a rising against the government, thereby provoking bloodshed. It accuses Entente agents of complicity, and says one of the French agents has been arrested in Petrograd.

The Soviet asks the population to arrest agitators who try to organize demonstrations near Red Army barracks. The proclamations are considered here official recognition of the trouble which started three weeks ago, when at a meeting of metal workers Lenine was accused of torturing workers and ruining Russia. When Lenine asked the metal workers whether they would prefer the former Czarist regime they are reported to have exclaimed:

"Let come who may—whites, blacks or devils themselves—just you clear out!"

Particularly alarming to the Russian leaders was the spread of the uprising to one of the oldest and most reliable centers of revolutionism.

Reds Admit Kronstadt Has Fallen

To Trotsky fell the task of suppressing the sailors whose adored leader he had once been.

Stockholm, March 17 [1921]. Cronstadt [Kronstadt] was taken by the Soviet forces at 2 o'clock in the afternoon, according to a Bolshevik news agency.

The arrival of the Cronstadt revolutionary committee and 800 soldiers at Terioki on the Finnish frontier, is confirmed.

The fighting for possession of the armed fortress was of a furious character and the attacking forces were ejected from the town at least once, according to reports received here.

For the assault . . . Trotzky had concentrated the whole of the new

Seventh Army, consisting of Red cadets from all the Russian cities and other troops, totalling 60,000.

The Cronstadt garrison consisted of between 15,000 and 16,000 men of whom 10,000 were sailors. They were exhausted through lack of sleep for several days.

Disturbances elsewhere were also put down, but Lenin had no illusion that anything had been solved. Never one to be corseted by impractical theory or commitment to vain programs, Lenin now did an about-face.

Lenine's Compromise
With Capital Approved

Riga, Latvia, May 27 [1921]. Premier Lenine of Soviet Russia won complete approval for his new policies at the final session to-day of the all-Russia trade union congress, before which he spoke, outlining plans to pull Russia through the present chaos by reforms, all of which are to be so controlled as to avoid complete return to capitalism.

According to limited extracts of Premier Lenine's speech received from Moscow, the reforms provide for the application of new capitalistic forms in the Soviet, and deal, among other things, with the management of problems relating to exchange of goods and the independence of the peasants.

The first move back toward capitalism in Russia came soon after the [Kronstadt] revolt, when the Moscow government lifted the ban on trading in foodstuffs.

Simultaneously, Lenine intensified his campaign for the conclusion of commercial agreements with several nations in preparation for the revival of trade. When statisticians at the All-Russian Congress of Trade Unions in Moscow last week, called to discuss the solution of Russia's economic crisis, brought out that production in Russia was only 2 per cent of normal the congress decided to insist upon immediate cooperative measures and the granting of foreign concessions in Russia in order to increase production. The conference voted to suspend the Bolshevik policy of confiscation . . . and to organize the country for the asquisition of raw materials through trade channels and the promotion of industrial enterprises.

Lenin in 1920.

LENINE CONCEDES FALL OF THEORIES

Lenine has frankly admitted the defeat of his own theories. In one recent address he said: "We must grant freer economic relations between workers and peasants. We hitherto have acted in a too military manner, and in some cases have gone too far in nationalizing trade. If some Communists thought that the organization of a socialist state was possible in three years they were dreamers. Freedom of economic relations means free trade and free trade signifies a return to capitalism. A practical solution of this problem is most difficult but must be found."

Cry for Food
Forces Change
In Red Creed

Berlin, June 1 [*1921*]. Confirmation of recent reports regarding the economic crisis in Soviet Russia and the intention of the Soviet government to denationalize industry and return certain plants to private hands was received by the "Tribune" correspondent in a full copy of the address delivered by Rykoff, chairman of the All-Russian Economic Council, at the recent congress of the local economic councils held in Moscow.

Rykoff exposes in the frankest manner the failure of the Soviet government's economic policies and predicts that unless productivity is increased and the vast Soviet bureaucracy radically curbed, the Soviet government will be unable to survive. Rykoff dwells particularly on the crisis in the iron, fuel and food industries, saying that the government needs 10,000,000 tons of iron in the near future, but that the maximum which it can hope to obtain is only between 200,000 and 300,000 tons.

LACK OF FOOD CRIPPLES WORKERS

He continues: "The food crisis, which became particularly aggravated in the last two months, reflects itself directly in the productivity of the workers. The aggravation of the present food and industrial troubles is due to the great failure of our economic organizations. There has been a great waste in our resources.

"In the last four years we have observed a constant decrease in the area of cultivation, with a constantly falling harvest and almost the entire disappearance of materials necessary for the development of industry, agriculture and export. The disorganization of the peasants' economies is the inevitable result of our food policy as conducted until recently."

Rykoff expects an improvement now that the system of requisition has been abandoned and a natural tax substituted. It is proposed to leave the greater part of the product in the hands of the peasants.

He admits that "this, of course, means the restoration of the institution of private ownership in the bourgeois sense of the word, and inevitably will lead to the development of a new and perfectly legal bourgeoisie," but consoles his audience with the assertion that the government at all times will be able to maintain severe control over industry wherever it appears necessary.

Rykoff puts out the promise that the government will act as the competitor of private enterprises by continuing operation of the larger enterprises not yet entirely destroyed.

Lenine's New Program Indorsed by Communists

Riga, June 1 [1921]. The congress of the Communist Party closed its sessions at Moscow on Monday [May 30] with a declaration of approval of the program expounded by Nikolai Lenine and his lieutenant Miliutin, Minister of Agriculture in the Soviet regime, who is now the ruling spirit in economic questions. The policy thus approved was outlined by Lenine and Miliutin in the course of the discussion and was accepted in silence by Zinovieff, Soviet Governor of Petrograd, who heretofore has been regarded as head of the irreconcilable element.

Premier Lenine's speech, as officially reported by the Soviet agency, explained that previous policies of requisition, etc., had been due to external conditions and to civil war, which had given no other choice than the adoption of these rigorous measures. But this necessity now being ended, he said, the task must be "the establishment of fixed relations between the workmen and the peasantry."

The policy as outlined by Lenine and Miliutin consists mainly in the following points:

First—collection from the peasants of a fixed amount of grain by a system of a tax in kind, estimated by Miliutin to amount to about one-third of the crop. The other two-thirds of the crop is to remain at the disposal of the peasant for trading through the newly restored coöperatives, whose power is to be extended. The former system of requisitions, which made the peasants the ardent and sometimes fighting foes of communism, permitted the peasant to keep only a small quantity of grain for personal consumption, while the state forcibly took the rest.

Second—retention in the hands of the state of the largest industries and means of transportation, particularly the leather, salt and textile industries. These latter are turning out manufactured goods now most needed by the peasants. They are to be sped up in order to satisfy the peasants' needs and the workmen are to be encouraged by a bonus system and other inducements, which will increase production. Supervision is to be under the trade unions, who will fix the rates of pay instead of the government as heretofore. These large industries and transportation facilities, as well as natural resources, such as metal, etc., are regarded as strong influences in maintaining the present regime.

Third—encouragement of small and medium coöperatives and private industries. Factories will be leased these smaller industries and even financial assistance will be given. The trades unions will fix the wages, the government retaining the right of factory inspection. Personal initiative of workers will be suitably rewarded and will supplant equal pay. Government officials in charge of factories who prove lax in their management will be strictly prosecuted. The chief purpose throughout will be to increase production.

Besides the foregoing, there will be general relaxation of prosecution and of hindrances to free trade.

In the course of his speech on Monday Lenine said the development of capitalism, through the small industries and agriculture, was not to be feared, for the reason that the proletariat always held firmly in its hands all the large sources of industry.

What emerged when the New Economic Policy, as the reforms were dubbed, took shape was, in Lenin's words, "state capitalism." Major enterprises, the transportation facilities, most natural resources, banking, and foreign trade remained in the hands of the Soviet government, while some small manufacturing concerns and most retail stores were yielded to private ownership. The farmers were permitted considerable latitude in trading their surpluses and were encouraged to produce by the offer of tax advantages for efficiency; later, they were given permission to hire farm labor and rent additional land. Trade unions were conceded the right to strike against the government, as well as against private employers. But over-all strict control was imposed.

The immediate problem of the famine and resultant epidemics had reached horrifying proportions during the summer of 1921, so the government sent out a plea for help to the world.

Hoover to Aid Russia
If She Opens Prisons

Washington, July 24 [1921]. In line with the announcement that the United States government would require the release of Americans held prisoner in Russia before any relief for famine sufferers would be forthcoming, Secretary of Commerce Herbert Hoover, who is also chairman of the American Relief Administration, to-day dispatched to Maxim Gorky at Petrograd, a statement of America's position.

Chairman Hoover said that the Russian authorities also would have to give assurances that American relief workers will not be interfered with in any way in their charitable work, and the hearty coöperation of the Russian people must be pledged before the American organization can enter upon the work of assisting the stricken children of that country.

Mr. Hoover's telegram to Mr. Gorky was similar to one dispatched six months ago, when the first offer to assist in relieving distress in Russia was made.

Russia Ready to Open
Cells to Get Food

Washington, Aug. 10 [1921]. Events moved swiftly to-day in the plans of the American Relief Administration to succor Russia's starving millions and obtain the release of all Americans held in Russia against their will. The chief developments were:

Herbert Hoover, chairman of the American Relief Administration, after a conference with President Harding, announced that the actual dispensing of relief would proceed immediately.

America and Russia came into their closest contact since the Red revolution with the opening conference in Riga between Walter Lyman Brown, European director of American relief, and Maxim Litvinoff, the Soviet envoy.

Mr. Brown insisted that all Americans now in Russia, whether in or out of prison, be permitted to leave as a condition of continuing negotiations. Litvinoff pledged that this would be done.

Six Americans liberated from Russian prisons, most of them half starved and in rags, reached Reval, Esthonia, making the total of Americans thus far liberated seven.

Ambassador Harvey, representing the United States in the Allied Supreme Council meeting in Paris, agreed to present to the Council full details of the American relief plans to aid the Council in determining its course in relation to famine relief.

By the end of 1921, the economy had begun to revive.

Changing Russia

A letter just received in London from Petrograd describes in detail many of the remarkable changes that are now taking place in Russia. . . . The writer, a highly educated man who at one time took an active part in politics, was imprisoned several times during the worst phases of the Bolshevik terror.

Business [he reports] is moving quickly, especially in Moscow. One enterprise after another is reviving in the form of coöperative associations. For example, the old Philipoff business is rising again—big bakeries, cafes and bakers' shops all over the town. The peasants have improved their condition; they are building; they eat better, and they are increasing their livestock. Their demand for manufactured goods is growing, and for that reason they will have to produce more themselves. All sorts of people have gone into the country from the towns—former hall porters, artisans, domestic servants and factory workers—and they have brought new interests and demands into the village. The old patriarchal muzhik is becoming a modern farmer.

Manners have grown coarse and rough; it is a hard time for the intelligentsia. The young people are particularly unpleasant; many of them are like fierce wolves.

The schools are in a wretched state; only one pen is allowed for six pupils and one pencil for the whole school. From the universities the best men have been driven out, and the mediocrities are triumphant. The lack of means and hunger and cold are terrible impediments to scientific work. Some of the students are very keen on their studies. Of late there have been disturbances among the students very like those under the old regime.

There are faint signs of a revival of journalism. Reviews are being published—"Nachaio," under the editorship of Radioff, Oldenburg and Platonoff; "Vyestinski Europi," a former Liberal review, has revived under the editorship of N. Kotliareski; and the "Economist." A business is being founded to publish books on technical questions and agriculture. And this in spite of the fact that it costs 12 rubles to set up one letter—three times as much as the author's fee. Paper is 6,000 rubles a pound.

We are now in a time of economic reaction and reaction of all kinds. There is a terrible individualism, greed, envy, open corruption and indifference to suffering. But the lower classes have risen. It is amusing, of course, how they try to dress up; barbers are in great demand. The peasant girls powder their faces and manicure themselves. On Sundays in the villages the women and girls parade about in silks and satins, white stockings and white shoes in imitation of the *ci-devants*. These are all signs of a great levelling process and the descent of the intelligentsia, for the intellectuals chop wood, load trucks and steamers and drive cabs— a very profitable business now.

There is a process of movement and change. . . . There is no returning to the past. Live in faith in the future, and don't torture yourself by expecting an immediate coming of brighter days.

The egalitarianism and the comparative latitude granted to private initiative in economic matters, were not, however, accompanied by an extension of political democracy or of political liberty. On the contrary. Menshevik leaders still living in Russia were forced to emigrate; the Socialist Revolutionary chiefs were arrested and put on trial, then, after serving a brief term in prison, were also banished from the country. At the X Congress of the Communist party, held in March 1921, a resolution was adopted for the prohibition of factional groups within the party, and that summer approximately one-third of the members were expelled. Despite the provision in the Constitution of 1918 stipulating that the elective All-Russian Congress of Soviets (Vtsik) was to be the supreme authority in Russia, with the Council of People's Commissars appointed by the Vtsik as the executive, the true authority was the Communist party. Indeed, power actually came to reside in the Political Bureau (Politburo) of the Party Central Committee. The regime was both authoritarian and highly centralized. The Cheka (reorganized in 1922 with a new name, State Political Administration, or GPU) continued its sinister ac-

In Lenin's program for political organization of the country, party functionaries were dispatched to towns and villages both to indoctrinate the populace and to act as ears for the government. (*Photo from European*)

tivities, although now that the civil war was over and the main political opposition eliminated, its record, for the time being at least, was less bloodstained. Poland and the Baltic provinces of Lithuania, Latvia, and Estonia, as well as Finland, which under the later Czars had restricted autonomy, were now independent, but the other nationalities that had attempted to win their freedom—the Armenians, the Georgians, and the Azerbaijani in the Caucasus; the Tatars, Kirghiz, and other Turks of Central Asia; the Ukrainians and White Russians in the west—had been forcibly brought back under the dominion of the Muscovite Russians.

The Bolshevik regime had, indeed, brought about a great social and economic leveling of the population, but in its authoritarianism, its centralized administration, its severe paternalism, and its disdain for the prerogatives of individual personality, it was notably reminiscent of the regime that had been overthrown in the chill days of March 1917.

Sources of Newspaper Articles, Headlines, and Cartoons

(Page numbers of this volume, in brackets, precede the references. References are to the New York *Tribune* except where otherwise noted.)

CHAPTER ONE.   [2:] *Herald,* Nov. 2, 1894, p. 3. [3:] Nov. 20, 1894, p. 1. [5:] *Herald,* Nov. 20, 1894, p. 9. [6:] *Herald,* Nov. 2, 1894, p. 3. [7:] Nov. 1, 1894, p. 1. [8:] Mar. 13, 1904. Part III, p. 3. Dec. 6, 1896, Part III, p. 4. [11:] Nov. 28, 1894, p. 2. [13]: Oct. 4, 1894, p. 6. The editorial was actually written on receipt of the news that Alexander III was dying. Minor corrections (in brackets) have been made to update it. [14:] Nov. 1, 1894, p. 1. [17:] Oct. 3, 1894, p. 6.

CHAPTER TWO.   [20:] *Herald,* Dec. 12, 1904, p. 3. [21:] Jan. 30, 1895, p. 1. Feb. 14, 1895, p. 1. [24:] Mar. 31, 1901, Supplement, p. 6. [25:] Mar. 2, 1899, p. 2. [26:] Mar. 6, 1901, p. 3. [27:] Mar. 16, 1901, p. 1. Mar. 18, 1901, p. 1. [28:] *Herald,* Mar. 19, 1901, p. 9. *Herald,* Mar. 20, 1901, p. 9. [29:] Mar. 13, 1898, Supplement, p. 7. May 17, 1901, p. 3. [30:] June 1, 1901, p. 9. April 27, 1902, p. 1. Mar. 29, 1903, p. 1. Mar. 30, 1903, p. 1. Aug. 7, 1903, p. 2. [38:] Aug. 8, 1903, p. 1. [39:] Apr. 28, 1902, p. 2. May 2, 1902, p. 3. Feb. 21, 1903, p. 1. [40:] July 29, 1901, p. 7. [41:] Feb. 10, 1904, p. 1. Feb. 11, 1904, p. 1. Mar. 10, 1904, p. 1. [42:] May 2, 1904, p. 1. May 4, 1904, p. 1. May 28, 1904, p. 1. June 6, 1904, p. 2. [43:] *Herald,* July 29, 1904, p. 3. [44:] Nov. 20, 1904, p. 4, combined with Nov. 22, 1904, p. 1. Nov. 23, 1904, p. 1. [45:] Nov. 26, 1904, p. 1. Dec. 12, 1904, p. 1. [47:] Dec. 27, 1904, p. 1, combined with Dec. 28, 1904, p. 1. [48:] Jan. 4, 1905, p. 2.

CHAPTER THREE.   [50:] *Herald,* Oct. 31, 1905, p. 3. [51:] Jan. 23, 1905, p. 1. Jan. 21, 1905, p. 2. [53:] Jan. 23, 1905, p. 1. [56:] Jan. 27, 1905, p. 1. [57:] Jan. 30, 1905, p. 1. Jan. 26, 1905, p. 1. Jan. 27, 1905, p. 1. Feb. 27, 1905, p. 1. [58:] Feb. 18, 1905, p. 1. Mar. 4, 1905, p. 1. [60:] *Herald,* June 29, 1905, p. 3. [61:] Aug. 9, 1905, p. 1, combined with Aug. 19, 1905, p. 1. [62:] Aug. 21, 1905, p. 2. Oct. 11, 1905, p. 1. [63:] Oct. 18, 1905, p. 1. *Herald,* Oct. 28, 1905, p. 3. [64:] *Herald,* Oct. 28, 1905, p. 3 (sic). [65:] Oct. 29, 1905, p. 7. [66:] Oct. 31, 1905, p. 1. [68:] Nov. 1, 1905, p. 1.

CHAPTER FOUR.   [70:] *Herald,* July 27, 1906, p. 3. [71:] Mar. 12, 1906, p. 2. [72:] Nov. 21, 1905, p. 1. [74:] *Herald,* May 11, 1906, p. 11, combined with May 11, 1906, p. 1. [75:] Mar. 25, 1906, p. 1. [77:] May 16, 1906, p. 4. May 27, 1906, p. 1. [78:] June 18, 1906, p. 1. [79:] July 5, 1906, p. 1. [80:] July 22, 1906, p. 1. July 23, 1906, p. 1. [81:] Aug. 1, 1906, p. 1. Aug. 3, 1906, p. 1. Aug. 5, 1906, p. 1. *Herald,* Aug. 5, 1906, p. 3. [82:] Aug. 26, 1906, p. 1. Aug. 27, 1906, p. 1. [83:] Oct. 20, 1906, p. 1, combined with Nov. 10, 1906, p. 7. [84:] Nov. 30, 1907, p. 30.

CHAPTER FIVE.   [88:] Mar. 16, 1917, p. 1. [90:] June 29, 1914, p. 1. [92:] July 24, 1914, p. 3. July 25, 1914, p. 1. [93:] July 26, 1914, p. 1. [94:] *Herald,* July 29, 1914, p. 3. July 31, 1914, p. 1. [96:] Aug. 1, 1914, p. 1. Aug. 2, 1914, p. 1. Aug. 3, 1914, p. 1. [97:] Aug. 5, 1914, p. 1. [98:] May 12, 1915, p. 3. June 4, 1915, p. 1. June 24, 1915, p. 1. [99:] Aug. 6, 1915, p. 1. Aug. 27, 1915, p. 1. [100:] *Herald,* Oct. 16, 1917, Part II, p. 1. [102:] June 21, 1915, p. 3. [103:] Mar. 21, 1917, p. 4. [104:] Jan. 3, 1917, p. 3. [105:] Jan. 21, 1917, p. 4. [106:] Jan. 29, 1917, p. 3. Feb. 13, 1917, p. 8. [107:] Mar. 16, 1917, pp. 1 and 2, combined with *Herald,* Mar. 16, 1917, p. 3. [114:] Mar. 18, 1917, p. 1. [115:] *Herald,* Mar. 17, 1917, Part II, p. 1, combined with Mar. 17, 1917, p. 1, and Mar. 16, 1917, p. 1.

CHAPTER SIX.   [118:] May 16, 1917, p. 1. [120:] Mar. 19, 1917, p. 1. [121:] April 14, 1917, p. 1 (cartoon). [122:] Mar. 23, 1917, p. 1. Mar. 23, 1917, p. 4. [123:] Mar. 25, 1917,

Part V, p. 1. [125:] Apr. 20, 1917, p. 5. [127:] Mar. 19, 1917, p. 2. [128:] Apr. 17, 1917, p. 4. Mar. 28, 1917, p. 1. [130:] Apr. 15, 1917, p. 1. [133:] Apr. 25, 1917, p. 6. [134:] Apr. 28, 1917, p. 4. [136:] May 4, 1917, p. 5. [137:] May 5, 1917, p. 1. [138:] May 5, 1917, p. 3. May 16, 1917, p. 1. [140:] May 20, 1917, p. 1. [141:] May 24, 1917, p. 1. [142:] May 29, 1917, p. 2. May 29, 1917, p. 1. [143:] June 3, 1917, p. 2.

CHAPTER SEVEN. [146:] Aug. 6, 1917, p. 1. [147:] *Herald*, July 2, 1917, Section II, p. 1. July 3, 1917, p. 1. [148:] July 2, 1917, p. 1 (cartoon). [149:] July 18, 1917, p. 1. [150:] July 19, 1917, p. 1. [153:] July 20, 1917, p. 1. [155:] July 21, 1917, p. 1. July 24, 1917, p. 1. [157:] July 27, 1917, p. 1. Aug. 5, 1917, p. 1. [158:] July 12, 1917, p. 3. [160:] Aug. 29, 1917, p. 3. [161:] *Herald*, Sept. 11, 1917, Part II, p. 1. [162:] Sept. 14, 1917, p. 1. [163:] Sept. 15, 1917, p. 1. [165:] Sept. 28, 1917, p. 7. [166:] Sept. 29, 1917, p. 4. Oct. 4, 1917, p. 5. [167:] Oct. 7, 1917, p. 6. [168:] Oct. 11, 1917, p. 1. [169:] Oct. 12, 1917, p. 1. Oct. 16, 1917, p. 1. Oct. 25, 1917, p. 3.

CHAPTER EIGHT. [172:] *Herald*, Nov. 9, 1917, p. 9. [174:] Nov. 3, 1917, p. 3. [175:] Nov. 8, 1917, p. 1. [178:] Nov. 9, 1917, p. 1 (cartoon). [180:] *Herald*, Nov. 9, 1917, p. 9, combined with Nov. 9, 1917, p. 1. [183:] Nov. 10, 1917, p. 1, combined with Nov. 12, 1917, p. 2. [185:] Nov. 12, 1917, pp. 1 and 2. Nov. 13, 1917, p. 1. [186:] Nov. 14, 1917, p. 1. *Herald*, Nov. 14, 1917, p. 9. [187:] Nov. 14, 1917, p. 2. [188:] Nov. 15, 1917, p. 1. Nov. 16, 1917, p. 1. Nov. 18, 1917, p. 2, combined with Nov. 17, 1917, p. 1. [190:] Nov. 18, 1917, p. 1. [191:] Nov. 9, 1917, p. 3. [194:] Nov. 22, 1917, p. 1. Nov. 26, 1917, p. 1. Nov. 22, 1917, p. 4. [196:] Nov. 29, 1917, p. 1. Dec. 2, 1917, p. 1. [197:] Dec. 10, 1917, p. 1. Dec. 11, 1917, p. 1. Dec. 21, 1917, p. 2. [198:] Dec. 30, 1917, p. 3. [199:] Dec. 20, 1917, p. 1. [200:] Dec. 30, 1917, p. 1. Dec. 23, 1917, p. 1 (cartoon). Dec. 31, 1917, p. 1. [201:] Jan. 3, 1918, p. 8, combined with Jan. 4, 1918, p. 8. [205:] Feb. 12, 1917, p. 1, combined with Feb. 13, 1918, p. 1. [206:] Feb. 19, 1918, p. 1. *Herald*, Feb. 24, 1918, p. 1.

CHAPTER NINE. [208:] Aug. 2, 1918, p. 4. [212:] Jan. 20, 1918, p. 1. [213:] Jan. 21, 1918, p. 1. [214:] Feb. 1, 1918, p. 2. [215:] June 13, 1918, p. 5. [216:] July 6, 1918, p. 4. July 18, 1918, p. 6. [217:] July 6, 1918, p. 4. [220:] July 28, 1918, p. 3. [222:] June 16, 1918, p. 3. [223:] July 7, 1918, p. 1. July 9, 1918, p. 1. [224:] July 7, 1918, p. 1. [225:] Mar. 16, 1918, p. 1 (cartoon). [226:] Mar. 12, 1918, p. 1. [228:] June 20, 1918, p. 1 (cartoon). [229:] Aug. 16, 1918, p. 1. [230:] Aug. 2, 1918, p. 4. [233:] July 21, 1918, p. 1. [236:] *Herald*, Sept. 4, 1918, p. 9, combined with Sept. 1, 1918, p. 3, and Sept. 2, 1918, p. 1. Sept. 4, 1918, p. 3. [237:] Sept. 10, 1918, p. 3. [239:] Sept. 27, 1918, p. 1. [240:] *Herald*, Nov. 11, 1918, p. 9.

CHAPTER TEN. [242:] Jan. 2, 1920, p. 1. [243:] Nov. 8, 1918, p. 1. Nov. 9, 1918, p. 1. [244:] Nov. 10, 1918, p. 1. [245:] Nov. 13, 1918, p. 1. Nov. 14, 1918, p. 1. Jan. 1, 1919, p. 1. Nov. 22, 1918, p. 1. [247:] Nov. 22, 1918, p. 3. July 22, 1919, Section VII, p. 3. [249:] Nov. 21, 1918, p. 1 (cartoon). [250:] Jan. 12, 1919, p. 1 (cartoon). [252:] Feb. 7, 1919, p. 1. Feb. 20, 1919, p. 6. [253:] Mar. 27, 1919, p. 1. Mar. 31, 1919, p. 1. [254:] Apr. 11, 1919, p. 1. [255:] Apr. 20, 1919, p. 1. [256:] Oct. 16, 1919, p. 1. [257:] Nov. 16, 1919, p. 1. [258:] Oct. 21, 1919, p. 3. [259:] Oct. 22, 1919, p. 4. Oct. 23, 1919, p. 9. [260:] Oct. 25, 1919, p. 3. Oct. 28, 1919, p. 1. Jan. 2, 1920, p. 1. [262:] Jan. 17, 1920, p. 1. [263:] Feb. 9, 1920, p. 2. Mar. 21, 1920, p. 3. Mar. 29, 1920, p. 4. May 9, 1920, p. 16. [264:] May 25, 1920, p. 4. June 14, 1920, p. 3. Aug. 5, 1920, p. 1. [265:] Aug. 5, 1920, p. 1. Aug. 18, 1920, p. 1. [266:] Aug. 14, 1920, p. 1. Aug. 21, 1920, p. 1. Oct. 6, 1920, p. 1. [267:] Nov. 15, 1920, p. 1.

CHAPTER ELEVEN. [270:] Oct. 7, 1920, p. 1. [275:] Feb. 28, 1920, p. 2. [276:] Mar. 29, 1920, p. 4. [278:] Feb. 6, 1921, p. 4. [279:] Feb. 25, 1921, p. 1. Feb. 27, 1921, p. 6. [280:] Mar. 3, 1921, p. 1. [281:] Mar. 6, 1921, p. 1. Mar. 18, 1921, p. 1. [282:] May 28, 1921, p. 2, combined with May 30, 1921, pp. 1 and 2. [284:] June 2, 1921, p. 1. [285:] June 2, 1921, p. 2. [287:] July 25, 1921, p. 1. July 26, 1921, p. 1. Aug. 11, 1921, p. 1. [288:] Dec. 25, 1921, Section II, p. 1.

Index

COLLEGE OF ALLEGHENY COUNTY
COMMUNITY
LIBRARY

ALLEGHENY
CAMPUS
808 RIDGE AVENUE
PITTSBURGH, PA.
15212